CW01664358

HISTORY

OF THE

KING'S GERMAN LEGION.

HISTORY

OF THE

KING'S GERMAN LEGION,

BY

N. LUDLOW BEAMISH, F.R.S.

LATE MAJOR UNATTACHED.

"Hah! Du vielleicht? mein alter Kriegsgefährte, mit dem ich einst meinen letzen Bissen theilte, als uns Alles mangelte—oder Du, dem ich in der Schlacht vom Tumibamba das leben rettete?—oder Du, dessen Sohn ich befreyte, als eben die Feinde ihn niederhauen wollten?"—KOTZEBUE

VOL.I.

The Naval & Military Press Ltd

Published by

The Naval & Military Press Ltd

Unit 5 Riverside
Bellbrook Industrial Estate
Uckfield, East Sussex
TN22 1QQ England

Tel: +44 (0) 1825 749494
www.naval-military-press.com

Cover image: The storming of La Haye Sainte by Richard Knötel, German artist and pioneer of the study of military uniform. La Haye Sainte was the crucial position at the centre of Wellington's position at the Battle of Waterloo.

In reprinting in facsimile from the original, any imperfections are inevitably reproduced and the quality may fall short of modern type and cartographic standards.

TO HIS EXCELLENCY

GENERAL CHARLES COUNT VON ALTEN,

G.C.B. AND G.C.H.

ETC. ETC. ETC.

To your Excellency as the most distinguished of those expatriated Hanoverian soldiers who shared with their brethren of Britain the laurels torn from the common enemy, this record of their services

Is inscribed by

Your Excellency's faithful servant,

N. LUDLOW BEAMISH.

INTRODUCTION

The *King's German Legion* was without a doubt amongst the very best troops commanded by Wellington in the Peninsula and at Waterloo. Two (out of many) outstanding deeds of valour spring immediately to mind — one involving *KGL* cavalry, the other *KGL* infantry.

On 23 July 1812, the day after the great victory of Salamanca in north-central Spain, six squadrons of *KGL* heavy dragoons under General Eberhardt, Baron von Bock (445 cavalrymen in all), in support of a Regiment of British light dragoons, caught up with three battalions of Général Count Maximilien Sèbaseien Foy's division (forming part of the rearguard of the gravely-wounded Marshal Marmont's smashed *Armée de Portugal*) on the slopes beyond the small town of Garcia Hernadez near the north bank of the River Tormes, and proceeded to drub them in a classic cavalry-against-infantry engagement. All three French formations were destroyed: one, uniquely, in a formed square, after a dying horse rolled into one of its faces thus creating a fatal gap, immediately exploited; the second succumbed, also in square, as survivors from the first battalion flung themselves into it seeking momentary sanctuary from the remorseless Hanoverian cavalry swords; the third, in column, after a further charge up-hill by the seemingly unstoppable Hanoverian horsemen, wielding their long straight swords, in their red jackets and old-fashioned black bicorne hats, secured by brass-scaled chin-straps.* In all, the French lost some 1,200 casualties (out of 2,400 infantrymen engaged) of whom a full battalion laid down their arms to the *KGL's* 127 at the close of this spirited action, which forced Foy to deploy his whole division (perhaps 8,000 men in all) into a defensive position. Had not the battle-tired British infantry been so far behind their questing cavalry-screen, Foy's doom — and probably that of the mass of French fugitives with him — would in all likelihood have been sealed. As it was, Foy was able to resume both his retreat and his covering rearguard role. But nothing could ever detract from the achievements of the 1st and 2nd Regiments of *KGL* Dragoons that hot summer's day.

The defence of the farmstead of La Haye Sainte to the fore of Wellington's centre on 18 June 1815 was entrusted to Major George Baring and the 2nd *KGL* Light Battalion, supported by

* A vivid, although fictional, account is to be found in Sharpe's Sword by Bernard Cornwell (Collins, 1983) pages 288 to 300.

elements of the 1st Light Battalion and the light company of the 5th *KGL* Line Battalion — perhaps 463 officers, NCOs and men in all. From shortly after midday until 6 pm, Baring and his handful of men repulsed attack after attack by the massively stronger I Corps of Général Drouet d'Erlon, particularly Quiot's division. Every assault was repelled despite the fires that were soon raging around the farmhouse and its out-buildings. It was only when Baring ran out of ammunition and failed to receive re-supply that at about 5.30 pm, as Marshal Ney in person led up a fresh attack, the *KGL* — now only 42 men still on their feet, was forced to give up its hard-held position. Seventeen officers had become casualties (four killed), 160 rank-and-file were dead or wounded, and a further 29 were missing. Wellington in his victory despatch stressed the all-importance of the defence of Hougoumont Château by the Guards in front of his right flank; but he owed an almost equal debt to the intrepid light infantrymen from Hanover who gave their all in the protracted (albeit overwhelmed), defence by the few hundred Hanoverians protecting the approach to the centre of his Allied Army.

The *King's German Legion* was formed from exiled subjects of King George III in his capacity as Elector of Hanover in 1803, following the French occupation of his Electorate. It in due course comprised ten battalions of the line, two light battalions, five cavalry regiments (three of dragoons and two of hussars) and batteries of both foot and horse artillery. As the years passed and native German replacements could not be found in sufficient numbers, men of many nations were drafted into its ranks. Standards did not drop, however, and in spain the *KGL* cavalry was regarded as the best for outpost work in Wellington's Anglo-Portuguese army. At Waterloo, the *KGL* present numbered six battalions of line infantry, two of light, four regiments of cavalry (16 squadrons in all) and three batteries of artillery, a total of 395 officers and 7,291 other ranks. By the day's close, of these 129 officers and 1,821 rank and file had become casualties.

Clearly, therefore, the *KGL* played a major part in the wars against Napoleon from 1803 onwards, and particularly between 1808 and 1815. It is typical of the enterprise of Richard Brown and Chris Buckland, that Ludlow Beamish's classic *History of the King's German Legion* is now being made available again after being many years out-of-print. Now new generations of readers will be able to appreciate what this *corps d'élite* represented to the war effort against the First French Empire.

Dr. David G. Chandler,

Head, Department of War Studies,
The Royal Military Academy Sandhurst.

18 August, 1993.

PREFACE.

The claims of the king's German legion to the notice of the historian are founded upon the distinguished services of that corps in the British army, during the whole extent of a period marked by the greatest exertions which England has ever made, and the most brilliant victories which her arms have ever achieved.

Deprived, by a tissue of untoward circumstances, of the means of redressing, in the ranks of her national armies, the wrongs which their country had sustained, the disbanded Hanoverian military sought that object in those of Britain, and sacrificing the ties of home and kindred to the more exalted feeling of national honour, became voluntary exiles in another land, and fought for the recovery of their own, under the banners of England.

The commencement and termination of the late

war are coincident with similar periods in the history of the king's German legion. Throughout the whole of the peninsular campaigns they bore an active part, and few of those memorable engagements, whose names now stand commemorative of British valour, have not been honourably shared in by some part of the corps.

Such are the pretensions of the German legion to a place in history. It will now be right to shew the authenticity of the work which professes to record their services.

A few years after the reduction of the king's German legion in 1816, three distinguished members of the corps, whose long and conspicuous services had given them a personal knowledge of events well calculated to effect their object, determined upon writing a history of the legion, and the work was actually commenced. These officers had, however, proceeded but a short way towards the completion of their task, when, for various reasons, they were led to discontinue it. This circumstance was, several years after, mentioned to me by a zealous and gallant member of the late corps, who at the same time proposed that I should continue and complete the work, which, on his promising to provide me with the necessary materials, I undertook to attempt.

To this officer,* therefore, and to the distinguished individuals alluded to,† who, upon my intentions being made known to them, liberally placed the result of their labours at my disposal, are the public indebted for the documents which form the basis of this history. A residence of more than twelve months in Hanover enabled me to add to these, other important documents, and the same occasion afforded me the advantage of personally communicating with many of the principal actors in the scenes which are here described.

To the gracious interposition of his royal highness the duke of Cambridge I am indebted for having obtained access to the Archives of the Hanoverian Guelphic Order, from which authentic source all accounts of the individual achievements of the non-commissioned officers and soldiers of the corps have been taken.

* Captain Christoph Heise, K.H. Royal Hanoverian Rifle-Guards.

† Major-general sir George Julius Hartmann, K.C.B. and K.C.H. Royal Hanoverian Artillery.

Colonel George Baring, K.C.H. Royal Hanoverian Grenadier Guards.

Colonel Ernest von Linsingen, K.C.H. Adjutant-general to the Hanoverian Cavalry.

The principal returns have been specially prepared for the work by captain Lewis Benne, formerly attached to the staff of the king's German legion, and now to that of his royal highness the duke of Cambridge. The original illustrations of the different uniforms were drawn by captain count Castell, of the third Hanoverian hussars.

Thus provided, it only remained for me to collate the several manuscripts, investigate the doubtful points, and unite the whole into an historical form.

Those who have attempted the compilation of history will readily believe that one part of this duty, namely, the investigation of facts, has not been unattended with difficulty. The frequent discrepancy between statements respecting the king's German legion in the several works on the Peninsular war, which have appeared in this country, and those that were furnished to me in manuscript by the officers of the corps, rendered it, in this case, peculiarly embarrassing; and I have been, in many instances, reluctantly obliged to reject the authority of standard works, whose authors, however correct in their relation of all matters connected with British regiments, have evidently been unprovided with that information which could alone enable them to be equally accurate with regard to the German legion. On these grounds a special account of the operations of the German troops during the late war may be allowed to claim an interest distinct from that which has been excited by the annals of the British army in general, during that period.

If, notwithstanding my efforts to be correct, some inaccuracies should have evaded my examination, I trust they will be attributed rather to that impenetrable veil with which truth is so often found encompassed, than to a want of diligence in prosecuting the inquiry; and that, if that extreme minuteness of detail, which in the history of a separate corps may, perhaps, be expected, be not invariably found, the words of the conscientious Barthelemy will be accepted in justification of such deficiencies:—" J'ai mieux aimé supprimer certains faits, que de ne les établir que sur des conjectures."*

Having found, during my residence in Hanover, that a difference of opinion existed there, both with regard to the comparative merits of the king's German legion in the British army, and with regard

* Mémoires sur Anacharsis.

to the manner in which the corps was disposed of after it had been placed under the Hanoverian government; feeling also that my own judgement was not unbiassed on these questions, I have studiously avoided entering upon them. The encouragement of party feeling is not the object of this work, and I have preferred leaving my readers, unschooled, to the simplicity of facts, to influencing their judgements with the prejudices of a partizan.

LONDON, June, 1832.

TABLE OF CONTENTS.

CHAPTER I.

CHAPTER II.

CHAPTER III.

CHAPTER IV.

CHAPTER V.

CHAPTER VI.

CHAPTER VII.

CHAPTER VIII.

CHAPTER IX.

CHAPTER X.

CHAPTER XI.

CHAPTER XII.

CHAPTER XIII.

CHAPTER XIV.

CHAPTER XV.

CHAPTER XVI.

CHAPTER XVII.

CHAPTER XVIII.

CHAPTER XIX.

CHAPTER XX.

CHAPTER XXI.

CHAPTER XXII.

APPENDIX.

List of the printed works and manuscripts to which reference is made in this Volume.

PRINTED WORKS.

No. 1. Darstellung der Lage worin sich das Hannöverische militair in den Monathen May, Juny, und July, 1803, befand. 1 heft 8vo. 1803.

2. Historische Berichtigungen des öffentlichen Urtheils über die durch die Französische Occupation des Kurfürstenthums Hannover daselbst veranlassten Militairischen Maasreglen. 2 heft 8vo. Niedersachsen, 1803.

3. Allgemeine Literatur-Zeitung, Nos. 55 and 57, Halle, 1804.

4. History of the reign of Geo. III., by Robert Bisset, L.L.D. 6 vol. 8vo. London, 1820.

5. The siege of Copenhagen; or, Documents comprehending an Official Detail of the Bombardment of that City, together with a Danish Narrative of the dreadful calamities suffered by the inhabitants in consequence thereof; the whole compiled from original British and Danish papers. By an Officer from Copenhagen. To which is prefixed an historical account of the City of Copenhagen. 1 vol. 12mo. London, 1808.

6. Bulletins of the Campaigns of the British troops, from 1807 to 1811, compiled from the London Gazettes.

7. History of the War in the Peninsula and in the South of France, from the year 1807 to the year 1814. By W. F. P. Napier, C.B. colonel H.P. forty-third regiment, and member of the Royal Swedish Academy of Military Sciences. Vols. 1, 2, and 3, London, 1828, 1829, and 1830.

8. Narrative of the Peninsular war from 1808 to 1813 by lieutenant-general Charles William Vane, marquess of Londonderry, G.C.B. and G.C.H. colonel of the tenth royal hussars, 2 vol. 8vo. London, 1820.

9. Letters from Flushing, containing an account of the expedition to Walcheren, Beveland, and the mouth of the Scheldt, under the command of the Earl of Chatham, with a topographical and statistical account of the Islands of Walcheren and Beveland. By an Officer of the eighty-first regiment. 1 vol. 8vo. London, 1809.

10. A short narrative of the late campaign of the British army, under the orders of the right honourable the earl of Chatham, K.G. with preliminary remarks on the topography and channels of Zealand, 1 vol. 8vo. London, 1810.

No. 11. Further strictures on those parts of colonel Napier's History of the Peninsular war, which relate to the military opinions and conduct of general lord viscount Beresford, to which is added a report of the operations in the Alemtejo and Spanish Estremadura, during the campaign of 1811, by major-general sir Benjamin d'Urban, 1 vol. 8vo. London, 1832.

MANUSCRIPTS.

GERMAN.

No. 1. Narrative of general Frederick von der Decken, G.C.H. Master-general of the Hanoverian ordnance, formerly lieutenant-general and colonel-commandant of the artillery, late king's German legion.

2. Narrative of colonel Ernest von Linsingen, K.C.H. adjutant-general to the Hanoverian cavalry, formerly captain in the first hussars, and major half-pay third hussars, late king's German legion.

3. Journal of colonel Ernest von Linsingen, K.C.H. &c. &c &c.

4. Correspondence of colonel Ernest von Linsingen, K.C.H. &c. &c. &c.

5. Narrative of colonel George Krauchenberg, K.C.H. inspector of the Hanoverian cavalry, formerly captain in the first hussars, and major half-pay third hussars, late king's German legion.

6. Narrative of sir Lewis Moeller, K.C.H. privy councillor of legation to the Hanoverian mission in London, and secretary to the royal Hanoverian Guelphic order.

7. Journal of the first light battalion, late king's German legion.

8. Narrative of colonel George Baring, K.C.H. commanding the first brigade of Hanoverian infantry, formerly captain in the first light battalion, and major half-pay second light battalion, late king's German legion.

9. Narrative of major-general sir George Julius Hartmann, K.C.B. and K.C.H. of the Hanoverian artillery, lieutenant-colonel late king's German artillery.

10. Journal of major Rautenberg, K.H. formerly captain in the first light battalion, and captain half-pay veteran battalion, late king's German legion.

11. Journal of the second regiment of hussars, late king's German legion.

12. Journal of the third regiment of hussars, late king's German legion.

13. Journal of major Heinemann, K.H. captain half-pay fifth line battalion, late king's German legion.

No. 14. Journal of major Christian Heise, captain half-pay third hussars, late king's German legion.

15. Narrative of the loss of the Augustus Cæsar transport, by major von Borstel, K.H. captain half-pay first line battalion, late king's German legion.

16. Narrative of doctor Rathje, surgeon in the Hanoverian service, and assistant surgeon half-pay second line battalion, late king's German legion.

17. Narrative of captain George Meyer, K.H. of the third Hanoverian hussars, captain half-pay third hussars, late king's German legion.

18. Journal of third line battalion, late king's German legion.

19. Narrative of lieutenant-colonel Quintus von Goeben, K.H. of the sixth regiment of Hanoverian cavalry, (lancers,) captain half-pay third hussars, late king's German legion.

20. Correspondence of the late major-general Martin, K.C.H. formerly major in the first light battalion, late king's German legion.

21. Journal of doctor Grosskopf, K.H. staff-surgeon in the Hanoverian service, and formerly surgeon in the third hussars, late king's German legion.

22. Journal of captain Schnath, adjutant, half-pay, first line battalion, late king's German legion.

23. Journal of lieutenant Tiensch, half-pay second line battalion, late king's German legion.

24. Journal of captain Stutzer, adjutant half-pay seventh line battalion, late king's German legion.

25. Notes of major von Holle, K.H. captain half-pay second line battalion, late king's German legion.

26. Narrative of lieutenant-colonel George von der Decken, K.H. of the Hanoverian hussar guards, captain half-pay first hussars, late king's German legion.

27. Notes of lieutenant-colonel William von der Decken, K.H. of the Hanoverian rifle guards, captain half-pay second line battalion, late king's German legion.

28. Guelphic Archives, being the attested memorials of the non-commissioned officers and soldiers of the late king's German legion, who claimed the Guelphic medal for extraordinary services during the late war.

29. Narrative of the late captain Bussman, captain half-pay king's German artillery.

30. Journal of eighth line battalion, late king's German legion.

31. Narrative of captain von Hohnstedt of the eighth regiment of Hanoverian infantry, captain, half-pay, sixth line battalion, late king's German legion.

Page 114, line 27, *for* " Freiderickswerk" *read* " Friederickswerk."
.. 115, .. margin, *for* " 1803" *read* " 1807."
.. 116, .. 6, *for* " Freidericksberg" *read* " Friedericksberg."
.. 119, .. 20, *for* " Oschenskiold" *read* " Castenskjold."
.. 122, .. 1, *for* " Linginsen" *read* " Linsingen."
.. 124, .. 1, *for* " Schnüring" *read* " Schneering."
.. 126, .. 18, *for* " adjutant-general" *read* " quarter-master-general."
.. 130, .. 3, *for* " twenty-six" *read* " sixteen."
.. 131, .. 6, *for* " first" *read* " seventh."
.. 131, .. 9, *for* " same regiment" *read* " first line battalion."
.. 131, .. 28, *for* " legion" *read* " battalion."
.. 135, .. 20, dele " his."
.. 137, .. 23, *for* " Magens" *read* " Magius."
.. 139, .. last line, *for* " two hundred and twenty-six" *read* " four hundred and sixty."
.. 141, .. 25, dele " all."
.. 163, margin, *for* " Gruben" *read* " Goeben."
.. 171, line 2, *for* " Puebla de Sante" *read* " Pueblo de San."
.. 171, .. 4, *for* " there" *read* " three."
.. 171, .. 6, *for* " Puebla" *read* " Pueblo."
.. 171, .. 24, *for* " brigadier-general" *read* " lieutenant-colonel."
.. 172, .. 10, *for* " Ribiadavia" *read* " Ribadavia."
.. 173, .. 4, *for* " which" *read* " who."
.. 179, .. margin *for* " journal" *read* " narrative."
.. 182, .. 1, *for* " compliment" *read* " complement."
.. 187, .. note, *for* " Fienck" *read* " Tiensch."
.. 189, note, The four line battalions were at this period in the actual command of the following officers:—

1st line battalion......major Bodecker.
2d do. ....lieut.-col. Brauns.
5th do. ....major Gerber.
7th do. ....major Berger.

.. 192, .. 5, *for* " Ragoa" *read* " Regoa."
.. 192, .. margin, *et passim*, *for* " Hölle" *read* " Holle;" *for* " first line battalions" *read* " second line battalion."
.. 209, .. 17-18, *for* " eighteen rank and file killed, two officers and nine rank and file wounded" *read* " nineteen rank and file killed, one officer, five serjeants, and forty-four rank and file wounded."
.. 216, .. 27, *et passim*, *for* " bombadier" *read* " bombardier."
.. 219, .. 7, *for* " regiment" *read* " corps."
.. 223, last line, *for* " Soult" *read* " South."
.. 227, line 1, *for* " Ruttern" *read* " Ruttem."
.. 228, .. 9, *for* " laying" *read* " lying."
.. 228, .. 23, *for* " Ost-Zobourg" *read* " Oost-Soubourg."
.. 240, .. 8, *for* " at" *read* " the."

Page 241, line 2, *et passim*, *for* " Liefkenshock" *read* " Liefkenshoek."
.. 259, .. 18, *et passim*, *for* " Fiurama" *read* " Fiumara."
.. 260, .. 3, *for* " Capo d'Arno" *read* " Capo d' Armi."
.. 261, .. 19, *for* " aid" *read* " aide."
.. 268, .. 28, *for* " Golegoa" *read* " Golegão."
.. 273, margin *for* " Liniungen" *read* " Linsingen."
.. 277, line 3, *for* " strength" *read* " number."
.. 277, .. 26, *for* " squadrons" *read* " Hanoverians."
.. 279, .. 20, *for* " da Bispo" *read* " do Bispo."
.. 284, .. 13, *for* " Louvea" *read* " Gouveia."
.. 285, .. 4, *after* " the" *read* " British."
.. 285, .. 14, *for* " Mongualde" *read* " Mangualde."
.. 286, .. 6, *for* " killed" *read* " wounded."
.. 286, .. 7, *for* " lieutenant Decken and four men were wounded" *read* " lieutenant Decken's horse was killed, and four men were wounded."
.. 286, .. 8, *after* " two" *read* " hussar."
.. 287, line 7, *et passim*, *for* " Mortagao" *read* " Martagao."
.. 288, .. 23, *for* " Dao" *read* " Dão."
.. 321, .. 19, *for* " Puente" *read* " Ponte."
.. 322, .. 6, *for* " Fons" *read* " Foz."
.. 327, last line of text, *for* " third" *read* " fifth."
.. 328, margin, *for* " Journal of colonel von Linsingen" *read* " London Gazette."
.. 328, line 13, *for* " Poco Velha" *read* " Poco Velho," after " morning" *read* " of the fifth."
.. 342, .. 7, *for* " his" *read* " the French."
.. 342, .. 14, *for* " Solana" *read* " Solano."

APPENDIX, No. VI. A.

First column, *for* " approved" *read* " approval."
Column rank and file, transfer the 38 recruits " deserted," to column " Total."

B.

Names of officers shipwrecked, *for* " Geogre" *read* " George," *for* " Farber" *read* " Färber."

Memorandum, *for* " 37" *read* " 337."

No. XI. B.

Names of officers wounded, *after* " lieutenant Ernest Poten severely" *dele* " arm amputated."

HISTORY

OF THE

KING'S GERMAN LEGION

Plate Section

Plate 1.

First Hussars.

Second Hussars.

Plate 2.

THIRD HUSSARS.

FIRST DRAGOONS. (1812)

Plate 3.

Second Dragoons. (1812)

First Dragoons. (1803)

Plate 4.

FIRST LIGHT INFANTRY.

Plate 5.

Second Light Infantry.

Plate 6.

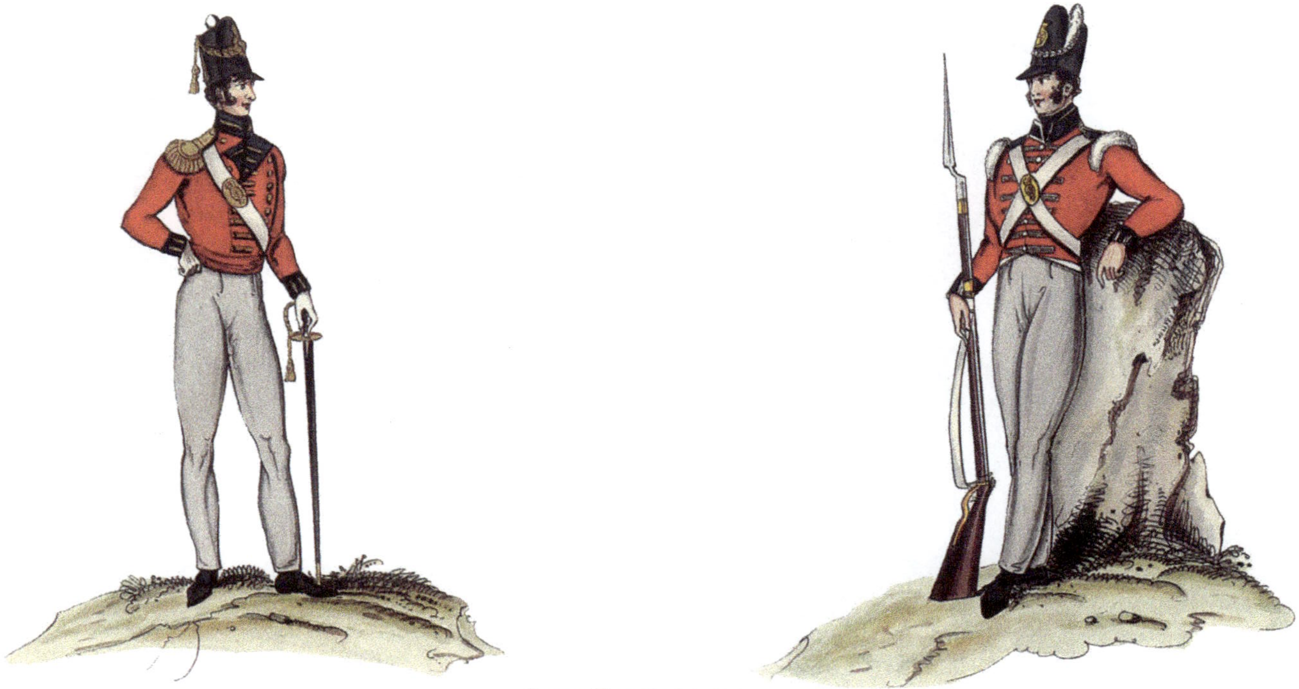

LINE BATTALIONS.

Plate 7.

Skirmishers.

Plate 8.

ARTILLERY

Plate 9.

PRIVATE OF FOOT ARTILLERY.

OFFICER OF ENGINEERS.

THE

HISTORY

OF THE

KING'S GERMAN LEGION.

CHAPTER I.

THE electorate of Hanover had not yet recovered 1803.
from the deep wounds which the French revolu- March.
tionary war, the support of an army on her frontier, and, above all, the occupation of her territory by Prussia, had inflicted upon the resources of the state, and the spirit of the people; when new misunderstandings between France and England threatened her with a renewal of those afflictions from which she had just been relieved.

Measures of mistaken economy, and an extreme apathy on the part of the Hanoverian government, had been for some years operating to lessen the military importance of the electorate, and now rendered it ill qualified to assume a defensive position; the army had been reduced, the for-

1803. March. tresses neglected, great part of the existing force suffered to return home on leave of absence, many vacancies in regiments, both among officers and men, had been allowed to remain unfilled, and a general relaxation of military discipline and military spirit had been permitted to engender.

Official Returns. In March, 1803, the nominal strength of the army, including cavalry, infantry, artillery, and engineers, amounted to 15,546: of these, however, more than one third were on furlough, and the effective force could not be fairly estimated at more than ten thousand men.

Such was the strength of the Hanoverian army, when M. de Talleyrand's celebrated *note verbale* to the English ambassador* sufficiently indicated the first consul's designs upon the electorate.

According to the principles of justice, good faith, and the acknowledged rights of nations, Hanover was justified in an expectation of being allowed to remain an undisturbed spectator of the impending contest; under the treaty of Basle she could claim neutrality, and, as an integral part of the German empire, the protection afforded her by the peace of Luneville. But such claims had little weight with the then ruler of France. Under the pretext that if

* Communicated to lord Whitworth at Paris, on the 11th of March, and which stated,—" If we do not receive satisfactory explanation respecting these armaments in England, and if they actually take place, *it is natural* that the first consul should march 20,000 men into Holland. These troops being once in the country, *it is natural* that an encampment should be formed on the frontiers of Hanover," &c.

the sovereign of two countries declare war as king of one, his other territory must necessarily be involved in the same contest, Napoleon justified his occupation of Hanover. 1803. March.

That such a calamity, however, was to be apprehended by the electorate, her prime minister, the baron von Lenthe, would not allow himself to believe: that he who had violated the most solemn engagements of the treaty of Luneville; who, instead of restoring the independence of Switzerland, Holland, and the Italian republic, was endeavouring to fix more firmly his despotic rule in those subjected countries;—he who, alike uninfluenced by national or personal honour, sought to evade his sacred promise to the German emperor, and withhold all indemnification to the grand duke Ferdinand for the loss of Tuscany;—he who had scarcely ratified the treaty of Amiens, when he took measures for its violation;—should now meditate a breach of faith with the empire by invading one of her provinces, baron von Lenthe persisted in considering a groundless and unwarrantable alarm; and notwithstanding the king's message to parliament of the 8th of March, the consequent preparations in England, (of which he, residing in London, must have been fully aware,) M. Talleyrand's *note verbale* of the 11th, and the still more decisive evidence of approaching war which an actual assembly of French troops in Holland furnished,—this unsuspecting statesman persevered in

1803. March. an opinion that no hostilities would take place, and succeeded in rendering his colleagues in Hanover equally insensible to the gathering storm.

But his majesty was far from encouraging so groundless an expectation, and it must ever be lamented, by all those who value the attachment of a loyal people, and the feelings of a brave and devoted army, that the energetic measures which were on this occasion devised by our benevolent sovereign for the defence of the electorate and the protection of her troops, should have been frustrated by the false confidence of his Hanoverian minister.

Narrative of general von der Decken, MSS.

So early as the end of March, major von der Decken, aid-de-camp to his royal highness the duke of Cambridge, (who, without being a member of the Hanoverian cabinet, served as lieutenant-general in that army,) was commissioned, at an interview with which he was honoured by his majesty in London, to acquaint his royal highness that his majesty's wishes were, first, that endeavours should be made to procure assistance from Prussia, in case of which being unsuccessful, the troops to be drawn towards Stade, and if then found unable to oppose any effective resistance to the enemy, that they should be there embarked for England.

His late majesty, then prince of Wales, and their royal highnesses the dukes of York and Clarence, strenuously supported the views of the king, and the English ministry sanctioned the preparation of transports for the conveyance of the Hanoverian troops, and their being taken into British pay on their arrival in England. 1803. March.

This considerate and judicious design was, however, totally defeated by the inflexible pertinacity of baron von Lenthe; and the non-interference of the British government in Hanoverian politics left that minister at full liberty to guide the helm of the electorate, and to dictate to his acquiescent colleagues a temporizing and pernicious policy.

However, after England had been one month in expectation of, and in preparation for, an event of which his majesty's message to parliament intimated the approach, baron von Lenthe decided that some precautionary measures on the part of Hanover were also advisable, and in furtherance of this view an official communication was despatched from London, on the 8th of April, addressed to field marshal von Walmoden Gimborn, then at the head of the Hanoverian army. This document stated that, "it appeared adapted to circumstances to employ the present time, usually devoted to the exercise of the troops, to call in all those on furlough, and to make arrangements for a camp of instruction, in order that the regiments might be brought together without exciting public attention, and thus, at all

Darstellung der Lage worin sich das Hannöveresche Militair in dem Monathen May, Juny, und July, 1803, befand.*

* This work is supposed to have been written by marshal Walmoden: it was published in Hanover, in the German and French languages, and nearly all the statements are verified by copies of official documents appended to the work."

1803. March. events, to prevent the scattered garrisons from being unexpectedly cut off':" it further empowered marshal Walmoden to take the steps necessary on his part for the execution of the proposed plan, which was stated to be, for the present, " solely limited to measures of precaution."

The official note which contained these instructions reached marshal Walmoden on the 19th, and on the following day he sought further instruction from the ministry respecting the prescribed arrangements, which not corresponding with his own notions of the best means to be adopted for putting the country into a state of preparation against danger, also feeling doubtful as to the extent of preparation intended to be made, led him to submit to the ministry the following queries:—

Darstellung, &c.

In what part of the country are the troops to be assembled?

Upon what place are they to fall back?

Is the fortress of Hameln to be put in a state of defence?

What are in general our means of resistance? and,

To what extent shall we be permitted to employ them?

The field marshal added his conviction that the execution of " the measures which the approach of danger would require, could not be effected in a short time," and concluded by stating that " he found himself obliged to press most urgently for a decision respecting the points of preparation alluded to, or to give up the possibility of being able to execute them with promptitude." 1803. April.

The reply of the Hanoverian cabinet, on the 22d, was as inconsistent as extraordinary.

" The ministry," say they, " entirely acknowledges the necessity for detailed determinations, which the object in view requires; nevertheless, as those determinations depend entirely upon the future developement of affairs, it would be not only dangerous but altogether impracticable to countenance them with too much warmth, and to fix positively upon points of detail. On the whole the ministry view two points as the most important to be first decided on; the one to avoid for the moment all that could *give umbrage*, or create notoriety, *(faire un éclat,)* by which what is feared might be brought on; the second to concert all the preparatory measures which are not contrary to the first point of view, and which might assist the execution of the king's orders." Darstellung, &c.

The field marshal, perceiving clearly that this note of the cabinet empowered him literally *to do nothing*, decided upon laying the state of his hereditary dominions before the king himself, and on the 27th addressed a letter to London, in which he unreservedly detailed the situation of the country.

" The army," said he, " is very different from what it appears on paper: it has been considerably

1803. April. Darstellung, &c.

weakened by desertion, which sudden changes and alarms will increase, and it is absolutely deprived of all means of being recruited. We shall be obliged to leave small garrisons in several places; the fortress of Hameln cannot be abandoned; and all the infantry that can be calculated on amounts to ten thousand bayonets: the cavalry want more than five hundred horses, part of which are employed by the horse artillery, from whom they cannot be taken, and even replaced would be useless, unless at the same time means are found to supply one hundred and forty men, which the cavalry want to complete," &c.

Meantime the designs of France became more developed, and the title of *armée d'Hanovre*, given to the troops which she had collected on the Dutch frontier, rendered their destination no longer doubtful.

Marshal Walmoden, therefore, delayed not in taking every step compatible with the restriction by which his exertions were bounded: the Elbe and Weser were reconnoitered, the necessary field equipage put in preparation, the repairs required at Hameln commenced, and on the 4th of May an exact account of what had been done was laid by him before the ministry, who were at the same time informed that, "in consequence of the interdiction of all preparations that might give '*umbrage*,'*

* The following anecdote, in explanation of the meaning attached by the ministry to the word "*umbrage*," was related to me in Hanover. The

he found himself incapable of making any further arrangements." 1803. May.

This declaration the marshal supported, on the following day, by a long and pressing note in which the ministry were plainly told that, "according to the principles which they had laid down, their measures literally amounted to *doing nothing;*" a considerable augmentation of the army was strongly urged upon them; the details consequent upon this measure brought to their notice; and, finally, they were requested to inform the marshal, who naturally felt that he would be held responsible for the execution of their plans, what were their absolute intentions with regard to the defence of the country. Darstellung, &c.

The ministry had already decided upon authorizing the assembly of the camp of instruction, suggested to them by the official communication from London, which has been already mentioned, when this note reached them; and marshal Walmoden was consequently, on the following day, empowered to undertake the arrangements necessary for the accomplishment of that object: no

general commanding the Hanoverian army having been instructed by the ministry not to suffer the troops to fire, and only in case of emergency "*to use the bayonet with moderation,*" Baron A——, one of that body, was questioned by a friend, "whether such orders had absolutely been given," and "what was meant by *using the bayonet with* CHRISTIAN *moderation?*" The minister, in reply, acknowledged "that the statement was substantially true," but declared "that the word '*Christian*' was an uncharitable addition of the public!"

1803. May. Darstel-lung, &c. notice, however, was taken of his observations respecting an augmentation of the army, and the camp of instruction appeared to be the utmost extent of preparation on which they were disposed to venture.

With reference to this measure, marshal Walmoden reported, on the 9th of May, that the regiments could not be brought together in less than three weeks. The intelligence from London now furnished a confirmation of the probability that war would be immediately declared, and that from Holland announced the approach of a French army. Walmoden, therefore, again addressed the ministry, and after detailing the arrangements which he had been enabled to make, recurred thus energetically to the important point of augmentation.

"The ministry have already been informed of the actual number of effective troops, and can judge what will remain after Hameln has been garrisoned with three thousand men; double the number remaining is necessary to support an obstinate and continued defence; the insufficiency of so weak a corps, however stimulated by duty its ardour and bravery may be, cannot escape the observation of the ministry. But we have resources; this is a fact not doubtful; they existed formerly, and we did not hesitate to have recourse to them under circumstances of much less danger than those which probably now await us. * * * *

"This is no question of war with foreign countries; we seek but to defend our own, to protect the property of individuals, our own homes, and to ensure our personal safety. Who would withhold his person and all his exertions from a co-operation in this defence? Arms and ammunition are not wanting; we have only to assemble the combatants. The field-marshal feels confident that they will be found if proper measures be taken to procure them."

1803.

May.

Darstellung, &c.

"If we should even be unable to assemble such an army as the electorate furnished during the seven years' war, we may at least calculate on collecting, in a short time, from twenty-eight to thirty thousand men.

"A corps of this strength would always render an absolute defence possible, and, even anticipating the most unfortunate consequences, that of being obliged to yield to a superior force, the position must be again laid down, that it is only with arms in our hands, and provided with a respectable force, that we can hope to obtain an equitable, and not a disgraceful capitulation."

This note was drawn up by marshal Walmoden in concert with his royal highness the duke of Cambridge, who, however, did not place much dependence upon the doubtful prospect of a capitulation, (more than once alluded to by marshal Walmoden,) but strongly advocated the more vigorous measure of determined resistance.

The deputies for the province of Calenberg

1803. May. Darstellung, &c.

(Calenbergsche Landstande) also advocated defensive measures; and to these united counsels the ministry at length yielded. An augmentation of the army from twenty-five to thirty thousand men was decided on, and the note of the 13th of May, which communicated to marshal Walmoden this acquiescence in his proposition, invited him, at the same time, to a personal communication with the ministry; a freedom of intercourse which, although so imperatively called for by the official activity and expedition which the state of the country demanded, had yet, up to this moment, never been offered to him.

1803.

May.

CHAPTER II.

On the 13th of May, therefore, about two months after the king's message to parliament was known in Hanover, the government of that country decided upon taking the first step of any value towards its defence, and the manner in which this was attempted to be put in execution was singularly unhappy. Darstellung, &c.

The belief implied in marshal Walmoden's note of the 11th of May, that no subject of the electorate would withhold his personal exertions from the defence of the country, if proper means were adopted for calling them into action, which opinion was afterwards supported by his verbal expressions to the same effect, was adopted by the ministry to such an extent as to induce them to issue a proclamation on the 16th of May, which set forth, "that, although the king, as elector and member of the German empire, had determined to observe the most strict neutrality with regard to the points of difference between the governments of England and France, yet as the movement of troops in Holland made evident the possibility of the existing negotiations not terminating pacifically, it was, therefore, necessary to ascertain, without delay, the Appendix, No. I. A.

1803. May. number of inhabitants capable of bearing arms; that, merely with this view, the magistrates were required to make out a complete list of all subjects of the government, and *solemnly to bind them to place themselves, in case of necessity, at its disposi-*

Appendix, No. I. A. *tion, for the defence and deliverance of the country, for so long a period as the necessity may exist and the defence of the land require.*"

"Any one avoiding this engagement by removing himself out of the country, should," it was added, "forfeit his property and patrimony without hope of pardon."

This proclamation, which was naturally interpreted to be a requisition for a *levée en masse* of the inhabitants, was received with marked dissatisfaction throughout the country: whole districts *(amts bezirke)* formally refused to comply with its demands; others required time to think, and employed that time in sending all their sons out of the country who were capable of bearing arms. The reports which poured in to the ministry from the authorities charged with the execution of their orders, soon communicated to them these fatal consequences of their incipient measure, and impressed them with the necessity of speedily interposing some preventative: another proclamation was, therefore, issued on the 24th, which explicitly declared that "the views of the government had never been directed to a *levée en masse*, and that in requiring a list of all subjects capable of bearing arms, they did so merely for the purpose of being able to call out the number of men necessary to complete the regular army, in which it was intended they should serve in the capacity of regular soldiers, for so long a period as the defence of the country required." 1803. May. Appendix No. 1. B.

This contradictory document served only to confirm the people in the opinion that a *levée en masse* was originally intended, and impressed them with no favourable opinion of the candour or firmness of their ministry.

Meantime, another communication from London added to the difficulties and discouragement which now seemed daily to present new impediments to the adoption of any vigorous or decided measures. This note, which was addressed to general Walmoden in reply to his statement of the 27th of April, acknowledged the painful feelings with which his representations had been received, and rendered justice to the zeal for the troops entrusted to his charge, by which these representations had been dictated; with regard, however, to that point on which it was so necessary that he should be precisely instructed, namely, whether, in case of invasion, an actual resistance was or was not to be made, it merely informed him that "the decision of this question must entirely depend upon the degree of utility which, under the circumstances, such a measure might be expected to afford; and Darstellung, &c.

1803. May. Darstellung, &c.

it would be superfluous to add that, if there was a probability of repulsing the enemy, and really defending the country, they should not hesitate in employing all possible resources to obtain this essential object. If, on the contrary, the too superior force of the enemy, and other too disadvantageous circumstances, should reduce them to feel satisfied with saving the most valuable effects, and that it should be necessary to limit themselves to withdrawing the corps into a position where there might be some probability of its receiving assistance, or effecting its embarkation, or, in fine, obtaining a less unfavourable capitulation, then the means to be employed should only be proportionate to these objects."

"However warm an interest," it continued, "his majesty may take in the safety and honour of his brave troops, the *paramount* attention which should be paid to the good of the country in general, and that of the subject, ought to prevent the adoption of measures, the weight of which would, without producing any general benefit, only augment those evils which are already inevitable. It is under this point of view that the ministry and the field-marshal should consider the subject: it is impossible, in consequence of the great distance, and the uncertainty respecting the events which may arise, to give here more precise orders. It is confidently felt that, if the troops be called upon, they will give new proofs of their bravery, and of their attachment to the king and his house, whose benevolent participation will be always insured to them," &c. 1803. May.

Discouraging and indefinite as these instructions were, they yet gave to marshal Walmoden and the ministry a power of deciding upon the course to be pursued; and although this latitude was coupled with a responsibility which gave every reason to apprehend that the result, and not the motive, of their measures would influence the public judgement upon them, they yet ventured to persevere in the preparations for defence, which had now been earnestly commenced. An augmentation of each infantry regiment to twelve hundred men, and a general enlistment for this supply were ordered and entered upon; the organization of a rifle corps, to be formed out of the game-keepers *(jagd-bedienten)* and other good marksmen, was authorized; conscriptions of horses were levied throughout the country; incessant exertions made to place Hameln in a state of defence; conspicuous endeavours shown by the officers of artillery to render that arm effective; in short, all that activity which a union of zeal, patriotism, and courage could give, was exhibited throughout the several military departments. Darstellung, &c.

But what years have destroyed cannot be made good in days; and a painful conviction was soon afforded that the decision of the ministry had been formed too late.

Major von der Decken, who, early in May, had

1803. May. been sent to Berlin for the purpose of endeavouring to obtain assistance from Prussia, returned from thence on the 30th of the same month, having been entirely unsuccessful in the object of his mission. Diplomatic intrigues, terminating in a strong note of Russia, which stated that the occupation of Hanover by Prussian troops would be considered by the autocrat as a declaration of war, were the immediate causes of this result; the duke of Brunswick also, who, it was proposed, should have the command of the allied army, declined the offer; and thus was the electorate, notwithstanding the boasted benefits of the Germanic confederation, the protecting solemnity of the imperial decree,* and her expected guardianship by the British government, thrown, finally, upon her own limited resources, and left single-handed to cope with the armies of France.

It was on this occasion that his royal highness the duke of Cambridge, in a letter addressed to baron von Lenthe, expressed those noble sentiments which will ever stand a bright example of princely feeling and patriotic devotion.—" *Rest assured,*" wrote his royal highness, " *that I will sacrifice my*

* In the imperial decree, addressed to the *Reichs Versammlung*, September 1, 1792, it is said,—" If an individual state or province of the empire be attacked by a foreign power, the whole of Germany is thereby attacked, and the confederation of the empire being thus involved, powerful assistance, from the united means of the empire, shall be afforded to the state attacked."

blood and life for a country to which I am so much attached." 1803. May.

But no sacrifice, however exalted, could repair the evils which misgovernment had brought on, or overcome the difficulties which, augmenting as the danger approached, now rose on every side around the measures of the ministry. The most effective young men, and those with whom their families could best dispense, having been prepared, by the proclamation of the 16th, for the enforcement of a *levée en masse,* and experience having taught them to regard with little apprehension the threatened consequences of evading the requisition, took advantage of the time which elapsed before the execution of the professed spirit of that proclamation was entered upon, to leave the country; the consequence of which abstraction from the number of eligible recruits, was, that, when the conscription absolutely began, the magistrates were in most places obliged to enrol only sons of farmers, boys of fourteen, nay, in many cases, fathers of families, and even then were unable to furnish their prescribed quota. Historische Berichtigungen.*

The severity of this alternative, also, produced universal dissatisfaction, and in some places absolute insurrection; the magistrates were personally

* Historiche Berichtigungen des offentlichen Urtheils über die durch die Französische Occupation des Kurfürstenthums Hannover daselbst veranlassten Militairischen Maasreglen. *Niedersachsen,* 1803.

This work is attributed to an officer of the late Hanoverian life-guards.

1803. May. Historische Berichtigungen.

insulted, and the new conscripts forcibly liberated. To quell these disorders it was necessary to send military detachments from the nearest garrisons, and thus was time lost, and the troops, instead of being occupied in preparations for active service in the field, were driven about the country to enforce compliance with the laws. To this cause of delay was added that produced by the apathy of individual magistrates, who treated a measure, on the expeditious effecting of which the preservation of the country might have depended, with the same phlegmatic tranquillity that they would observe towards an ordinary judicial proceeding, and considered the delay of a few days quite as unimportant in the one case as in the other.

The supply of horses was attended with equal difficulty; no general returns of the horses of the country were in possession of the government, and a protracted examination and selection of them was, therefore, ordered. This alone was an operation which required some weeks: then came petitions from individual *bauers*, to be exempted from the proposed levy: these had to be considered and reported upon, (for none of the usual forms and delays of office could be dispensed with;) and thus, when hours were of value, whole days were uselessly sacrificed. At length, horses were taken from the plough wherever they could be procured, and distributed among the cavalry, artillery, and train.

A most unaccountable ignorance, both of the

force and position, as well as of the designs of the enemy, existed among the authorities in Hanover. The French troops on the Yssel, which did not exceed twelve thousand ill-appointed combatants, without artillery, and having but a few squadrons of badly-mounted cavalry,* were magnified into an army of thirty thousand men; these, it was supposed, would not pass the Ems before the Hanoverian ministry had been allowed time and opportunity to negotiate, or should any hostile movement be commenced by them, that it would be confined to occupying the mouths of the Elbe and Weser, taking possession of Hamburgh and Bremen, and, perhaps, that part of the electorate situated near these places: the ministry, therefore, judged it prudent to abstain from any *offensive* measure, and decided that, even if it were positively ascertained that the French were advancing towards the frontier, their movements should be met by a deputation, having for its object the obtaining, by negotiation, favourable terms for the electorate.

1803. May.

Darstellung, &c.

The former suppositions were soon found to be fallacious, and the rapid advance of the French army rendered the execution of the measure with which it had been decided to meet that event, immediately necessary: two deputies, M. von Bremer, chief of the tribunal of justice, and lieutenant-colonel von Bock, of the regiment of

* Allg. Literatur-Zeitung, 1804.—Num. 55, p. 437.

1803. May. life-guards, were, therefore, selected, and commissioned to proceed forthwith towards the frontier, and endeavour to meet the French head-quarters either there or on their entrance into the country. At the request of Messrs. von Bremer and Bock, commercial counsellor Brandes was permitted to accompany them; and, supposing the march of the French army to be directed upon Quakenbrück, Wildeshausen, and, perhaps, Osnabrück, these three gentlemen left Hanover.

Darstellung, &c.

In order to gain further information respecting the enemy's line of march, the deputies took the road by Nienburg, Suhlingen, and Diepholtz, on which they soon ascertained that, instead of the French being, as was supposed, in march for Wildeshausen, they were moving upon Quakenbrück, at which place the head-quarters had absolutely arrived, the advanced guard being on the road to Diepholtz.

The departure of the deputies did not cause any relaxation in the defensive measures which had been commenced. On the 30th of May, the foot-guards left Hanover for Nienburg, and on the same day prince Schwartzburg's regiment repaired to Neustadt; a number of undrilled recruits, great part of whom had not yet been clothed, a few chasseurs, and one battery of horse-artillery, followed these regiments, marshal Walmoden's intention being to unite the whole on the right bank of the Weser, and form a line of defence extending from the junction of that river with the Aller to Stoltzenau. 1803. May.

Meantime, accounts of the enemy's continued advance towards the frontier followed each other with rapidity, and every succeeding hour rendered the situation of the electorate more critical; the reports made to marshal Walmoden by the different colonels of regiments, and from the *employés* of the army in general, as well respecting the measures which were in progress as those which could only have been commenced, determined him to order the transport of recruits to be discontinued; a mass of undisciplined men would, he conceived, prove rather an incumbrance than an acquisition to the army; it was, also, impossible to furnish them with ammunition and appointments, and he therefore felt justified in taking a step apparently inconsistent with his former suggestions. Darstellung, &c.

On the 1st of June his royal highness the duke of Cambridge took the command of the troops which had been brought together at Nienburg, amounting to about four thousand men; and his royal highness made immediate dispositions for surprising the enemy's advanced posts on the night of the 2d.

But, on the 2d of June, the deputies returned to Hanover with the appalling intelligence that the French commander, general Mortier, had been instructed to require the surrender of the whole

1803. June. Historische Berichtigungen.

Hanoverian army as prisoners of war, the object of the first consul being, as he informed them, to procure as many prisoners as possible, in order that he might be provided with the means of regaining, by exchange, those French troops which the English might capture during the approaching war.

In not insisting upon the troops becoming prisoners of war, general Mortier stated that he would be departing from his instructions, and suffering himself to be guided by the advice and opinion of the generals whom he had consulted, and who thought with him that the advantage of avoiding considerable losses on both sides, and the sacrifice of so many brave men, would justify him in thus departing from the express orders of the first consul.

The deputies were pressed to give a final answer, and were forewarned that the march of the French troops would not be discontinued, and that if the least resistance was made to them, and the French general had once crossed the Weser, he should no longer feel himself bound by any offer which he had previously made.

Darstellung, &c.

The whole effective force at general Walmoden's disposal might, at this moment, be confidently calculated at two thousand seven hundred cavalry and six thousand three hundred infantry; and the regiments coming from the Göttingen country were already in march, and would have reached the

Weser in a few days; neither marshal Walmoden, however, nor the ministry felt sufficient confidence in this force to trust to it either for the defence of the country against the invading army, or for the obtaining, by the successes with which its first offensive efforts were almost sure to be attended, more favourable conditions than those which Mortier had already proposed; and they therefore decided that the deputies should be sent back to the French head-quarters fully empowered to conclude a convention on those terms, at the same time endeavouring to moderate Mortier's demand if possible; which negotiation having been decided upon, his royal highness the duke of Cambridge was recalled from Nienburg. Between this place and Neustadt the prince was met by the deputies, now proceeding with their final instructions to the French head-quarters; and having learned from them that they were empowered to concede to that proposition of general Mortier which rendered it obligatory on the Hanoverian army not to serve against the French during the war, his royal highness, in accordance with a previous declaration which he had made, "never to become a party to such an engagement," placed his commission, on the following morning, at the disposal of the ministry, and the same day left the country for England.

1803. June. Darstellung, &c.

Notwithstanding the disposition which the government exhibited to terminate their labours

1803. June.

by negotiation, and the preliminaries which had absolutely commenced, the invading army continued to advance; and this determination to take advantage of the forbearance imposed upon the Hanoverians, led at length to an affair of outposts, in which the intruders received a just correction.

About three o'clock in the afternoon of the 2d of June, the advanced vidette of a cavalry piquet of thirty-two men, under the command of lieutenant von Linsingen, which was stationed near the village of Borstel, on the high road between Nienburg and Suhlingen, gave notice that the enemy were advancing. Lieutenant von Linsingen, agreeably to the course which he had been ordered in such a case to adopt, rode forward with a trumpeter bearing a flag of truce, and stated to the officer in command of the enemy's party, "that the French and Hanoverian authorities were already in treaty, and that the conference was likely to terminate in a capitulation on the part of the Hanoverians;" adding a request that the officer in command of the detachment would suspend hostilities until the result of the negotiation had been made known. The French officer replied by taking lieutenant Linsingen and his trumpeter prisoners, and forthwith attacking the Hanoverian piquet, which, deprived of its commander, fell back upon a detachment of the same strength, that was stationed as reserve in the rear, under lieutenant Krauchenberg. This officer, igno-

Narrative of colonel von Linsingen, MSS.

1803. June.

rant of what had passed, but seeing enough to convince him that, as far as the outposts were concerned, it was no affair of diplomacy, quickly drew the united detachments behind a small bridge, and prepared to check the enemy's advance. The French cavalry followed, and their advanced horsemen passed the bridge; but no further indulgence was shewn them by Krauchenberg, who, charging with impetuosity, drove the whole back on their support. The enemy were, however, too strong to admit of this attack being followed up with any chance of success, and, sending a few skirmishers after them, he retained his position. The French now re-assembled, and having brought off their wounded, again tried to force a passage; but in vain. Three several attempts were defeated, and seeing that no opening was likely to be effected by them across this part of the stream, they sent a detachment higher up to seek another passage. Krauchenberg, aware that this could be easily found, and his party thus surrounded, was about to retreat, when the brigade of the ninth and tenth dragoons, with two guns, and a light company of infantry, came up to his support. The Hanoverians now assumed the offensive, and the enemy as quickly commenced their retreat. Krauchenberg followed them to Borstle, where, apprehending an ambuscade, he drew off, and returned to his former position, having lost in the whole affair two men killed, and nine men and seventeen horses wounded. The casualties of the enemy could not be ascertained.

Narrative of colonel Krauchenberg, MSS.

1803. June. in consequence of their wounded having been brought off, but it must have at least equalled that of the Hanoverians.

Thus terminated the only collision of military force which attended the entrance of the French army into the electorate; for general von Hammerstein, who commanded the advanced corps, finding that he could not maintain his position beyond the Weser, ordered the troops under his command to retire behind that river; and on the 3d of June the following convention was signed by the Hanoverian deputies, and the French commander at Suhlingen.

Convention of Sublingen. I. The electorate of Hanover, as well as the forts appertaining thereto, shall be occupied by the French army.

II. The Hanoverian troops shall retire behind the Elbe. They will engage themselves, upon word of honour, not to commit any hostility, or bear arms against France or her allies, for so long a time as the war between France and England shall last. They shall not be absolved from this engagement until after having been exchanged for as many general officers, officers, non-commissioned officers, soldiers, or sailors of France, as England may have at her disposition.

III. No individual of the Hanoverian troops shall leave the place in which his residence shall have been appointed, without the knowledge of the general-in-chief.

IV. The Hanoverian army shall retire with the

honours of war. The regiments shall take with them their field-pieces. 1803. June.

V. The artillery, powder, arms, and ammunition of all kinds, shall be placed at the disposition of the French army.

VI. All effects whatever, belonging to the King of England, shall be placed at the disposition of the French army.

VII. All the public chests shall be put under sequestration, with the exception of that of the university of Göttingen.

VIII. Every English military person or agent of whatever kind, in the pay of England, shall be arrested by the orders of the general commanding in chief, and sent to France.

IX. The general commanding in chief will reserve to himself the power of making such changes in the government, and other authorities constituted by the elector, as he shall judge fitting.

X. All the French cavalry shall be remounted at the expense of Hanover. The electorate will provide alike for the pay, clothing, and subsistence of the French army.

XI. The worship of different religions shall be maintained upon the same footing on which it is at present established.

XII. All persons, all property, and the families of the Hanoverian officers, shall be placed under the protection of the French.

XIII. All the revenues of the country, as well

1803. June. the electoral domains as the public contributions, shall be placed at the disposition of the French government. Previous engagements will be respected.

XIV. The actual government of the electorate will abstain from exercising any kind of authority in the country occupied by the French troops.

XV. The general commanding in chief will levy upon the electorate of Hanover such contributions as he shall deem necessary to supply the wants of the army.

XVI. Any article upon which doubts may arise shall be interpreted favourably to the inhabitants of the electorate.

XVII. The preceding articles shall not prejudice any stipulation which may be made in favour of the electorate between the first consul and any mediating power.

Done at the head quarters at Suhlingen, the (14 *Prairial, an* xi.) 3d June, 1803.

Provided the first consul approves (*Sauf l'approbation du premier consul.)*

(Signed.) The lieutenant-general commanding in chief,

ED. MORTIER.

F. VON BREMER, judge of the electoral court of justice and provincial counsellor.

G. VON BOCK, lieutenant-colonel, commanding the regiment of Hanoverian life-guards.

CHAPTER III.

THE same day on which the convention was signed at Suhlingen, but before its details were known in Hanover, marshal Walmoden left the latter place for Celle, to take the command of the army. In the afternoon of the following day he was joined by colonel von Bock, who delivered to him a copy of the first five and seventeenth articles of the convention.

1803. June. Darstellung, &c.

As these six articles contained all that had any direct reference to the military, it was, perhaps, not material that the remaining ones should be immediately communicated to marshal Walmoden; but allowing him to remain ignorant of the condition added by general Mortier—to proceed with the fulfilment of the convention, uninformed of a clause which completely suspended its validity, was a most unpardonable and altogether unaccountable omission on the part of lieutenant-colonel von Bock, and one which, if it did not absolutely cause the disasters with which the Hanoverian army were soon after overwhelmed, materially hastened their approach.

In the full conviction that a valid document, equally binding upon the two contracting parties, had been signed at Suhlingen, Walmoden

1803. June. Historische Berechtigungen.

proceded to comply with the conditions which it imposed upon his army. The artillery was given up to French commissaries; orders for the immediate surrender of Hameln were sent to the officer who commanded that fortress; and so scrupulously, both in spirit and in letter, was this convention fulfilled on the part of the Hanoverian government, that the military stores of Stade and Harburg, which, agreeably to orders given before, but executed after, thesigning of the convention, had absolutely arrived in Lauenburg, were, on the reclamation of general Frere, returned to the arsenals from whence they had been removed, and the pontoons, on a like demand of general Mortier, were also given up to the French.

Thus deprived of their artillery and pontoons, the stores of two arsenals, and their only fortress, the Hanoverian troops proceeded to comply with that article which stipulated that they should retire behind the Elbe. Their route lay through the town of Lüneburg, and over a great part of that vast uncultivated country which bears its name.* Here, where money could scarcely supply the wants of an individual traveller, provisions and quarters for fifteen thousand souls, and from eight to nine thousand horses, were immediately required. The new formed magazines could not be made available to this

* The *Lüneburgher Haide (Lüneburgh Heath)*, which, with the exception of the province of Meppen, is the most desolate part of the Hanoverian dominions.

purpose, for they had been established on the Weser and Aller, and both time and means of transport for their conveyance were wanting; the French, also, laid claim to these stores under the authority of the convention: the commissariat were, therefore, obliged to depend upon whatever corn and forage the individual *amts* in the vicinity of the line of march might have at hand, and their own personal exertions in forming magazines wherever it was possible to collect supplies.

1803. June. Historische Berichtigungen.

In a desolate and unfruitful country, this operation would, under the most favourable circumstances, have been attended with difficulty; but when to the naturally ungenial soil, was added the discontent and disaffection of its possessors, the increase of impediment may well be imagined. Such a feeling had now arisen in the district of Lüneburg. A confused association of the idea, "arrival of the French," with that of "subversion of all order and civil government," pervaded the minds of the country people; an insurrectionary spirit was in many places openly exhibited, and the magistrates saw their orders derided, and their personal safety endangered. Abandoned, as a great part of the peasantry believed themselves to be by the army, they no longer acknowledged its claims upon their resources, and upon the only means which they possessed of supplying their own wants, and appeasing the expected demands of a rapacious enemy.

For these reasons it was that whole amt-districts

1803. June. Historische Berichtigungen.

not only refused delivering to the commissariat the supplies which they had at hand, and for which they were offered immediate and liberal payment, but in some places took forcible possession, and prevented the distribution, of those stores which had been already collected for the use of the troops.*

In such cases no alternative remained but to retake the articles in a similar manner, and thus it became necessary to resort to extremes, rarely called for but in an enemy's country. The difficulties under which the commissariat laboured, were also much increased by the obligation which was imposed on them at the same time to provide for the wants of the army during its march, and to prepare for its reception and abode in Lauenburg. The necessity for this double duty naturally divided their labours, and prevented the troops from immediately experiencing the full benefit of the arrangements that were made; however, the indefatigable zeal of the several officers of this department, and particularly the able and quickly concerted measures of commercial counsellor Heise, prevented either men or horses from suffering any material privation during the whole of the march.

But the cause and general nature of this movement towards the Elbe was too humiliating to the

* Some of the Lüneburgher *Bauers* are said to have accompanied their resistance to the requisitions, which were made upon them, with the following *naïf* observation, "*Sie wüssten ja nicht ob Bonaparte es haben wolle.*" You don't know but Bonaparte may want it!

feelings of a brave and loyal soldiery not to be productive of the most injurious effects upon their discipline, and desertion became frequent. Believing that the country was lost, knowing that it had been abandoned to the enemy without a struggle, and finding themselves reduced to a state of neutrality, many fancied that they were justified in throwing off their allegiance, and escaping from those duties which seemed so little likely to be attended with credit to themselves or benefit to the country.

1803.

June.

Historische Berichtigungen.

According to a preliminary understanding with the French commander, the space of ten days was to be allowed for the troops to effect their passage of the Elbe; but so desirous was Mortier to gain possession of his easy conquest, that before half that period had elapsed, French detachments appeared on the Hanoverian line of march, and the town of Lüneburg was, on the same night, occupied by troops of both armies. To such a collision, under all the irritating circumstances connected with their retreat, it was desirable that the Hanoverians should not be exposed; the march, therefore, was precipitated, and its difficulties were consequently increased.

The Elbe was to be crossed at three different points, to which the several regiments now hurried; but although the greater part of an enormous baggage-train had been shipped at Lüneburg,

1803. June. Historische Berichtigungen.

and from thence conveyed down the Ilmenau to the right bank of the Elbe, the passage of that river was not effected in less than five days, and even then several regiments had not yet reached the army.

On the 9th of June, marshal Walmoden established his head-quarters in the town of Lauenburg, and immediately proceeded to make a suitable disposition of his troops. On the 13th, lieutenant colonel von Bock, who had returned to Hanover for the purpose of superintending all minor details connected with the military, transmitted to him a complete copy of the convention of Suhligen; and this communication, which reached Walmoden on the 14th, first informed him of the clause with which Mortier had qualified his ratification of that document.

On the 15th of June, the French general informed colonel Bock that he had that day received the first consul's ratification of the convention of Suhlingen, on the condition that it were also ratified by the king of England, to whom, for that purpose, it had been sent.

This portentous intelligence, which was immediately communicated to marshal Walmoden, gave rise to the most painful apprehensions in the mind of that general, who clearly saw, in this specious conduct of Napoleon, an attempt to invalidate a convention, on the faith of which his army were already in possession of all the advantages which, under its authority, they were entitled to claim. 1803. June.

The first consul's conditional assent was communicated by M. de Talleyrand to lord Hawkesbury in the following terms :—

" Milord,

" Après un léger engagement avec les troupes de S. M. britannique, l'armée française occupe le pays d'Hanovre.

" Le premier consul n'ayant eu en vue que d'obtenir des gages pour l'évacuation de Malte, et de travailler à accomplir l'exécution du traité d'Amiens, n'a point voulu faire éprouver toutes les rigeurs de la guerre aux sujets de S. M. brittanique. Cependant, le premier consul ne peut ratifier la convention conclue entre l'armée française et celle de S. M., dont j'ai l'honneur de joindre ici copie, qu'autant qu'elle sera pareillement ratifiée par S. M. brittannique, et dans ce cas le premier consul me charge expressément de déclarer qu'il est dans son intention que l'armée du roi d'Angleterre en Hanovre soit d'abord echangée contre tous les matelots ou soldats que les vaisseaux de S. M. ont fait ou sont dans le cas de faire prisonniers.

" Le premier consul verrait avec peine que S. M. brittannique, en refusant de ratifier la dite convention, obligeât le gouvernement francais a traiter le pays d'Hanovre avec toute la rigueur de la guerre, et comme un pays qui, livré a lui-même, abandonné

1803. June. par son souvrain, se serait trouvé conquis sans capitulation, et laissé à la discretion de la puissance occupante.

" J'attendrai avec empressement, milord, que vous me fassier connaître les intentions de S. M. brittannique.

" Recevez, milord, l'assurance de ma plus haute consideration.

" (Signé) CH. MAU. TALLEYRAND."

Narrative of Sir L. Möller, MSS.

When this letter reached London, transports for the conveyance of the Hanoverian army to England lay ready at the Nore, and were to have sailed for the Elbe on the 13th or 14th inst., but anxious as was the king that their destination should be fulfilled, and indignant as the paternal monarch could not but feel on being informed of the humiliating conditions to which his brave Hanoverian troops had been subjected, his majesty was led to believe that a faithful observance of the terms of the convention would, however justifiably they might be resisted, now best serve the general interests of the electorate: the sailing of the transports was consequently countermanded, and the following reply to the communication of M. de Talleyrand despatched by his majesty's commands on the 15th inst.

" SIR, Downing-street, June 15th.

" I have laid before the king your letter of the 10th instant.

1803. June.

"I am commanded by his majesty to inform you that as he has always considered his character of elector of Hanover as distinct from his character of king of the united kingdom of Great Britain and Ireland he never can consent to acquiesce in any proceeding by which he shall sanction the idea that he is liable in justice to be attacked in the one capacity, for the line of conduct which he may have felt it to have been his duty to adopt in the other.

"This principle is not now advanced for the first time; it has been recognized by most of the powers of Europe, and by none more particularly than by the French government, who, in the year 1795, in consequence of his having acceded to the treaty of Basle, acknowledged the neutrality of his majesty in his capacity of elector of Hanover, at a time when they were engaged in a war with him as king of Great Britain.

"It has been further confirmed by the conduct of his majesty on the occasion of the treaty of Luneville, and by the arrangements which have lately taken place relative to the German indemnities, and to the constitution of the empire, which have been solely guaranteed by some of the principal powers of Europe, but to which his majesty, as king of Great Britain, was no party. Under these circumstances, his majesty has determined, in his character of elector of Hanover, to appeal to the empire, and to those powers of Europe who have guaran-

1803. June. teed the Germanic constitution, and thereby his rights and possessions as a prince of that empire.

"Until his majesty shall be informed of their sentiments, he has commanded me to say, that in his character of elector of Hanover, *he will scrupulously abstain from doing any act which can be considered as being in contravention to the stipulations contained in the convention that was concluded on the 3d of June, between the deputies appointed by the regency of Hanover and the French government.*

"I desire you to accept the assurances of the high consideration with which

"I have the honour to be, &c. &c.

"HAWKESBURY."

But this reply did not correspond with the expectations of the first consul, who, doubtless, calculated upon his majesty's unqualified refusal to sanction the convention of Suhlingen, and, consequently, upon being provided with a pretext for declaring it invalid; he, therefore, had recourse to the expedient of misinterpreting the expressions contained in lord Hawkesbury's reply, and general Mortier, having previously put his troops in motion for the Elbe, made requisitions of boats, and commenced planting batteries on that river, thus proclaimed this new ground of proceeding.

"EDOUARD MORTIER, lieutenant-general, &c. à son excellence M. le feld-maréchal comte de WALMODEN, &c. 1803. June. Darstellung, &c.

"Armée d' Hanovre, au quartier général à Lüneburg,
"le 11 messidor, an 11 de la republique Française.

"MONSIEUR LE MARÉCHAL,

"J'ai eu l'honneur de prévenir votre excellence, que le premier consul approuverait dans son entier la convention de Suhlingen si le roi d' Angleterre consentait lui-même à la ratifier. Il m'est donc pénible d'avoir à vous apprendre que lord Hawkesbury a fait connoître au citoyen Talleyrand, minister des rélations extérieurs, que sa majesté brittannique *se refusait formellement à cette ratification.*

"Votre excellence se rappelera qu'en 1757 pareille convention fut conclue à Kloster Zeven, entre M. de Richelieu et le duc de Cumberland; le roi d'Angleterre n'ayant pas voulu y adhérer, donna l'ordre à son armée de recommencer les hostilités.*

"C'est pour éviter le renouvellement des scènes qui eurent lieu alors, que mon gouvernement me charge de prévenir votre excellence que le refus de sa majesté brittanique rendait nulle la convention de Suhlingen.

* This was not a parallel case; for the duke of Cumberland's army was composed of troops in the pay of *England*, under the command of an *English* general.

1803. June. "Il est évident, M. le maréchal, que l'Angleterre sacrifie indignement vos troupes, dont la bravoure est reconnue de l'Europe entière ; mais il n'est pas moins que tout projét de defense de votre part serait illusoire, et ne ferait qu'attirer de nouveaux malheurs sur votre pays.

"Je charge le général Berthier, chef de l'état major général, de vous faire part de mes propositions ; je dois insister pour que votre excellence veuille bien me faire dans les vingt-quatre heures une réponse catégorique.

"L'armée que j'ai l'honneur de commander, est prête et n'attend que le signal du combat.

"Veuilles, M. le Maréchal, recevoir l'assurance de ma consideration distinguée.

"Ed. Mortier."

It is almost unnecessary to observe upon the misrepresentation which this letter contained; but if any doubt could reasonably have existed as to the nature of the king's intentions respecting the convention of Suhlingen, his majesty's express orders that the terms of that convention should be strictly observed on the part of the Hanoverian army, which orders were, immediately after the departure of lord Hawkesbury's reply, transmitted to marshal Walmoden and the ministry in Lauenburg, sufficiently proved the false and unworthy light in which the crooked policy of the French

Narrative of Sir L. Möller, MSS.

usurper had placed the upright intentions of the British monarch. 1803. June.

General Berthier, who was the bearer of the above communication, submitted to marshal Walmoden at the same time the following programme for a new convention. Darstellung, &c.

I. The Hanoverian army shall repass the Elbe, lay down their arms, and proceed to France; they shall retain their baggage, and the officers their swords. The latter shall be allowed to retire into any part of the continent, but not to England.

II. The Hanoverian army shall march past with all the honours of war; provisions shall be secured for the troops, and carriages for the baggage.

III. The capitulation shall not be submitted to the ratification of the two governments.

A deputation from the electoral provinces (Messrs. von Lenthe and Wangenheim) had already prepared marshal Walmoden for the appearance of such conditions as this document contained; and having, at the same time, in the name of their whole body, energetically besought him to employ every means of averting the total ruin with which the country was threatened, he felt that he could not, with due regard to the sentiments of the representative body, send a specific reply without first taking the opinion of the general officers of his own army on the new terms, to which he was called upon to consent. He, therefore, answered general Mortier's letter to that effect; but at once stated, verbally, to

1803. June. Darstellung, &c.

the bearer of the communication, that he would never consent to the troops being taken to France; with which assurance general Berthier departed.

Twenty-four hours were given to marshal Walmoden to send in a categorical reply, and in the mean time head-quarters having been removed to Gülzow, he requested that the generals of his army would assemble at that village on the morning of the 31st.

Mortier's communications having been laid before this body, its demands were, without a dissentient voice, declared inadmissible; and Walmoden now gladly beheld his line of conduct simplified to the employment of those vigorous and decided measures which had been long and anxiously desired by his troops.

The position occupied by the Hanoverian army in Lauenburg possessed great natural advantages. The broad Elbe, overhung by steep and commanding heights, defended the front; the rivers Steck-nitz and Bille ran along the flanks; and these were further protected, on the one side by the neutral territory of Mecklenburg, and on the other by those of Hamburgh and Denmark.

With a corps of thirty thousand men, this position could doubtless have been made most formidable; but the small number and impaired condition of the Hanoverian army rendered them unable to derive the full benefit of its locality. The effective force now under the command of the marshal, consisted of two thousand sabres, seven thousand bayonets, fifty three-pounder amusettes, being the regimental guns, and a few howitzers, which, as *pièces d'honneur*, the French general had allowed him to retain. For the service of this force only two days' ammunition was at hand, and any stores which might by possibility have been obtained from Hamburg and Lübeck, could not arrive in time to supply the immediate deficiency which hostilities protracted beyond that period would necessarily cause.

1803.
July.
Historische Berichtigungen.

Although so defective in artillery and ammunition, the inferiority in number of Walmoden's force as compared with that of his opponent, was not considerable. Mortier had not, it has been generally believed, more than twelve or thirteen thousand men under his command; but then the French general had adroitly possessed himself of the means of conveying these troops to the opposite side of the Elbe; he was also far superior in artillery, and an army of reserve, under general Dessoles, was reported to be in march to his assistance.

Still the result of the council of war was received throughout the army with general feelings of satisfaction, and the contest which appeared now inevitable was anxiously but fearlessly awaited.

These expectations were, however, soon destroyed; for before colonel von Bock had com-

1803. July. Darstellung, &c.

municated to general Mortier the decision of the council of war, less humiliating terms were proposed to Walmoden, through the medium of the deputies von Lenthe and Wangenheim; on the morning of the 3d these were again modified, and the following conditions were finally forwarded to the Hanoverian head-quarters by lieutenant-colonel von Bock, as those on which general Mortier proposed to conclude a new convention.

I. The troops shall lay down their arms on this side the Elbe, at a place that shall be hereafter fixed upon.

II. The cavalry shall give up their horses to one or more deputies of Hanover, furnished with all the necessary power.

III. Colonels of regiments shall provide their troops with furloughs for one year.

IV. The soldiers shall return home, but not wear their uniform.

V. The regiments shall pass the Elbe, and move from thence in such a manner as not to meet the French troops in march.

VI. The officers and soldiers shall preserve their effects and baggage, and the former their swords.

VII. The support of the officers without fortune shall be attended to. *(L'on soignera l'entretien des officiers sans fortune.)*

Although much more favourable than either of the preceding propositions, more so indeed than those that were eventually acceded to, the dissolution of the Hanoverian army still forming the basis of the demand, Walmoden persisted in refusing assent to any terms of which this condition formed a part. He, therefore, answered general Mortier to that effect; but wishing, at the same time, to shew his willingness to meet the views of the French general, suggested to him the sufficient security which the return home of those men who had lately been called in, the delivering of hostages, or other individual and definite security, would give to his government, without the total dismemberment of the Hanoverian army.

Either this reply was not considered by general Mortier sufficiently explicit, or the French commander was willing to give marshal Walmoden more time to consider the subject; for colonel von Bock, to whom the letter was entrusted, had already been some time absent, when a French officer, bearing a flag of truce, appeared at the outposts, and having been conducted to the Hanoverian head-quarters, laid the following note before marshal Walmoden.

" Quartier-general à Lüneburg le 14 Messidor an 11 (3d July, 1803.)

" Le lieutenant-général Mortier a l'honneur de saluer le maréchal de Walmoden. Il le prie de vouloir bien lui faire connoître si son excellence a pris une décision relativement aux dernières propositions, qu'il a eu l'honneur de lui communiquer.

1803. July. "Le general Mortier prie Mons. le Maréchal de recevoir," &c.

To this Walmoden briefly replied by referring general Mortier to his last letter, adding, that it was impossible for him to accept, without some alteration, the conditions which had been proposed, both his reasons and regret at which, he thought he had fully explained in his reply.

Historische Berichtigungen. A crisis in the negotiation appeared now to have again arrived, and the departure of the French officer who was the bearer of the last note, produced a general conviction in the Hanoverian army that the following day would open upon a desperate conflict. Marshal Walmoden shared in this opinion, and accordingly gave orders that the head-quarter baggage should be ready to move off, and his own horses to be mounted at an hour's notice; he recommended his officers to take a few hours' rest in their clothes, and laid down himself alike prepared to answer the demands upon his exertions which an attack of the enemy would, he fully expected, soon render necessary.

1803.

July.

CHAPTER IV.

BUT an unlooked-for event soon destroyed this anticipation. Historische Berichtigungen.

The probable proximity of the attack requiring an early preparation of the troops, the heavy cavalry brigade, consisting of the life-guards, garde-du-corps, and second heavy dragoons, who were encamped near Lauenburg, was, at midnight, ordered to saddle. No sooner had this order been pronounced, when suddenly from one end of the brigade to the other was heard the pass-word* of, "the troops will not saddle!" *(Es soll nicht aufgesattelt werden.)* The officers, thinking it prudent to appear at first unconscious of this symptom of insubordination, simply exhibited astonishment at the order being so slowly complied with, and succeeded in making the few individual men whom they met, procced, at least apparently, to the fulfilment of their duty. By degrees, however, the mutineers assembled in large bodies, in the middle of which, the most hardy, their persons being concealed by the darkness of the night, gave vent to their feelings in unequivocal terms, and openly

* The order to saddle is given in the words "*Es soll aufgesattelt werden.*"

1803. July. Historische Berichtigungen.

declared "that no further duty ought to be done until it was known for whom they were really to fight and have their bones broken—why the country had been abandoned, and the army shut up in a corner, where, sooner or later, they must be in one way or other destroyed;—who, since the whole income of the country was in the enemy's power, would pay their pensions to those soldiers who might become crippled in the approaching battle: finally, until it was known whether the soldiers from whom the exertions of war for no kind of purpose were required, would be given, at least, their full war allowances, and not be suffered to starve upon their scanty peace allowances under the sweat of their brows and the loss of their blood."

With these and similar expressions were the officers assailed, who mixed among the insurgents, and by threats, exhortations, prayers, and promises, endeavoured to calm their irritation and bring them back to their duty. These efforts had been partially successful, and the garde-du-corps had nearly all complied with the order to saddle, when a new subject of complaint brought the former angry feeling into action with an increased impulse.

A few men of the second cavalry regiment had, at the beginning of the disturbance, gone to the left of the brigade, where the life-guards were encamped, and endeavoured to kindle, as zealously as the officers laboured to extinguish in that regiment, the flame of insubordination. Observing their efforts, and the injury which they were effecting, cornet Jansen, a high-spirited young officer of the life-guards, went up to them, and demanded what their business was with that regiment at so late an hour. The men made no reply, but endeavoured to escape, upon which Jansen cut at them with his sword, and wounded three of the party sufficiently to make evident to their comrades the chastisement which they had undergone.

1803.
July.
Historische Berichtigungen.

Exaggerating these appearances, the men of the second regiment now became furious, and cried out for revenge upon the officers of the life-guards. In vain did the most resolute of their superiors endeavour to counteract this design; in vain did they succeed in drawing off a few of the more tractable from the mass and making them return to their tents; the threats and imprecations of their comrades soon changed their good intentions, and in a few minutes more than two hundred men, armed with their swords and threatening the most violent proceedings, had assembled. Before, however, any further step towards the excesses to which these manifestations appeared likely to lead, had been taken by the mutineers, the powerful remonstrances of their respected colonel, von Dzierzianowsky, succeeded in subduing their rage, and thus prevented a scene which would probably have led to the most fatal consequences.

But although the personal exertions of this zealous officer defeated the intentions of his

1803. July. Historische Berichtigungen.

misguided corps, they were insufficient to check the general spirit of discontent which an exaggerated report of the cause of the excitement had spread throughout the camp. Major general du Plat, who commanded the left wing, accompanied by colonel the prince of Schwartzburg, now arrived on the spot. By this time an outward appearance of quiet had been assumed, and a squadron of the life-guards marched, by the general's order, to the relief of an outpost; a gloomy, stubborn, and mutinous spirit was, however, still perceptible, and in this state Walmoden found the three regiments whose reported insubordination caused him to appear before them about day-break on the morning of the 4th.

The field-marshal addressed the brigade with all the energy with which a painful consciousness of the disgraceful nature of their conduct, and of the pressing danger of the moment, inspired him. He promised them an investigation into their complaint if it was properly brought forward, and satisfaction, if it proved to be well founded. He reminded them of the fame which they had earned in former wars—stated to them the probability of being immediately attacked—and, finally, demanded of them whether they would fight or surrender as prisoners of war. A gloomy silence followed this appeal, and the outward demeanour of those to whom it was addressed, showed too clearly how ineffective it had proved. A report now reached the marshal that the enemy were about to cross the Elbe at Artlenburg. This, which afterwards proved to be a false alarm, could not but augment the difficulties with which events, already embarrassing, had surrounded him; he, therefore, resolved again to summon a meeting of the generals of his army, and to submit to them the expediency of assenting to the modified terms which Mortier had last proposed.

1803.

July.

Historische Berichtigungen.

Before, however, Walmoden left the camp, some individual soldiers of the disaffected regiments hurried after him and expressed their contrition and readiness to return to their duty, and soon after a field officer and a captain of the second regiment officially reported to him that that regiment awaited his orders to turn out and oppose the enemy;* but the marshal's confidence in his army had been shaken; he feared that the mutinous spirit which had been yet but partially exhibited might prove contagious and become general; that a knowledge of the late commotion might reach the French head-quarters, and lead to demands still harder than those which had been yet put forward, and which the disorganized state of his army might render him unable to resist;—in fine, perplexed, disheartened, and despairing of that re-establishment of discipline and good spirit among his troops, upon which he could alone depend for success in the unequal con-

* Allg. Litt. Zeitung, Februar. 1804, No. 57, p. 455. Minerva, November, 1803, p. 325.

1803. July. Historische Berichtigungen.

test with which he was threatened, he did not allow himself to be influenced by the symptoms of returning order which the disaffected regiments now exhibited, but retained his intention of summoning another council of war, and again submitting the guidance of his conduct to the generals of his army.

These officers accordingly assembled at Haidekrug about five o'clock in the afternoon, and the conditions on which Mortier had last proposed to treat having been laid before them, they declared themselves unanimously of opinion that, "provided the proposed conditions were observed, and no worse substituted, his excellency might conclude a convention with the French general."

Appendix, No. II.

Supported by this opinion, which was formally drawn up and signed, Walmoden addressed a note to Mortier early on the following morning, accepting the terms which had been last offered, and requesting permission to send an officer of his staff to concert the necessary details with the French general. Mortier replied by expressing his readiness to comply with the marshal's request, but subsequently proposed that the details should be arranged by Walmoden and himself on the Elbe, which was acceded to, and a boat having been moored in the river for the purpose, the conference was fixed for the same afternoon.

Darstellung, &c.

The fates seemed, however, opposed to this finishing stroke of the French general; for just as he left the Hanoverian shore, a squall of wind sprang up, and the little sail-boat in which he had embarked, being badly managed, was in imminent danger. Another accidental circumstance threatened still more the personal safety of the general. On the departure of the boat from Artlenburg, the French had omitted to make the usual signal of a flag of truce, and the officer who commanded the Hanoverian artillery on the opposite bank had not been informed of the approaching conference. Seeing, therefore, a vessel in full sail making for the right bank, with an enemy's crew on board, the officer considered that he would be only acting in obedience to his orders by firing upon the apparent invader. He accordingly directed a gun upon the vessel and fired two shots, one of which is said to have hit the bark without doing much injury. This salutation was now about to be strengthened by a charge of grape, when a staff officer gallopped up and arrested the fire by communicating the pacific state of affairs.

1803. July. Historische Berichtigungen.

Thus escaping from the perils of two elements, Mortier reached the boat, and the two commanders proceeded to draw up the details of the new convention.

This document, which has been respectively called the Elbe, Artlenburg, and Lauenburg convention, was thus worded.

Elbe Convention.

" The king of England having refused to ratify the convention of Suhlingen, the French consul feels himself obliged to consider that convention

1803. July. as not having been concluded. Lieutenant-general Mortier, commanding in chief the French army, and his excellency the count Walmoden, commanding in chief the Hanoverian army, have consequently agreed upon the following capitulation, which shall be immediately put in execution, without being submitted to the ratification of the two governments.

" Art. I. The Hanoverian army shall lay down their arms, which shall be given up, together with all their artillery, to the French army.

" II. All the Hanoverian cavalry horses, together with those of the artillery, shall be given up to the French army by one of the members of the government. A commission nominated by the general in chief shall be immediately sent to make the necessary arrangements for this purpose.

" III. The Hanoverian army shall be disbanded; the troops shall pass the Elbe and return to their homes; they shall bind themselves by word of honour not to bear arms against France and her allies until after they shall have been exchanged by as many French military of equal rank, as may be taken prisoners by the English in the course of the war.

" IV. The Hanoverian generals and officers shall retire upon parole to those places which they may select for their residences, provided that they do not leave the continent. They shall keep their swords, and take with them their horses, effects, and baggage.

"V. A nominative control over all the individuals which compose the Hanoverian army shall be given to the general commanding the French army with the least delay. 1803. July.

"VI. The Hanoverian soldiers sent to their homes shall not wear uniform.

"VII. Subsistence shall be issued to the Hanoverian troops until their arrival at home. In like manner forage for the officers' horses shall be also allowed.

"VIII. The sixteenth and seventeenth articles of the convention of Suhlingen* shall be applicable to the Hanoverian army.

"IX. The French troops shall immediately occupy that part of the electorate of Hanover situated in the province of Lauenburg.

"Done in duplicate on the Elbe, this sixteenth Messidor, year eleven of the French republic (5th of July, 1803.)

"The lieutenant-general commanding the French army in chief,

"Signed. { ED. MORTIER.
Marshal count von WALMODEN."

Owing to the hurry of the moment and the variety of details to be entered into, many stipulations which a regard for the future welfare of the Hanoverian army would naturally have dictated to marshal Walmoden, were either settled verbally, or altogether omitted. Among others, that which Historische Berichtigungen.

* See page 30.

1803. July. provided for the future subsistence of the officers and soldiers was unfortunately entrusted to the former mode of adjustment, and the advantage afterwards taken by the enemy of this inadvertency, in withholding or deferring the payment of the promised subsistence, placed many individuals in circumstances at once unexpected and distressing.

The mutinous conduct of the three cavalry regiments having been the immediate cause of marshal Walmoden taking the opinions of his generals on the expediency of submitting to the conditions upon which this convention was founded, it seems fitting that we should here inquire into the motives which led to so violent and open a demonstration of indiscipline and disloyalty.

Fairly to effect this object, it will be necessary to bring under review the general condition and temper of the army from the period of its arrival in the province of Lauenburg until the fatal morning of the 4th July.

It has been stated that the march of the army towards the Elbe was attended with considerable desertion. That this breach of faith with their country and the discontented feeling which led to it should have become more general among the troops after they had crossed that river, may well be imagined. Banished from their homes and families without having been allowed to make one effort to avert that condition—forced to leave all that they held most dear to the doubtful protection

1803. July. Historische Berichtigungen.

of a lawless enemy—shut up in a corner of the land from whence they could only be liberated by gallant exploits in which they were themselves denied a participation, it cannot be a matter for surprise that discontent and despondency should have taken strong possession of their minds. The long existing laxity in discipline had also engendered among them a habit of criticising and censuring the orders of their superiors; and the fatigues and inconveniences consequent upon their present situation, which were, perhaps, sometimes unnecessarily though unintentionally increased, gave frequent occasion to such comments. To all these causes of dissatisfaction was added that contained in the regulation respecting their pay and allowances, which were not, as they expected, placed upon the war establishment; and so far did the perverseness produced by this latter cause of complaint carry them, that although the commissariat had provided amply for the wants of the army and offered provisions to the men at the first cost, they preferred buying in the neighbouring towns and villages at double the price charged by the commissariat, articles which they conceived ought to have been furnished to them gratis.

The forage was also deficient both in quality and quantity. The horses were altogether deprived of straw; the ration of hay was reduced to three pounds per diem; and although that of oats was at the same time increased to ten pounds, the quality of

1803. July. Historische Berichtigungen.

the corn was so indifferent as to render it no equivalent for the reduction in the former article. The cavalry horses were consequently thrown out of the good condition in which they had previously been, and for the preservation of which the German dragoon is so justly celebrated, and the spirit of the rider sank with the condition of the animal, on whose powers his own efficiency in the day of battle depended.

The elements themselves appeared to be in league against the soldiers' constancy. Cold and rainy weather, unnatural to the time of year, had followed the encampment of the troops, and this they the more severely felt in consequence of the meagre supply of blankets which had been issued to them, and the impossibility of obtaining even the substitute of straw.

Exemplary as was the conduct of the officers in general during this trying period, some imprudent individuals of that body were unguarded enough to allow themselves a freedom of expression respecting the convention of Suhlingen, and the present humbled condition of the troops, which could not fail to increase the irritation of minds already too well disposed to receive exciting impressions; and their open abuse of those authorities to whose measures they considered the late convention chargeable, no doubt fed that suppressed spirit of revolt which at last exploded.

The general discontent of the army was first expressed by numerous and frequent desertions. 1803. These occurred both in the infantry and cavalry, July. some regiments losing more than a hundred men in Historische Berichtigungen. the space of three weeks; nor was, as is commonly the case, this loss confined to the idle and disorderly, but the choicest, best conducted, and most confidential soldiers left their ranks.

The local position of the three heavy cavalry regiments peculiarly exposed them to the impression thus general throughout the army. Encamped between the towns of Lauenburg and Glüsingen, where the greatest body of troops was united, and in more direct communication with their native provinces than the other regiments, they became early acquainted with the various dispiriting reports and lamentations which the friends and kindred of the soldiers daily spread among them. The citizens of Lauenburg, also, with whom these regiments had frequent intercourse, and who felt themselves oppressed by the unaccustomed burthen of their presence, spared no exertions to seduce them from their duty. However, the result of the council of war of the 1st of July, when Mortier's demand that the army should surrender and be marched to France was positively rejected, was hailed by these regiments with the same satisfaction, good spirit, and anxious desire to regain, by a contest, that position from which the late convention had thrown them, as animated the rest of the troops; but the communication made

1803. July. Historische Berichtigungen.

by the deputies on the 2d,—that of the French general on the following day—the distorted and exaggerated manner in which intelligence of these varied propositions reached them,—and, finally, the doubt and perplexity in which the whole proceeding appeared to be enveloped — caused their former feelings to return in aggravated force.

On the 1st of July, for instance, the troops were informed that the enemy required they should proceed to France as prisoners of war. The thought of this was most appalling to them. Many veterans knew, by sad experience, the miseries which such a condition involved, and pictured them to their uninitiated comrades, who in consequence burned with the desire of revenging themselves upon the enemy, and hesitated not to encounter death rather than submit to demands attended with such frightful results. But on the following day this excitement was at an end. Even before the new terms then offered were made known to the troops, it had been falsely reported among them that the *officers only* would be required as prisoners. Hence arose a belief that they were called upon to fight merely for the honour of their superiors; and when on the 2d the certain information reached them, that no prisoners of war whatever were required by the enemy, they began altogether to doubt whether this condition had been ever proposed, and to suspect that it had been mentioned for the sole purpose of urging them to a contest in which the honour of their superiors was alone concerned. 1803. July. Historische Berichtigungen.

The soldier, also, could not reconcile it to his simple notions of consistency, that no effort to defend the country had been made at Suhlingen, and that now, when the prospects of success had been so much diminished, a desperate engagement was to be fought, which, in all probability, would leave both the country and the army abandoned to the devastating consequences of an unsuccessful contest.

That these various and just causes of dissatisfaction, suffered to take root and become entwined in the minds of troops over whom the strictness of military discipline had been long relinquished, should have kindled the flame of mutiny, and led at length to its bursting forth in an act of open resistance to authority, cannot be a matter of surprise; and the same reasons forbid us to make it a subject of censure.

The conduct of marshal Walmoden both previous to and during the eventful period of the French invasion of Hanover, has called forth much and severe animadversion. The reduction of the army has been attributed to his influence, and its inefficiency to his inertness; his advocacy of resistance has been pronounced insincere; military talent has been denied him; a predetermined

1803. July. intention to avoid all hostilities has been laid to his charge, and even his personal courage has been questioned.

As in, perhaps, all cases of unqualified and wide-extended censure, these imputations contain much of untruth and exaggeration. So far from the inefficient state of the Hanoverian army being attributable to the influence or inertness of Walmoden, it is a well attested fact, that, long previous to the period now under consideration, he submitted to his majesty a plan for the entire reorganization of that army, as the only means of restoring it to an effective condition; and at the same time, feeling himself, it is to be presumed, too old* and infirm for so arduous a situation, proposed to resign the command of the army in favour of his royal highness the duke of Cambridge.

But the interference of baron von Lenthe prevented the first part of the proposed arrangement from being carried into execution, and his majesty being at the same time unwilling that his royal highness should be yet engaged in the labours of public business, the marshal still continued to discharge the duties of commander-in-chief.

Of the nature of Walmoden's views and intentions respecting the defence of the electorate, the letters which have been already quoted furnish the best developement. His anxiety that bold, effec-

* Walmoden was then upwards of sixty.

tive, and decided measures should be adopted immediately upon the first intimation of impending danger, is there clearly evinced, as well as his undisguised condemnation of the temporizing policy exhibited by the Hanoverian ministers. 1803. July.

That, after his strenuous efforts to infuse vigour into their councils, to point out the resources of the country, and to shew the inadequacy of the means with which he had been provided, had been unproductive of good effect; after his zeal had been discouraged, and his exertions neutralized, and when he found himself left at last with an army which he felt convinced was unequal to fulfil the task that was likely to be required of it;—that under these circumstances Walmoden should have voluntarily continued in his command, may, perhaps, be a matter of surprise; but his doing so can be alone ascribed to the high sense of public duty with which he was impressed; and unfitted as his advanced age and limited military experience may have rendered him for the critical situation into which he was suddenly thrown, upright, conscientious, and truly patriotic motives cannot fairly be denied him.

The evident desire to effect the peace of the electorate by amicable means, which so strongly marked his proceedings after the French had passed the Hanoverian frontier, has probably

1803. July. led to the imputations upon his personal courage; but this charge appears to be entirely without foundation. For many years the Hanoverian ambassador at Vienna, the marshal's experience had been more in diplomatic than in military transactions; extreme caution, also, was a conspicuous feature in his character, and this quality, increasing with age, tended to produce in him an indecision of purpose which rendered him totally unequal to meet the rapid succession of unfavourable events which followed the march of the French army; but his uniformly gallant conduct during the campaigns of 1793–95 in Holland, where he commanded a corps of Hanoverian troops, and, after the departure of the duke of York, the whole Anglo-Hanoverian army, places his personal courage beyond all question.

Controuled by the restrictions of the ministry—limited in his sphere of action to passive measures of defence — expressly prohibited from giving "*umbrage*" to the enemy, and being himself strongly impressed with the conviction that the general welfare of the country, and not the particular interests of the army, should be his paramount consideration, he adopted that course which under the circumstances he conceived best calculated to attain this object. That his dependance upon conciliatory measures led him into an extreme of forbearance which raised the hopes and increased the demands of the enemy in proportion as his system became developed, the facts which have been recorded too clearly testify. What might not an opposite course have effected? It has been generally allowed that the first engagement with the French advanced corps must have terminated favourably to the Hanoverians; Mortier himself admitted the probability of such a result—and to what important consequences might not so propitious a commencement have led? The French general boasted, certainly, of his "army of reserve," and endeavoured to shew how fruitless any success that might attend the first efforts of the Hanoverian arms would be rendered by the superior numbers which would ultimately be opposed to them: but this vaunted reserve proved, on its arrival, to be an ill-clothed, worse-appointed, and undisciplined band of conscripts, without artillery, cavalry, or magazines! The probable increase of the Hanoverian army is also to be considered—every day brought new levies to its ranks; and, unwillingly as many individuals might have left their homes and families when the unchecked progress of the French seemed to prefix the stamp of hopelessness to a cause in support of which the hazard of their lives was required,—one successful action, one reasonable prospect of the invaders being driven back, would doubtless have reconciled them to the demand on their exertions; and instead of the gloom and dissatisfaction which every where prevailed,

1803. July.

Allg. Lit. Zeitung. No. 55, 1804.

1803. July. the tide of public opinion might have so turned in favour of resistance, as to have supplied the army with zealous volunteers in place of discontented conscripts.

Thus encouraged to maintain the neutrality of the north of Germany, Prussia could no longer have stood by a passive observer of its violation, but complying with the request of the Hanoverian government, would doubtless have hastened to its assistance, and vigorously supported the further operations of those troops whose first effort offered so fair a prospect of ultimate success: England would soon have added the strong arms of her naval and military force, and instead of upholding the cause of freedom through the long struggle of the peninsular war, would have encountered the usurper in a more friendly territory;—then might that land, where Varro's veteran legions yielded to the patriotic bands of Armin, have been also distinguished by the baffled efforts of ambitious France, and the first step towards the liberation of Europe.

CHAPTER V.

WHILE the eventful incidents which have been detailed were passing in Lauenburg, the greatest anxiety concerning the fate of his Hanoverian soldiers reigned in the breast of their affectionate sovereign. 1803. July.

It has been shewn how, dissatisfied as was the king with the convention of Suhlingen, and the tame submission of the electoral ministry to the demands of the invader, his majesty, believing that a faithful observance of the conditions which had been imposed upon the troops by the convention would now best serve the interests of the electorate, had authorized lord Hawkesbury to state, that "until informed of the sentiments of the empire and those powers of Europe who guaranteed the Germanic confederation, his majesty, as elector of Hanover, would scrupulously abstain from doing any act which could be considered as being in contravention to the stipulations contained in the convention of Suhlingen;" and that the king had, in accordance with these sentiments, issued express orders that the convention should be strictly observed on the part of the Hanoverian army, and had consequently countermanded the transports which were

1803. July. intended for the conveyance of that army to England. When, however, on the 8th of July, intelligence had reached London that Mortier had put his troops in motion for the Elbe, and, violating the convention in virtue of which he had secured most important advantages, now put forth new and most unwarrantable demands; the former design of removing the army to England again became an object of royal solicitude.

His majesty's wishes were anticipated by an active member of the Hanoverian diplomatic body in London. Mr. Lewis Moeller, secretary to the department,* who was to have accompanied the transports to the Elbe in the first instance, and had remained keenly watching the progress of events, saw at once the importance of the present moment, and repairing to Windsor on the evening of the 9th, requested that he might be permitted to proceed on his original mission, and endeavour to effect the embarkation of the troops.

The king entered with much warmth into the views and feelings of his zealous servant, and provided him on the following day with a requisition to the admiralty for the necessary number of transports. In anticipation of the king's approval, the secretary had prepared a short proclamation to authorize the removal of the troops, which his majesty readily signed, declaring, with much satisfaction,

* Now Sir Lewis Moeller, K.C.H. privy counsellor of legation, and secretary to the royal Hanoverian Guelphic order.

"that it was the only document unauthenticated by 1803.
the counter-signature of the minister, to which he July.
had ever subscribed."

Thus all things seemed favourable to the execution of the plan; but scarce had its details been entered into, when accounts from Lauenburg threw doubts over its fulfilment: soon came the mortifying intelligence that a second convention had been concluded between the French and Hanoverian armies. This destroyed the operation altogether, and the transports were again and finally countermanded.

Moeller's exertions in the cause of his countrymen were not, however, on that account discontinued. Some vessels had been appointed to convey to England the electoral stud and other property of his majesty, which had been removed for safety to Mecklenburg, and with these he conceived the design of embarking. In this province he felt sure of meeting with many officers and soldiers of the disbanded army, whose future prospects he hoped, by means of the king's proclamation, and his own personal assurance of the royal sentiments, to place before them in a more cheering light, and thus direct their steps towards England. His majesty assented to the departure of the secretary, as also to the issuing of an order from the admiralty, which he had suggested, authorizing all British vessels cruizing off the German coast, to take on board and convey to England any Hanoverian officers, non-commissioned officers, or men, who might solicit

1803. July. that indulgence. This was immediately forwarded, and having been acted upon without delay, materially aided the emigration of the troops.

Provided with his majesty's proclamation, Mr. Moeller sailed from the Nore on the 19th of July, and on arriving in Mecklenburg had the gratification to find that his hopes had been well founded: many officers would immediately have embarked with him for England, but considered, on reflection, that by secretly disseminating the cheering intelligence of which he was the bearer, they would best promote an object in the success of which they were so deeply interested.

Narrative of colonel von der Decken. MSS.

Meantime lieutenant-colonel von der Decken, who, on a visit to England in April, had been given reason to suppose that he would be empowered to raise a corps of foreign troops for the English service, had been officially established at the head of a recruiting department in London, with authority to raise a corps of foreigners not exceeding four thousand men.

At this department, therefore, Moeller recommended those officers and soldiers of the late army whom he met in Mecklenburg, to present themselves, and the gratifying assurance of his majesty's considerate sentiments, which he conveyed to them, joined to their own well grounded confidence in the generous feelings of the monarch, soon pervaded the scattered ranks of the disbanded Hanoverians, and prepared the way to their reunion under the banners of England. 1803. July.

The principal impediment to the emigration of the troops was raised by their own ministry and general officers, the most of whom, apprehensive that such an infraction of the third article of the Elbe convention would be visited upon the conquered country by a more severe treatment of the inhabitants, endeavoured to deter them from leaving the continent.

But the situation of the disbanded soldiers in their own country was too galling, and the prospect which offered itself to them in England too favourable, to allow of their long hesitating as to the course which they should pursue. The insulting demeanour of the French military—the painful aspect of their native land—the doubtful and distant prospect of her emancipation—gradually operated to overcome their natural reluctance to abandon their friends and families, and led them finally to place their whole dependance upon British protection.

The hurried and careless manner in which the last convention had been concluded, much favoured the scheme of embarkation. No promise not to serve against France had been required of the troops; in fact the Elbe convention was never officially communicated, and first became known to them through the public papers; they were, therefore, in nowise bound to observe its restrictions.

1803. July. A rescript in the king's name was also published by the several British ministers at the German courts, which explicitly absolved his majesty's Hanoverian subjects from the observance of all conventions which his ministers or generals might, without his majesty's ratification, enter into with the French. Thus no moral objection to the departure of the troops can be said to have existed.

To this step the French did not offer any serious impediment—perhaps the known loyalty of the troops prevented any over-anxiety to detain them on the part of the new government; and a free passage through Holsteen having been generously granted by the king of Denmark to those Hanoverians desirous of embarking for England, little difficulty presented itself to their progress to the coast.

But although the French prudently abstained from employing any forcible means of preventing the departure of men, whose abode, as civil inhabitants, in their new possession might have been dangerous to its peace, they omitted not to tempt them with offers which were calculated to procure their stay, under the more advantageous condition of military service. A corps to be called the "French Hanoverian Legion" was proposed to be organized, and in this the disbanded officers and soldiers were invited to enrol themselves; but, attractive as this proposition doubtless was to those officers whose professional incomes had alone afforded to themselves and families the means of support, honour and loyalty maintained their influence over the general body, and two only* were induced to take service in the ranks of the French. 1803. July.

Lieutenant-colonel von der Decken was, as has been stated, empowered to raise a corps of foreigners for the British service, not exceeding four thousand men. The letter of service which invested him with this authority, was issued from the commander-in-chief's office on the 28th of July, and held out to the Hanoverians nearly all the advantages which government offered to recruits enlisted for British regiments. Lieutenant-colonel Decken was to have the rank of colonel, and fifteen guineas for each recruit on approval, the bounty being seven pounds, twelve shillings, and six pence.

It was, however, stipulated that if four hundred approved recruits should not have been raised within three months from the date of the letter of service, it should be at the option of his majesty to order the levy to be discontinued: the king also reserved to himself the power of putting an end to the present agreement upon giving two months' notice.

The same day on which the letter of service was issued to colonel Decken, a similer authority was given to major Colin Halkett, of the Dutch service, empowering him to raise, on nearly the same conditions, a battalion of infantry with an establishment

* One lieutenant and two ensigns of the disbanded army entered the French service; but one of these was a native of Denmark.

1803. July. of four hundred and fifty-nine men, and offering him the rank of lieutenant-colonel should he increase the number to eight hundred men.

The first individuals of the late Hanoverian army who landed in England were major von Hinüber, captain Offney, and cornet Augustus Heise. These officers left Lauenburg immediately after the Elbe convention had been concluded, and were forthwith put in requisition by colonel Decken to assist in the formation of his new corps.

Journal of 1st light battalion, MSS. The town of Lymington, in Hampshire, was appointed the place of rendezvous for the recruits, whose examination and outfit were here carried on. Officers were also stationed at Plymouth and Harwich, from which ports the men were forwarded to Lymington.

The commencement of the recruiting was far from promising. On the 8th of August not more than seven men had been enlisted. The British government, therefore, thought it advisable to give more publicity to the king's design, and his royal highness the duke of Cambridge having expressed his readiness to take the command of the corps which it was intended to raise, the following proclamation was made public.

"10th August, 1803.

"His majesty George the Third, king of the united kingdoms of Great Britain and Ireland, has been pleased to grant letters of service to colonel baron Decken, for raising a corps of light infantry for the British service, which is to be called the KING'S GERMANS, and which, when completed, will be under the command of his royal highness the duke of Cambridge. All foreigners, and especially all brave Germans, are therefore called upon to enlist in the said corps. They will receive a very considerable bounty, and are to enjoy the same pay and prerogatives as the regular regiments in the British line.

Journal of 1st light battalion, MSS.

"Those who are disabled during the war are also to have pensions. Each recruit is to engage for seven years, and for half-a-year after the signature of a future definitive treaty of peace, after which he will be discharged, and is then to receive an adequate sum of money to defray his expenses home."

Advantageous as were the terms which his majesty's proclamation offered, little immediate effect appears to have been produced by it, and serious apprehensions began to be entertained that colonel von der Decken would be unable to comply with that condition of his letter of service which limited the period allowed him for the raising of four hundred men, to *four months*. In this event, the men which should have been already enlisted were to be distributed throughout the British West India regiments, and the result of the first ten weeks' recruiting was so unpromising, that such a consequence appeared far from improbable.

1803. Sept. Journal of 1st light battalion, MSS.

Towards the end of September, however, colonel Decken's prospects brightened; the design of the English government had become known in Hanover, and the Hanoverian officers spared no exertion to promote its fulfilment. Several hundred recruits were now expected in England, and these arrived at Lymington so suddenly and in such numbers, that the depôt was soon overstocked, and it became necessary to remove a part of the men to Parkhurst barracks in the Isle of Wight.

So favourable a change in the progress of the recruiting had now taken place, that it was no longer found necessary to continue the stations at Plymouth and Harwich; and major von Hinüber, who had been in superintendence at the former place, was therefore removed to the Isle of Wight, where, on the 13th of October, he took the command of the King's German Regiment, as the new corps was first entitled.

The increasing emigration from Hanover appears, about this time, to have alarmed the French. On the 6th of October a proclamation was issued by the executive commission, warning the magistrates not to encourage recruiting for the English army, and requiring them to give information against all persons found to be so engaged. This was followed, on the 10th, by another proclamation, in which the inhabitants were informed that any one who was engaged in recruiting for the English army, or induced others to enter into the English service,

Appendix, No. III. A.

would be given up to the French military tribunal, 1803.
and punished, according to its laws, with *death.* October.
This formidable warning was read for three succes- Appendix, No. III. B. & C.
sive Sundays in the public churches; but notwithstanding the severity of the threatened sentence, and the imposing manner in which it was denounced, the agents of the new corps continued their exertions, and except in one instance appear to have evaded the vigilance of the French. The case in question was that of a sergeant named Ahrens, who was apprehended and brought to trial on the charge of *embauchage*, or secret recruiting, of which Appendix, No. III. D.
he was found guilty; but the majority of his judges being against the extreme punishment of death, the sentence was commuted to *fifteen years' imprisonment in irons!*

The number of officers who had now arrived in England was so much greater in proportion than that of men, that it was not possible at once to provide them with suitable appointments in the new levy, and therefore to obviate this inconvenience to the individuals, the British government liberally allowed each Hanoverian officer, from the day of his arrival until that of his gazettement, two thirds of the pay to which British officers of similar rank were entitled.

On the 3d of November, the number of recruits at the Isle of Wight amounted to four hundred and fifty, and the continuance of the levy was consequently secured.

1803. December. The original plan of forming a regiment only was now extended, and a corps consisting of cavalry, infantry, and artillery was proposed to be raised. The better to effect this object, the independent levies of colonel von der Decken and major Halkett were ordered to be discontinued, and the men that had been already enlisted by those officers to be incorporated as the basis of a legion, which his majesty was pleased to authorize should be raised by his royal highness the duke of Cambridge.

Appendix, No. IV. This corps was not to exceed five thousand men, which were to be enlisted, if possible, for ten, but certainly for not less than seven years. The other conditions of the letter of service, by virtue of which his royal highness was empowered to raise the legion, were nearly similar to those by which colonel von der Decken and major Halkett had been restricted. His majesty also held himself free to discontinue at pleasure the new corps or any part thereof, even although the period of enlistment should not have expired.

Journal of 1st light battalion, MSS. Meantime, major von Hinüber had been busily engaged in dividing and regulating the fast increasing numbers of his command at the Isle of Wight, which was, in the middle of November, removed to Hilsea barracks, and before the end of that month numbered about a thousand men.

From these, the men fit for the cavalry and artillery services having been withdrawn, two light regiments and the foundation of one line battalion were formed. The light brigade being intended for a rifle corps, were clothed in green, while the line battalion was furnished with a uniform nearly similar to that worn by the British royal regiments of infantry. *(See Plate.)* 1803. December.

The organization of the cavalry and horse-artillery was commenced at Weymouth; that of the foot-artillery, at Hilsea. From the men intended for the cavalry service, and the most of whom were volunteers from the late Hanoverian army, four troops of heavy, and four of light, dragoons were formed; the heavy cavalry were clothed like the British royal regiments of heavy dragoons, the light regiment as the English hussars; the uniform of the artillery and engineers was in every respect similar to that of the same corps in the British service. *(See Plate.)*

The artillery were also principally furnished with recruits from the late Hanoverian army, and these, together with other foreigners who had already been in that branch of the service, arrived in such numbers before the end of the year, that one horse and one foot battery were by that time formed.

Thus, in less than six months from the period of the dissolution of the Hanoverian army in Lauenburg, its scattered elements had been re-united in England, and now formed the basis of that corps which was henceforward to bear the name of THE KING'S GERMAN LEGION.

1804.

February.

CHAPTER VI.

The foundation of the new corps having been thus laid, its superstructure rose rapidly to completion; and notwithstanding the difficulties which a foreign country, foreign commanders, and a foreign language presented to its organization, several squadrons, battalions, and batteries were in a short time ready to take the field.

Narrative of colonel v. Linsingen, MSS.

In the month of February two additional troops were added to the two cavalry regiments, which before the end of the year numbered each four hundred and fifty horses. Quartered at Weymouth and Dorchester, under the command of major-general von Linsingen, this brigade became an object of his majesty's notice, and was many times honoured with the royal inspection during the sojourn of the king at his usual summer residence. The heavy regiment, in particular, was a marked favourite with his majesty, who not unfrequently appeared in the uniform of that corps.

Narrative of colonel Baring, MSS.

The formation of the infantry regiments was naturally much sooner effected than that of the cavalry. In April, a second line battalion had been formed; in May, the foundation of a third, and a few months afterwards, that of a fourth battalion was commenced;

1804. July.

both of these regiments were completed before the end of the succeeding January, when, also, the frame-work of a fifth battalion was at hand.

Narrative of general Hartmann, MSS.

The formation of the artillery, although necessarily attended with much greater difficulty than either of the other arms, was proportionately successful. In July, a second foot battery had been completed; the formation of a third foot and of a second horse battery was immediately commenced, and both were completed in the course of the following spring.

Narrative of colonel Baring, MSS.

The four battalions of infantry which had been already completed, were formed into a light and line brigade, the former under colonel von Alten, the line brigade under colonel von Langwerth; and these regiments, after having been a short time encamped in the new forest, were, together with the first foot battery of artillery, removed to Bexhill, on the coast of Sussex, at which place it was intended to establish the general infantry depôt of the legion.

The barracks here did not, however, afford room sufficient for the numbers that now required accommodation, and earthen huts were ordered to be built for that purpose. These were quickly thrown up by the troops, who occupied their straw-roofed tenements before the end of the year.

In January, 1805, the King's German Legion consisted of the following corps.

1805.

January.

CAVALRY BRIGADE.

MAJOR-GENERAL VON LINSINGEN.

1st dragoons ....colonel von Bock.
1st hussars ....colonel Victor von Alten.

LIGHT INFANTRY BRIGADE.

1st light battalion ....col. Charles von Alten, brigadier.
2d light battalion ....lieutenant-colonel Halkett.

FIRST LINE BRIGADE.

1st line battalion.............colonel von Ompteda.
2d line battalion ....colonel von Barsse, brigadier.

SECOND LINE BRIGADE.

3d line battalion ....colonel von Hinüber.
4th line battalion ....colonel von Langwerth, brigadier.

ARTILLERY.

COLONEL COMMANDANT—COLONEL VON DER DECKEN.

(ADJUTANT-GENERAL TO THE KING'S GERMAN LEGION.)

MAJOR, FREDERICK VON LINSINGEN.

1st horse battery............captain G. J. Hartmann.
2d horse battery ....captain Röttiger.
1st foot battery ....captain Brückmann.
2d foot battery ....captain Kühlmann.
3d foot battery ....captain Heise.

ENGINEERS.

Captains Berensbach, Prott, Meinecke.
Lieutenants Hassebroik, Appuhn, Schweitzer.

The cavalry brigade and captain Hartmann's battery of horse artillery formed part of a corps of eight thousand men, which was encamped near Weymouth during the summer, under the command of his royal highness the duke of Cumberland.

Although for the first time called upon to manœuvre in conjunction with English regiments, to whose words of command they had not been yet habituated, the Hanoverians proved not less efficient than their British comrades. The light cavalry movements in particular met with the marked approbation of the inspecting generals, as did the correct and steady firing of the artillery.*

1805. July. Narrative of colonel v. Linsingen, MSS.

The camp was frequently visited by the king, the prince of Wales, and other members of the royal family. His majesty would often tarry near the German regiments: he also occasionally attended their parades for divine service, and by these and similar marks of condescension made his Hanoverian subjects deeply sensible of the royal favour.

The continental coalition against French ascendancy, which the active policy of Mr. Pitt this year effected, opened a prospect to the new-raised corps which spread universal joy throughout its ranks. Austria and Prussia had joined in a league with England against France; the British government were to send an army to the north of Germany to aid the operations of the allies, and the completed regiments of the legion were to form part of that army! No intelligence could have been more wel-

* The several regiments of the legion were at first permitted to follow the Hanoverian system of exercise and manœuvre, and only in mounting guard and all movements relating to parade, were required to conform to the British regulations, which they did not entirely adopt until 1808. The artillery were put under the board of ordnance from the 1st August, 1806.

1805. November. comed by the Hanoverians. The liberation of their country—the return to their homes—the restoration of their sovereign—were at once vividly pictured as the results of the expedition, and could not fail to present a brave, patriotic, and warm-hearted soldiery, with the most brilliant prospects of the approaching campaign.

But quickly and completely were these expectations destroyed. — Mack surrendered at Ulm, on the 17th of October; Buonaparte gained the battle of Austerlitz on the 2d of December; the treaties of Presburg and Vienna were soon after signed, the coalition was thus lamed, and Prussian troops took possession of Hanover.

Little, however, was so rapid and fatal a termination to the triple league anticipated, when lord Cathcart's expedition embarked for the Elbe. This army, about eighteen thousand strong, six thousand of which consisted of the king's German legion, sailed from Ramsgate in the month of November, under the command of general Don, and a most unpropitious commencement to their active career the legion experienced; for scarce had the transports in which they were shipped reached the open sea, when they encountered a gale of wind which dispersed the whole corps. The hussars were driven to the coast of Holland; half the heavy cavalry regiment was forced back to England, one of their transports narrowly escaping capture under the batteries of Calais, from which it was only

Narrative of colonel Baring, MSS.

saved by a sudden shift of wind; and three companies of the fourth line battalion were cast ashore on the island of Wangerode in Oldenburg. No lives, however, were lost, and in the beginning of December the whole corps, with the exception of that part of the heavy cavalry regiment which was driven back, and did not return, landed in the Hanoverian territory.

Lord Cathcart arrived on the 25th, and took the command of the army, establishing his head-quarters at Bremen. Those of general Don, under whom were the legion, were fixed at Verden.

In order to oppose the movements of the Austrio-Russian army, the French had evacuated the whole Hanoverian territory, with the exception of the fortress of Hameln, where a strong garrison still remained. The Russians had invested the place, and the first line brigade, first foot battery, and one engineer officer of the legion, were sent to co-operate with the Russian corps.

But the allies were too late in the field. Before the British troops left England general Mack had capitulated; before they reached the Elbe, Napoleon was at Vienna; and before lord Cathcart had established his head-quarters at Bremen, the "battle of the three emperors" had decided the fate of Austria. All hostile movements in the north of Germany were consequently suspended, and the British-Hanoverian army was ordered to return to England.

1806. January. Narrative of colonel Baring, MSS.

This intelligence produced general disappointment among the troops. To the legion, as may be well supposed, the tidings were peculiarly unwelcome, and the sudden and complete annihilation to all their hopes caused by the order for embarkation, joined to the wily machinations of some of their own evil disposed countrymen, had so powerful an effect upon the private soldiers, that many of them were induced to forsake their standard and return to their homes.

Landing in Germany under the full conviction that an opportunity would be given them of contending for the restoration of Hanover on her own soil, the sudden destruction of this prospect caused a proportionate degree of mortification and disappointment. A glance at their country—a hasty interview with their friends, and then the tame abandonment of both to Prussian dominion, little realized the sanguine expectations with which they had embarked. The inhabitants of Bremen, also, who in consequence of the blockade of the Weser were ill-disposed towards England, encouraged the discontented feeling which this disappointment produced, by representing, in the most forbidding colours, the fate which was likely to await them on their return. That they were destined for colonial service, and would never be permitted to return to their own country, was strongly dwelt upon, and the "*barbarians*" and "*cannibals*" of the East and

West Indies would, it was affirmed, be the inhabitants of their future quarters. 1806. January.

Giving credence to these and similar reports, the men who had any interest in Hanover felt naturally disinclined to re-embark, and many returned to their homes. The desertions were principally amongst the cavalry, several of whom, having a little property in the country, were more sensible to the impression that was sought to be made upon them, and left their regiments in bodies of tens, twenties, and upwards, taking with them their horses and appointments. Many, however, soon repented of their misconduct, and availed themselves of the general pardon which was soon after issued by Lord Cathcart.*

Narrative of colonel Baring, MSS.

Notwithstanding these desertions, the legion was considerably augmented during its short stay on the continent. Colonel von der Decken, who held the chief controul over the recruiting department, had gone to Hanover in November, with the local rank of brigadier-general, for the purpose of superintending the proposed augmentation of the legion to eighteen thousand men. In furtherance of this object, he established recruiting depots at Stade and Hanover, to which places volunteers soon poured in, and the following increase to the corps,

* A free pardon was offered by lord Cathcart to all deserters who should report themselves to the commander of the English fleet at Bremerlehe before the 10th of March, which pardon was afterwards extended by his majesty to the end of the year.

1806. February. which was effected before the end of February, proved the success with which the arrangements of the general, and the exertions of the officers under his command, had been attended.

Narrative of colonel v. Linsingen, MSS.

A second regiment of heavy dragoons, and a third regiment of hussars, each about six hundred and fifty strong, were formed. The second hussars, whose formation had been commenced in England the preceding June, was completed to the same strength, and the quick re-embarkation of the army alone prevented the formation of a fourth regiment of cavalry.

Narrative of colonel Baring, MSS.

Each of the infantry battalions which had been already raised were augmented to a thousand men; a fifth, sixth, and seventh, line battalion were raised; three hundred men, as a foundation for an eighth battalion, were also enlisted, and a fourth battery was added to the corps of artillery.

By the middle of February the whole had embarked, and in a few days the fleet arrived at Portsmouth. Here the cavalry, the three last raised regiments of infantry, and the artillery were landed, while the light-battalions and the two first line brigades were ordered to proceed to Ireland.

Narrative of colonel v. Linsingen, MSS.

The first heavy and first light regiments of cavalry were also destined for the same country, and embarked at Liverpool for Dublin in the month of April; the head-quarters of the former were stationed at Gort, in the county of Galway; those of the latter at Tullamore in the King's County.

The second dragoons marched to Northampton, where, under the command of colonel von Veltheim, the regiment was completed. The men that had been enlisted for the second hussars joined that regiment at Canterbury, where, under the command of colonel Victor von Alten, its head-quarters were established. 1806. April.

The third hussars were quartered at Guilford under colonel von Reden.

The two last raised regiments of cavalry had been partially mounted in Hanover, but want of transport room made it necessary that many of the horses should be disposed of previous to embarkation, and the few that were brought to England were there replaced by English horses, with which both the cavalry and artillery of the legion were all ultimately provided.

The fifth and sixth regiments of infantry were formed into the third line brigade under colonel von Drieberg, and marched to Winchester, where they were joined in May by the seventh and eighth battalions, now formed into the fourth line brigade under major general von Dreschel.

The artillery were stationed at Porchester barracks, under the command of major Röttiger.

The advantages of the royal military academy at Woolwich not being open to the officers of this corps, an establishment for professional instruction, at the private expence of the regiment, was set on Narrative of general Hartmann, MSS.

1806. May. foot by its commanding officer, major Röttiger, whose exertions proved of material service to the legion at large; for not only did this establishment furnish the artillery with efficient officers and non-commissioned officers, but many officers of the other regiments of the legion received from it their first lessons in theoretical instruction.

Journal of major Rautenberg, MSS.

It has been mentioned that the two light battalions and the first and second line brigades were ordered to proceed to Ireland. On the 6th of May these regiments sailed for Cork, but scarce had they lost sight of the English coast when a violent gale of wind sprung up and drove them into the Atlantic. The gale lasted nearly three days, and finally obliged the transports to put in to Bantry Bay, on the south-west coast of Ireland, where in the Harbour of Beerhaven they anchored on the 13th.

So long a voyage not having been anticipated, their stock of provisions proved here deficient, and recourse was had to the inhabitants of the coast for fresh supplies. To their dismay the Germans found that the peasantry of these parts, providently reserving any cattle which they might possess, as a means of paying the rent of their tenements, subsisted almost entirely upon fish and potatoes, and were consequently little qualified to provide the strangers with more substantial nourishment. From this state of abstinence the troops were, however, relieved on the 20th, when, the easterly wind subsiding, they sailed for Cork, and anchored in Cove-harbour on the following day, 1806. May.

The two light battalions went to Bandon, the first regiment of the line to Kinsale, the second to Middleton, and the remaining brigade was quartered at Clonooney-barracks * in the Queen's County.

After the Prussians had obtained possession of Hanover, they threw so many impediments in the way of general Decken's arrangements for continuing the recruiting, that the depots at Hanover and Stade were given up, and that officer returned to England; he was, however, enabled to send over five hundred additional men previous to his departure from Germany.

The first line brigade had been but a few weeks in its new quarters, when it was ordered to embark for Gibraltar, at which fortress the first and second line regiments landed at the end of June.

This change brought the third line brigade to Ireland, where it relieved the two light battalions; of these, the first regiment went to Tullamore in the King's County, the other to Kilbeggan in the neighbouring county of Westmeath.

The greater part of the legion had now been removed to Ireland, and found no reason to be dis- Narrative of colonel v. Linsingen, MSS.

* A temporary barrack capable of containing two thousand men, which was then situated about seven miles from Birr (Parson's Town) and one-and-a-half miles from Banagher: it has since been demolished.

1806. June. satisfied with the change. To both officers and men Ireland presented advantages which the sister island did not afford them. The hospitality of the inhabitants; the cheapness of provisions; the readiness with which a stranger, and particularly a military man, was admitted into the family circles of the gentry—formed an agreeable contrast to the parallel circumstances in England. There, indeed, the country towns were so crowded with troops, that general attention to the military could scarcely be expected from the residents; and he who was not fortunate enough to be provided with letters of introduction, had little chance of being invited to partake of their hospitality. In Ireland, on the other hand, the garrisons were smaller, and the gentry, ever more ready to form acquaintances than the English, make those advances* which are so agreeable to a stranger, and could not but prove highly gratifying to the officers of a foreign corps.

The Hanoverians became acquainted with Irish hospitality to its fullest extent; the houses of the more wealthy residents were open to them; at the grand entertainment or more humbly family party, they were equally welcomed; the ladies taught them English, and the gentlemen bore with their German;—festivities denoted their presence, and lamentations their departure.

* This quality is well expressed by the German word—*zuvorkommend* (literally, coming first), for which I know of no synonyme in our language.

That this friendly intercourse should have led to more near alliances may well be imagined, and the subsequent change of condition of several officers of the corps proved that the fair daughters of Erin were not insensible to the merits of their foreign guests. 1806. July.

With more complete satisfaction could we dwell upon the sojourn of the German legion in Ireland, did not an unfortunate event, which about this time occurred, mingle some painful recollections with this period of their history.

Journal of major Rautenberg, MSS.

The light companies of some Irish militia regiments had been formed into a brigade, and stationed at the town of Birr in the King's County. In the month of July this brigade was broken up, and the several companies of which it was composed were ordered to join their respective regiments. Agreeably to this order, four companies, being those of the Derry, Monaghan, Limerick, and Sligo regiments, marched into Tullamore, where, as has been stated, the first light battalion and one squadron of the first dragoons of the legion were quartered. On their entrance into the town, the militia officers were met by a deputation from those of the legion, who, wishing to return a similar civility which had been paid to one of their battalions by the Irish officers at Birr, begged that they might be favoured with their company at dinner. The invitation was declined on the plea of fatigue, and the militia pro-

1806. July. ceeded to take up their quarters in Tullamore for the night.

Appendix No. V. About seven o'clock in the evening a man belonging to the German light battalion, who was peaceably crossing the bridge that formed one end of the main street of the town, was knocked down by one of the militia, who was immediately joined by several of his comrades. Three other Germans, who were accidentally passing, and came up to see what was going forward, met with a similar fate.

Narrative of general v. Linsingen, MSS. Major-general von Linsingen, who, in the absence of general Dunne, commanded the district, happening to be at the moment about to leave the officers' dinner-room in the adjoining hotel, was attracted by the noise which this outrage occasioned, and seeing from the inn window that two or three of the German light infantry were surrounded by a crowd of militia soldiers, hurried to the spot, and in the best English he could command, entreated them to desist. For the moment his interference was effective; but two of the Germans had been already wounded with bayonets and stones, and a determination to repeat the assault appeared evident on the part of the militia. The major-general, therefore, sending to the barracks for a patrole, repaired to his quarters, and made the officer commanding the militia acquainted with what had occurred. This officer immediately waited upon

1806. July. Narrative of general v. Linsingen, MSS.

general Linsingen, who ordered him forthwith to parade his men for roll-call, and sent similar instructions for the first light battalion of the legion to colonel von Alten.

The patrole from the barracks now came up and seized one of the militia, who appeared to be a ringleader in the business. About twenty of his comrades then collected for the apparent purpose of rescuing him, and were about to charge the Germans with fixed bayonets, when captain von Düring of the first light battalion, who was parading his company in a square of the main street, moved it down upon the charging party, which had been momentarily stopped by the expostulation of brigade major von Kronenfeldt, and caused them to retreat behind the bridge. Here they faced about, and fired upon the Germans, seven of whom were wounded. Upon this, captain Düring pressed forward and drove them across the bridge and into the lanes beyond it; meantime colonel von Alten's battalion had been formed up in the main street.

The militia had now nearly all retired from this part of the town; but taking shelter in the houses, and at the corners of the streets, they still continued to fire upon the Germans, and lieutenant baron Marshalk was dangerously wounded by a musket-ball in the chest.

On the militia first beginning to fire, general Linsingen had ordered out a party of the first

1806. July. dragoons, which now arriving, he placed himself at their head, and charged the only body that still held out. This was the party which captain Düring had driven across the bridge, and which still kept a bold front in the lower part of the town. The German dragoons felt naturally irritated at the unprovoked treatment which their comrades had received, and shewed little mercy towards the aggressors. These, however, received them with a heavy fire; but not being able to withstand the violent reprisal of the cavalry, soon after dispersed, and here the affray, which lasted about half an hour, terminated.

Journal of major Rautenberg, MSS.

Three officers, (lieutenants Peters, Alten, and Marshalk,) twenty-two men, and five horses of the legion were wounded in this unfortunate disturbance; one of the wounded men afterwards died, and baron Marshalk, who had been shot through the lungs, was for a length of time not expected to recover.

Of the militia nine only were wounded, one of whom afterwards died, which small number of casualties, in proportion to that of the legion, was to be attributed to the latter being unprovided with ammunition, while the militia were all loaded with ball.

These serious results caused a long and minute investigation into the cause of the affray to be made by the government. A court of inquiry was convened at Tullamore, the report of which not being deemed satisfactory, was followed by a second investigation, under the immediate superintendence of general Floyd, the commander of the forces in Ireland; but both failed in ascertaining the exact cause of the provocation;* it was, however, fully proved that to the militia alone the fatal consequences which have been recorded were justly attributable. 1806. July. Journal of major Rautenberg, MSS.

The court of inquiry pronounced the conduct of two of the Irish officers reprehensible, and the one most censured was brought to a court martial on the principal charge of having been present at, and not using his best exertions to suppress, the disturbance. The charges were, however, not substantiated, and the officer was acquitted; but eight of the men, fifteen of whom were also tried, were sentenced to severe punishment as ringleaders in the affray.

The conduct of the Hanoverians under the peculiarly trying circumstances in which they were placed during the whole of this affair, was a theme of general commendation, and the official reports

* Various reasons have been given for the hostile feeling of the militia towards the Germans;—revenge for a punishment, which had, a short time before, been inflicted upon one of their body for stealing a pipe from one of the German light infantry; a belief that the arrival of the latter in Ireland was the cause of the militia light brigade having been broken up; the faithlessness of some former "*sweethearts*" of the Irishmen in Tullamore, on the arrival of the legion in that town, have been severally stated as the cause of aggression, and, taken collectively, will probably account for the affray.

1806. July. were in the highest degree favourable to them. General Linsingen, however, felt doubtful as to the impression which might have been made upon the mind of the king respecting the German troops, and addressed a letter to lieutenant-colonel Taylor, his majesty's private secretary, on the subject. From his reply, which completely relieved the general's mind, by informing him of the nature of the official reports, we have been permitted to make the following extract:—

"Windsor, August 4th, 1806.

"My dear general,

"I had the pleasure of receiving, yesterday, your obliging letter of the 28th of July, and I lose no time in acknowledging it, as I am anxious to release your mind from any uneasiness in regard to the impression which may have been made here by the unfortunate occurrence at Tullamore. The king had received lieutenant-general Floyd's and the solicitor general's first report; and their further reports, with the proceedings of the court of inquiry, have been laid before his majesty; and I am happy to assure you that every document speaks in the most favourable terms of the conduct of the Hanoverian officers and men in the business, and throws the whole blame on the militia light companies. The reports endeavour to do justice to your personal exertions, and to the activity and steadiness of the cavalry, and the lord lieutenant corroborates the testimony of general Floyd and the solicitor-general, as to the general excellent conduct of colonel Alten's battalion, including all the Hanoverians, and as to the popularity which they have so justly acquired among the inhabitants. I sincerely regret that, so early, your residence in Ireland should have been marked by a circumstance so unpleasant to a brave old soldier; but, however distressing, I can assure you that it has proved most honourable to yourself, and all those of the German legion who were concerned in it." 1806. July.

* * * * * *

" I communicated to the king the contents of your letter, and received his majesty's commands to assure you, that all that has come to his knowledge is highly to the credit of yourself and the Hanoverian officers and men, and tends to confirm him in the high opinion which he has ever had of the discipline and good conduct of the corps, which, his majesty is persuaded, will be conspicuous upon every occasion as upon this.

" The two light battalions have probably received their order to prepare for embarkation for Sicily, and I must only observe that this removal was decided upon before any information had been received of the affray at Tullamore. They are going upon what will, I think, prove a very interesting and very active service."

* * * * * *

The order for embarkation alluded to by colonel

1806.
December.

Taylor reached the light brigade in the beginning of August, when the first battalion marched to Middleton, and the second battalion to Mallow; but an arriving at these towns, it was made known to them that their departure from Ireland was, for the present, deferred, and they were soon after removed to their old quarters at Bandon, the third line brigade going to the King's County. In the following spring, however, these battalions were again in march; for the whole of the infantry, two regiments of cavalry, and four batteries of artillery of the legion, were, in the month of April, ordered to hold themselves in readiness to embark for the continent.

1807.

April.

CHAP. VII.

Although the continental coalition had been prematurely maimed, and the confederate army had evacuated Hanover, the chivalrous king of Sweden, under whose orders its operations were to have been carried on, still upheld the cause in which he had zealously embarked; and having rejected with disdain Napoleon's wily proposals for peace, although presented to him with the tempting condition of territorial aggrandisement, was now preparing to defend his territory of Pomerania from the attacks of the French.

General von Essen, the governor of that province, had, early in the spring, compelled the enemy to raise the siege of Stralsund, and repass the Swedish frontier; but on the 16th of April Mortier drove him back behind the Pene with considerable loss, and the contending parties concluded an armistice. Ten days' notice of the renewal of hostilities had been first agreed upon by the two generals, who afterwards extended this period to one month; the king of Sweden, however, who arrived at Stralsund early in May, and was there promised by general Clinton prompt and effectual assistance from England, declared that he would only acknow-

Bissett's reign of Geo. III.

1807. April. ledge the first stipulation of the armistice, and ordering the fortifications to be improved, and new works to be constructed in the neighbouring island of Rügen, awaited the arrival of the promised aid from England.

Journal of major Rautenberg, MSS.

This consisted of two regiments of light cavalry, eight battalions of infantry, and four batteries of artillery of the king's German legion, the whole amounting to about eight thousand men, of which lieutenant-general lord Rosslyn was appointed to the command.

It has been stated that the German battalions in Ireland had received orders to prepare for embarkation. These regiments sailed from Cork on the 29th of May, and with the usual luck of the legion on such occasions, encountered the next morning an adverse wind. The fleet were obliged to put into Mount's bay on the coast of Cornwall, where a serious calamity had well nigh befallen a part of the second light battalion.

The Northumberland transport, on board of which were lieutenant-colonel Halkett and three companies of his regiment, struck, in endeavouring to reach her anchorage, upon the Runnell stone rock, and sprung so great a leak that her preservation became hopeless. The sea was rushing rapidly through the opening, and the fate of all on board would, probably, have been soon identified with that of the vessel, had not one of the gun-brigs which formed the convoy hurried to her assistance, and by the great exertions of all parties concerned, succeeded in conveying the entire crew of the sinking vessel to an adjoining transport; to which they had scarcely been removed, when the Northumberland went down, taking with her the baggage and arms of colonel Halkett's detachment.

Journal of major Rautenberg, MSS.

On the 31st the transports were enabled to leave their place of shelter, and on the 7th of June the fleet anchored in the downs. Here they were joined by the second and third hussars, the fifth line brigade, the first battery of horse artillery, and the first, second, and fourth batteries of foot artillery of the legion, which had been embarked at Portsmouth and Ramsgate, and completed the force with which it was intended to assist the Swedes. This corps sailed in two divisions on the 19th of June and 1st of July, under the command of major generals von Linsingen and Drechsell, and by the 8th had reached the island of Rügen. In consequence of the low shore, the debarkation of the cavalry was attended with much difficulty, the greater part of the transports being obliged to anchor nearly two miles from the coast. By means, however, of a float which was provided with a trap-door, the horses were thrown into the water, through which they were led ashore from boats, and by the 15th the whole corps had safely landed. Part of general Drechsell's division, (which reached its destination on the 10th,) consisting of the sixth, seventh, and eighth line battalions, under colonel du Plat, were on the 14th sent over

Journal of 2d hussars, MSS.

1807. July.

to Stralsund, into which fortress the Swedes, after having been attacked in their lines by marshal Brune on the expiration of the armistice, had been forced to retire.

This brigade was placed under the orders of general von Essen, the governor of Pomerania, and took the daily piquet duty alternately with the Swedish troops.

Journal of major Rautenberg, MSS.

Nothing of importance occurred until the morning of the 6th of August, when about three o'clock in the forenoon the French commander sought, under cover of a strong division of his army, to push the investing corps closer to the fortress, which movement the little garrison resisted by a vigorous sally, the three battalions of the legion occupying the advanced works. The contest lasted for several hours; but the Swedes were finally obliged to yield to superior numbers, and again to retire within their walls.*

While colonel du Plat's brigade was thus employed at Stralsund, the two cavalry regiments, the light infantry brigade, and the first horse battery of artillery of the legion, were engaged in observing the opposite coast of the island of Rügen,

* This was one of many spirited sallies made by the garrison of Stralsund; but the utmost efforts of so small a corps could ultimately avail little against an army of seventy thousand men; and after destroying the magazines, and spiking the cannon, the king of Sweden committed Stralsund to the care of its citizens, and on the 19th of August transferred his troops and stores to Rügen, where, early in September, the little army capitulated.

and the vigilance of the German piquets caused the French to abandon an attempt to land on the point of the peninsular Inder, which they made in armed boats on the night of the 30th of July.

1807. August. Journal of 3d hussars, MSS.

But an event was in preparation which soon deprived the king of Sweden of his German allies.

A powerful naval and military armament had been fitted out by England for the purpose of ensuring compliance with a demand which the wavering conduct of Denmark, her inability to resist the ambitious views of France, and the positive information that Buonaparte had determined upon occupying Holstein with a military force, compelling Denmark to close the passage of the Sound against the British, and employing the Danish navy in the invasion of Great Britain and Ireland, had caused the government of those countries to make upon the sovereign of Denmark.

Declaration of his majesty, London Gazette.

His majesty's ministers required the temporary deposit of the Danish fleet in one of the British ports, on the solemn stipulation that it should be restored to Denmark in the same condition as that in which it should be delivered to the British admiral on the conclusion of a general peace.

This demand was rejected; the English fleet arrived in the Sound on the 3d of August; the prince royal of Sweden declared that he would adhere to the line of policy which he had hitherto pursued; and after a fruitless effort to shake this resolution had been made by Mr. Jackson the

1807. August. envoy, the naval and military commanders proceeded, according to their instructions, forcibly to effect that object which negotiation had failed to obtain.

Journal of major Rautenberg, MSS. To the British land forces that were employed on this occasion, and which amounted to about two thousand men under the orders of lieutenant-general lord Cathcart, it was deemed necessary to add lord Rosslyn's corps; pursuant to which arrangement colonel du Plat's brigade rejoined the main body of the legion at Rügen on the 8th of August, and on the 13th the whole were under weigh for Zealand. Here they joined the fleet which had arrived from England on the 3d, under admiral Gambier, and found that the first hussars and first line brigade had also come out. The latter had been suddenly sent from Gibraltar on the 10th June, and reached the Downs in time to accompany the other troops. Thus, with the exception of the two heavy dragoon regiments, the second horse battery, and third foot battery of artillery, the whole of the legion were employed in this expedition.

The three hussar regiments which constituted the entire cavalry force of the army, were united into a brigade, and placed under the orders of major general von Linsingen.

The infantry formed the second division of the army under lieutenant-general the earl of Rosslyn, and were thus brigaded.

1st brigade,	colonel du Plat, 6th, 7th, and 8th line battalions.	1807.
2d	,,	colonel von Drieberg, 3d, 4th, and 5th line battal.	August.
3d	,,	colonel von Barsse, 1st and 2d line battalions.	
4th	,,	colonel von Alten, 1st and 2d light battalions.	

To this division major-general von Drechsell and brigadier-general von der Decken were attached. Journal of major Rautenberg, MSS.

The legion artillery were under the immediate command of major Röttiger, the horse battery being commanded by captain A. Sympher, the three foot batteries by captains Gesenius, Tieling, and Heise; these four batteries, together with a similar force of English artillery, were under the chief command of major-general Bloomfield, to whom colonel Harding was second in command.

Colonel d'Arcy was the chief officer of engineers, major Fletcher second in command, under whom, of the legion, were captains Prott and Berensbach, lieutenants Meinecke, Appuhn and Schweitzer.

With the exception of one brigade which anchored higher up the Sound to make a diversion, the whole of the English infantry, the first line brigade of the legion, and two batteries of artillery were landed on the morning of the 16th at the village of Wedbeck, about eight miles from Copenhagen, and occupied the heights without meeting with any resistance. Towards evening, about forty horses of the first hussars were also landed, and under their escort the commander-in-

Journal of the army under lord Cathcart, London Gazette, 1807.

1807. August. chief proceeded to reconnoitre the approaches to the capital.

Journal of the army under lord Cathcart. The only opponents with which the detachments met were a troop of armed peasants, and these were easily made prisoners; however, on their providing the general with the information which his lordship required, and promising not to appear again in arms, they were permitted to depart, and the detachment continued its march, unmolested, to Jägerborg, where it found accommodation in a cavalry barrack which had been that morning abandoned by the Danes.

The army followed in three columns in the same evening, and on the following morning Copenhagen was completely invested, both flanks of the army resting on the sea.

About noon the advanced piquets of the left wing were attacked, and that part of the line was at the same time cannonaded with grape and round shot from the enemy's gun-boats in the harbour. The piquets repelled the attack and kept possession of their posts, and the English gun-brigs and bombs having opened a fire upon the enemy's gun-boats, obliged them, after a long cannonade, to retire into the harbour. A detachment of the second hussars, which, as well as the remainder of the first hussars and English artillery, had just then landed, came into fire on this occasion.

On the 18th, the garrison of Freiderickswerk surrendered to a squadron of the legion, after as bloodless, if not as ludicrous an expedition as ever terminated in the capture of a fortress. 1807. August.

Captain Krauchenberg of the first hussars, whose spirited conduct as lieutenant of the late Hanoverian cavalry has been already noticed, being in command of the advanced guard of a squadron of that regiment which had been sent out to reconnoitre under the orders of brigadier general von der Decken, learned that a convoy of a hundred and eighty waggons, loaded with ammunition and protected by a strong escort, was on its way to the fortress of Friederickswerk, about sixteen miles distant; and thinking that a good opportunity of making a capture was thus presented to the hussars, he proposed to, and obtained the consent of, general Decken to attempt to cut off the convoy.

The squadron accordingly proceeded to Krigume, but it was here ascertained that the convoy had already passed through on its way to Friederickswerk. Krauchenberg was not, however, disposed to give up the intended capture, and now proposed attempting to take the fortress by surprise.

The day was far advanced and the horses were much fatigued. General Decken, however, assented to the proposition of his enterprizing squadron officer, and the detachment moved on towards Friederickswerk, which was stated to be a strong position defended by a corps called the volunteers of the place, which had been raised by the crown prince

1807. August. himself for the protection of the powder-mills and arsenal there.

About one in the morning the squadron had arrived within half a mile of the place, and here general Decken halted with the main body, while captain Krauchenberg and lieutenant Schaumann, with a few men, rode forward, and succeeded in surprising the enemy's advanced picquet. Krauchenberg now sent the officer of the picquet to the commandant of the fortress with the imposing announcement "that general von der Decken, at the head of an army of ten thousand men, was in full march upon Friedericksswerk, and had sent him forward to summon the place, which," he added, "would assuredly be taken by storm if the governor did not immediately surrender!"

Major Tschering, the governor and aid-de-camp to the prince-royal, seeing, no doubt, the hopelessness of his being able to stand the assault with which he was threatened, sought only to moderate the demands that might be made upon him; and having expressed his firm conviction that his countryman general von der Decken (for the commandant was also a German) would grant him honourable terms of capitulation, empowered captain Krauchenberg to state his readiness to treat immediately with the general for the surrender of the place.

This being communicated to general Decken, he

kept the squadron stationary just long enough to allow for the supposed advance of his imaginary army, and then galloping up with all the clatter and parade which the hussars could make, presented himself to the simple-minded commandant, who did not long hesitate in agreeing to the terms that were offered to him by the general. Eight hundred and sixty men, thirty-two of whom only were regular troops, surrendered, upon conditions that they should not serve again during the war, or until exchanged ; and a great quantity of powder, guns, and small arms, were also placed at the disposition of the captors.

1807. August.

General von der Decken's Report.

As general Decken was unprovided with the means of transporting so large a quantity of stores, he was obliged to be satisfied with the promises of the governor and his officers that neither powder nor stores should be given to the Danes, and to content himself with carrying off four guns and half the arms of the garrison.

Every thing had been thus amicably arranged, and the squadron was on its return about five o'clock, in the morning, when the appearance and noise of crowds of armed peasants shewed that the expedition was no longer likely to proceed without interruption. The return of day-light had opened the eyes of the commandant, and it was soon known that the fortress of Freiderickswerk had surrendered to a squadron of German hussars instead of an army of ten thousand men. The peasants had, therefore, turned

1807. August. out—perhaps at the instigation of the governor—from all the neighbouring villages, and armed, some with rifles, the greater part with pitch-forks, made a show of opposing the return of the cavalry. Some thousands collected on a height, and a few shots were fired, but from too great a distance to have any effect on the squadron; and lieutenant Ernest Poten galloping up to them at the head of a few men, the greater part dispersed, leaving fifty men and five horses in the hands of the hussars.

General von der Decken's Report. Hearing that all the woods and villages which lay in the direction of his march were similarly beset with armed peasants, the general changed his road, and took the squadron away to the left, by which judicious detour he gained the open country, and brought the hussars and their trophies back in safety to Jägersborg. The prisoners, after having been chastised with the back of the sword, and set right with regard to the presence of the English troops in their country, were all liberated.

The fleet which bore lord Rosslyn's corps from Rügen anchored, on the 15th, in Kioge Bay, where, on the 21st, the whole of the infantry and two batteries of artillery were landed. The cavalry and two remaining batteries of artillery were sent round to Charlottenlund, and disembarked there on the 18th and 19th.

The duty of the three cavalry regiments and of the horse artillery of the legion was to observe the country in rear of the besieging army by a chain of posts from Sorgenfrey and Kollekalle, which was supported by the first line battalion; the whole being under the direction of brigadier-general von der Decken. Each cavalry regiment also furnished a squadron or more to the divisions before Copenhagen. The first hussars provided the centre, the second hussars the left, and the third hussars of the legion the right wing; the latter regiment was also employed in observing the great roads leading from the capital to Roeskilde and Kioge. At Roeskilde the Danes were said to have collected some troops, and a squadron of the third, under captain Küper, was sent on the night of the 21st to reconnoitre and endeavour to surprise them. About half a league from Roeskilde the squadron surrounded the Danish videttes, and at day-break surprised their outposts, which consisted both of cavalry and infantry. Sixteen of the enemy were killed, and three men and forty-five horses captured. The rest taking to flight, captain Küper pursued them to the gates of Roeskilde, from whence a fire of infantry obliged him to retire. His loss amounted to only four men and two horses wounded.

1803. August.

Journal of 3d hussars, MSS.

The troops which had occupied Roeskilde now retired to Geveningen, between which place and Ringstedt the Danish militia were concentrated and encamped. Kioge was also evacuated, and its

Journal of the army under lord Cathcart.

1807. August. citizens, who had begun to organize themselves into a corps, were disarmed by the Germans.

Journal of the army under lord Cathcart. On the 23d, lord Rosslyn's corps joined the army, and took its position in second line, covering the centre.

On the 24th, the army advanced, and the centre occupied a road running to Freidericksberg, parallel to the defences of the place, the suburbs between that point and Copenhagen being also occupied by the besieging army.

The enemy's piquets now fell back to the lakes or inundations in front of the place, and those of the British took possession of the abandoned positions. In the afternoon the garrison appeared on all the avenues leading from the town, apparently with the design either to recover their ground, or to burn the suburbs; and the several generals of the besieging army immediately drove them in, each in his own front. At the same time they seized all the suburbs on the north part of the lakes, establishing themselves, in some places, within four hundred yards of the ramparts.

On this occasion, major Halkett, with three companies of the second light battalion of the legion, captured a redoubt in a manner which reflected much credit upon that officer and the men whom he commanded.

Narrative of gen. sir H. Halkett. MSS. A reconnoitering party of the second light battalion had, unobserved by the Danes, crept into some of the gardens near the town, and discovered

Narrative of sir H. Halkett, MSS.

that the enemy were busily engaged in bringing guns into a newly-finished redoubt. Being close under the walls of their citadel, the Danish piquets considered themselves quite secure; and major Halkett thought that the circumstances were favourable to an attack being made upon them. He, therefore, sent an officer to the camp, requesting that two companies of the second light battalion might be sent up, and a third placed in reserve. The troops in advancing received the fire of the citadel, but were soon covered by the hedges which enclosed the gardens. Here they were met by the Danish riflemen; but the good dispositions which the two captains von Düring and du Plat made of their men, enabled them to reach the redoubt, which immediately opened its fire upon them. The work was instantly attacked, and, with the assistance of the reserve company under captain Bösewiel, was carried, the Danes making a sharp resistance. The riflemen who had opposed the advance of the Germans, finding that the redoubt was taken, retired towards the citadel, which, together with the crown batteries and block ships, now poured its fire upon the redoubt, and caused the whole British line to get under arms. Lieutenant-general Sir David Baird, to whose division the second light battalion was at this time attached, soon joined the troops in the redoubt, and although it had been attacked without his orders, he appeared gratified at major Halkett's success, and acceded to his request

1807. August. Narrative of Sir H. Halkett, MSS.

to be allowed to keep possession of his conquest. The commander-in-chief, however, on being informed of what had occurred, sent positive orders for the troops to fall back, as he did not consider the position tenable. But general Baird's report produced a change in the opinion of lord Cathcart, and the Germans now received orders to advance and again possess themselves of the post from which they had been inconsiderately withdrawn. Meantime, the Danes had received reinforcements, but the force which supported the second attack ensured its success, and the redoubt again yielded to its former victors.

This capture, united with the general success of the investing corps on the same day, led to new lines of approach being taken up; the works in progress were abandoned, and a parallel within eight hundred yards of the place, and nearer to it on the flanks, was immediately commenced.

CHAPTER VIII.

EIGHT hundred of the legion under colonel von Reinboldt, of the fifth battalion, having been sent forward, on the morning of the 25th, to close in the investment, the Danish garrison sallied out with much vigour and in considerable force. The attack was gallantly met and repulsed by the legion detachment, and the Danes were driven back at all points, but not without loss to the Hanoverians, from sixty to seventy of whom were killed and wounded. Among the latter was captain von Düring of the first light battalion.

1807. August. Journal of major Heinemann, 5th line battalion, MSS.

The following day major-general sir Arthur Wellesley, who commanded the reserve, was sent with that corps and eight squadrons of cavalry, the sixth battalion, and the horse artillery of the legion, into the interior of the country for the purpose of dispersing a *levée en masse*, which, as well as some regular troops, were reported to be assembled in the neighbourhood of Kioge, under the command of the Danish general Oschenskiold.

Journal of the army, under lord Cathcart.

The reserve consisted of the forty-third, fifty-second, and ninety-second regiments under brigadier general Stewart, the first battalion ninety-fifth under colonel Beckwith, and captain Newhouse's battery

1807. August. of horse artillery; the cavalry force was made up of detachments from the legion hussars, the first and third regiments furnishing each three, and the second hussars two squadrons. The squadrons of the first and second hussars, one squadron of the third, the forty-third foot, five companies of the ninety-fifth, the sixth battalion, and half the horse artillery of the legion, were placed under the orders of major-general von Linsingen, (the infantry forming a brigade under colonel von Hohnstedt,) and formed the right of sir Arthur Wellesley's corps, from which, on the 28th, it was detached for the purpose of turning the enemy's left flank by Roeskilde, while sir Arthur proposed to attack him in front by the coast road to Kioge.

Sir A. Wellesley's Report. For this place both divisions marched on the morning of the 29th. Upon general Wellesley's approach, he found that the enemy was in force in front of the town, and the skirmishers of the third hussars, which formed his advance, were cannonaded from a few guns which defended the front of the enemy's line; but these the British and German horse artillery soon caused to retire. The Danes had three or four regular battalions formed in one line, with cavalry on the flanks, and apparently a large body was beyond the town and rivulet which ran before it.

About nine o'clock, the time at which the two generals had agreed to make their concerted attack, sir Arthur Wellesley's corps deployed in one line, the right of which was flanked by the two squadrons of the third hussars, under colonel von Reden, and the left by the sea. In this position sir Arthur remained for more than an hour, hoping to hear that general Linsingen had crossed the rivulet; but no communication arriving from that general, and the enemy appearing to be in motion on his left, sir Arthur Wellesley no longer delayed the attack, but advanced in echelon of battalions from the left, covered by the ninety-fifth riflemen and the fire of his artillery. 1807. August. Sir A. Wellesley's Report.

The ninety-second, under lieutenant-colonel Napier, led the attack, which was supported by the forty-third and fifty-second, and the enemy soon retired to an entrenchment which he had formed in front of a camp on the north side of Kioge.

This entrenchment the ninety-second prepared to storm, and the enemy made a disposition of his cavalry on the sands to charge them. Sir Arthur therefore moved colonel von Reden's hussars to the left flank, and placed the forty-third in second line, upon which the ninety-second carried the entrenchment, and the enemy retreated in disorder into the town.

Colonel von Reden now led forward his hussars; the ninety-fifth, and afterwards the whole of the infantry followed, and the enemy fled in all directions.

Upon crossing the rivulet sir Arthur Wellesley

1807. August. found general von Linginsen upon his right flank, and both divisions now joined in pursuit of the enemy.

General v. Linsingen's Report. The march of general Linsingen's division had been delayed by the difficulties which it experienced in crossing a rivulet between Gungard and Kioge. Much wood and a large morass rendered this impracticable at the one pass of Yderholm, and the bridge at the other pass of Littenge Garde had been broken down; and although the pioneers of the sixth battalion of the legion under the direction of brigade major Münter repaired this bridge with so much expertness that in twenty-five minutes the infantry were able to pass in single file, so much time elapsed before the division could move forward, that general Linsingen did not arrive at Kioge until the Danes were already in full retreat.

Journal of major Heise, 3d hussars, MSS. Although the Danish regular troops fled with precipitation, throwing away their arms and appointments, the new levies shewed much spirit. Some of these raw recruits fired upon the cavalry from the windows of the houses in Kioge, and suffered themselves to be bayonetted by the infantry; others took shelter behind the sheaves of corn in the fields, and from thence fired on their pursuers. The greater part of these were either cut down or made prisoners, but not without loss to the legion hussars. Lieutenants Rudorf of the first, and Jansen* of the third regiment were wounded, the former mortally; and sixteen men and twenty-two horses of both regiments were wounded; the third being the principal sufferers. 1807. August.

General v. Linsingen's Report.

Major-general von Linsingen now continued the pursuit with his cavalry and artillery; the latter, commanded by captain von Witzleben, was brought to bear upon a column of infantry that was retreating towards the shore, and the Danish artillery in vain attempted to prevent its destructive effects; meantime the cavalry under colonel Victor von Alten had taken eighteen waggons loaded with ammunition, arms, and accoutrements; soon after which major Plessen's squadron of the first hussars captured about fifty waggons carrying various stores, and the pursuit was continued without intermission.

Major-general Oxholm, the second in command of the Danish troops, who had joined them the preceding evening from the southern islands, with four battalions, attempted to make a stand in the village of Herfolge. This place colonel Victor von Alten was ordered to attack, and while the horse artillery opened a fire upon the church-yard in which the enemy had collected, and some of the ninety-fifth riflemen assailed it in flank, colonel von Alten,

* Lieutenant Jansen received a flattering letter, accompanied by a case of handsome pistols, from sir Arthur Wellesley, in token of his distinguished conduct on this day.

1807. August. lieutenant Schnüring, and sixteen of the second hussars rapidly advanced, and major-general Oxholm, count Wedel Jarlsburg, several other officers, and four hundred men laid down their arms. The hussars had only one non-commissioned officer killed, and one man and one horse wounded.

The cavalry and horse-artillery continued the pursuit towards Soeder, where many prisoners were made. General von Linsingen now moved this part of his force, towards Giesler in order to press upon the enemy's right flank, and observe his retreat, of which soon losing sight, they were ordered to fall back and unite with the ninety-fifth and advanced posts in covering sir Arthur Wellesley's head-quarters at Kioge.

London Gazette. The loss of the Danes on this day was altogether considerable. Many fell, and nearly sixty officers and eleven hundred men were made prisoners. The remainder of their army now crossed over to the islands Laaland and Falster, and the British were suffered to continue the investment of Copenhagen uninterrupted by any further movements in the interior.

Journal of the army under lord Cathcart. Nearly all the British batteries had been finished and two-thirds of the ordnance mounted, when, about four o'clock on the morning of the 31st, a sortie, commanded by general Peyman in person, was made by the garrison, towards the Glüsing garden, on the British right. Although stopped by a piquet of the fiftieth regiment,

1807. Sept.

the Danes persevered for some time, but were finally repulsed by the piquets of the first division. Sir David Baird and the Danish general were both slightly wounded on this occasion.

Journal of the army under lord Cathcart.

On the 1st September, the mortar batteries being nearly ready for action, lord Cathcart and admiral Gambier summoned the place. General Peyman requested a passport to enable him to obtain the decision of his Danish majesty; this was refused, and at half-past seven in the afternoon of the 2d of September, all the besiegers' batteries were opened upon Copenhagen.

The first general flight of shells set fire to the town in several places; but by the exertions of the inhabitants the flames were extinguished, and the fortress returned the fire of the batteries with vigour. The bombardment was thus continued for twelve hours without producing any overture on the part of the garrison; towards night, however, the fire grew slack, and that of the besiegers was consequently abated; but on the following morning the Danes threw a quantity of shells from the place, and the British batteries again poured destruction into the town. The flames again burst forth; the

Siege of Copenhagen, &c.*

* The Siege of Copenhagen, or Documents comprehending an Official Detail of the Bombardment of that City, together with a Danish Narrative of the dreadful Calamities suffered by the Inhabitants in consequence thereof. By an Officer from Copenhagen. London, 1808.

1807. Sept. tower of the great church, which had been some time on fire, fell with a dreadful crash, and spread destruction around it; the fire engines, destroyed by the shells and frequent use, now became unserviceable, and the people fled in terror to the island of Amack, the road to which exhibited indescribable scenes of horror and misery. Three hundred and five houses and one church had now been burnt to the ground, and the total demolition of the city would have inevitably followed, had not general Peyman sent out a flag of truce, requesting an armistice of twenty-four hours, to afford time to treat for a capitulation.

Lord Cathcart's despatch. This proposition was declined by the British commanders, as tending to produce unnecessary delay, and the works were continued; but the firing ceased, and lieutenant-colonel Murray, deputy-adjutant-general to the British army, was sent to explain to the commandant that no proposal of capitulation could be listened to unless it was accompanied by the surrender of the fleet.

This basis having been at length admitted, major-general sir Arthur Wellesley, sir Home Popham, and lieutenant-colonel Murray were appointed to meet the Danish authorities, and propose the articles of capitulation. These were drawn up on the night of the 6th, and ratified by the respective commanders-in-chief on the following day; and at four o'clock in the afternoon of the 7th of September, lieutenant-general Burrard, who was second in command of the British army, took possession of the citadel. 1807. Sept.

During the siege, an effort was made by major-general Stricker, the commandant of Cronborg, to shake the allegiance of the German Legion, to whom, on the 4th, he addressed an insidious proclamation. "You, Hanoverians," it said, "we consider as innocent people, forced to accomplish the cruel commands of your government. But you will be the sacrifice; it is yet time to save your lives. Being Hanoverians, you are long since discharged from your duty and faith towards the treacherous government of England. Do not obey the commands of this inhuman and bloody ministry in order to subjugate an innocent nation. Let us associate ourselves together. The Danes will always receive you like friends. You will find the most secure refuge at Copenhagen or Cronborg. Hasten hither! The Danes, the faithful Danes, who will shew you kindness, security, and support, promise you in the most solemn manner, at the conclusion of the war, to lead you in safety to your native land. Siege of Copenhagen, &c.

"Hanoverians! hearken to the voice of friendship and reason!" * * * * * *

But this effort of the Danish general was completely unsuccessful; for instead of the Danes gaining adherents from the legion, a considerable number of foreigners from various parts of the continent

1807. October. who had entered the Danish service to avoid the conscription of Napoleon, now offered their services to the British, and were enrolled in the Hanoverian legion. By these means, not only were the deficiencies in the corps made up, but the establishment increased.*

Lord Cathcart's despatch. The capitulation required that the citadel should be restored to the Danes, and the British troops embarked, within six weeks from the day on which it had been ratified; and no sort of infraction of the agreement having been made by the Danes, who acted most honourably in the strict fulfilment of their engagement, the British commander decided upon commencing the embarkation of the army.

Accordingly, on the 13th of October, the eight line battalions of the legion, and on the following day the two light battalions, were embarked at the arsenal. The shipment of the cavalry and artillery

* The following strong illustration of German honesty, which occurred during the siege, is mentioned in the Journal of major Heise of the third hussars, and appears not unworthy of record.

On one of the British attacks upon the suburb, this officer, then a lieutenant, was posted with twenty-two men of the regiment in front of an apothecary's shop, where also spirits were sold. For this part of his stock in trade the apothecary found several customers among the hussars, but the continued discharge of grape from the citadel much disturbed the circulation of the glass. Still more, it might be supposed, would it have interfered with the after process of remuneration. This, however, was most conscientiously performed, and notwithstanding the uninterrupted fire from the citadel, the Germans were to be seen most methodically drawing our their purses, and presenting the apothecary with the value of his drams.

followed, and by the 21st the whole army was under weigh for England, accompanied by the Danish fleet. 1807. October.

The appearance of this immense armament,—one thousand sail, among which were forty-five line-of-battle ships, fifteen frigates, and numerous other smaller vessels of war of various descriptions,—crowding with swelling canvass into the narrow passage of the Sound, was a grand and imposing spectacle. The king of Sweden stood on the shore at Helsingborg as the British pendants passed, and each ship of war saluted his majesty with a discharge of twenty-one guns.

But the fair wind, which at starting filled their sails, changed to an adverse gale when the fleet entered the Categat, and increased during the night of the 22d to such a degree, that on the following morning not more than three or four vessels were to be seen together, the rest being scattered in various directions over the German ocean. Narrative of major Heise, MSS.

The weather continued tempestuous for several days; at length the fleet, after having been driven about the North Sea for more than a week, re-united at Yarmouth. Unfortunately, there were no orders for the troops to be landed here, and on the 8th of November the transports were again under weigh for their destinations of Portsmouth and Ramsgate.

But the elements continued to oppose their return: an adverse and violent gale again separated

1807. November. the fleet, and this second storm brought with it the most fatal consequences to the Hanoverians.

Narrative of major Heise, MSS.

One transport, containing twenty-six men and horses of the third hussars, struck, during the night, upon the Goodwin sands, and sprung a leak. The pumps soon became choked, and the water rising rapidly in the vessel, all clung to the masts, despairing of succour. The master, seeing that there was no chance of saving his ship, conceived the design of escaping with the sailors, and leaving the hussars and horses to their fate; he accordingly had the boat lowered down, and succeeded in getting into her, with four of his crew, and putting off from the vessel unobserved by the soldiers. When but a short distance off, they were perceived by the hussars, some of whom attempted to jump into the boat; but of these only two reached her and were saved, while the transport going down on the sands, took with her the rest of those who had been left behind.

Another small transport, with eighteen horses of the same regiment on board, was run foul of by an East Indiaman, which carried away the entire stern of the transport, and scarcely had the people escaped in the boats, when the vessel, with all the horses, went down.

The horses and baggage of two transports of the second hussars, as well as a gallant officer of the same regiment, captain Ludolphus Baring, also perished; the Hope transport, with forty sick on board, was also lost; another transport, called the Eagle, on board of which were eight officers, a hundred and seventy-two non-commissioned officers and soldiers, and the chaplain, with his wife and children, of the first line battalion, was never heard of after the gale, and is supposed to have gone down in the Queen's channel. Nearly three companies of the same regiment, under lieutenant-colonel von Ompteda, only escaped shipwreck to fall into captivity, and their perils are worthy of detail. These troops were embarked in the Augustus Cæsar transport, which, in the night of the 27th October, came into violent contact with the ship of war Inflexible, of sixty-four guns. The bowsprit of the man-of-war bearing down upon the larboard side of the transport, passed through her main chains, and carried away her mainmast; the masts, yards, and rigging of both vessels then got foul of each other, and the smaller ship, thus entangled, became exposed to the tremendous thumping of the man-of-war, which threatened soon to reduce her to a wreck. Every effort was made on both sides to get clear, but the darkness of the night and the heavy sea rendered this extremely difficult, and nearly an hour had passed before the vessels could be disengaged. Meantime five of the officers,* and about a hundred non-commissioned officers and men of the legion,

1807. November. Appendix No. VI.

Loss of the Augustus Cæsar, transport, MSS.

* Captain Laroche, Lieutenants von Borstel, Schlütter, Heine, and Ompteda.

1807. November. Loss of the Augustus Cæsar transport, MSS.

ventured to attempt escaping from the transport into the Inflexible. This was a hazardous experiment, as well in consequence of the violent concussion of the vessels, as of the number of spars that were falling about; however, although many were wounded, with the exception of one man, the whole gained the deck of the ship.

By this time the transport presented a deplorable appearance. Of her three masts, the foremast alone remained standing; large breaches down to the very edge of the water had been made in both her sides; twelve out of fourteen guns which she carried had been either torn away, or forced through the deck into the hold; her boats were driven from their fastenings and damaged, and the whole of her bulwark had been carried away.

Thus disabled, she was totally incapable of following the fleet, which on the morning of the 30th was completely out of sight, and the wind coming on to blow a gale from the westward on the following day, she was driven before it towards the coast of Holland. Land was first seen on the morning of the 31st, and now the apprehension arose that the ship might be dashed upon the beach, for they could find no holding ground at sufficient distance from the coast to be secured against a land attack, and the vessel had drifted within half gunshot of the shore, before she could be brought to anchor.

The sea broke over her with violence, and it

did not seem probable that her shattered hull would hold much longer together; at noon, however, the gale subsided, and some hope of safety was entertained. But now came the perils of the land, for the Dutch, having descried the vessel, had brought down a few guns to the shore, and from these soon opened a fire upon the luckless transport. The English signal of distress was then made, which caused the firing to be for a time suspended, but towards evening it was resumed, and continued until the master of the transport had been made by signal to understand that he was required to hoist a lantern at the mast head, which being done, the firing ceased, and the vessel, which had received but little additional injury from the ill directed shots, was left unmolested until morning. A Dutch naval officer then came off to the transport, and demanded the surrender of all on board as prisoners of war. Colonel von Ompteda felt that he had no alternative but to submit to this requisition, and his whole force, amounting to nine officers, and more than two hundred non-commissioned officers and soldiers, were, together with the crew of the vessel, disembarked and marched to the Hague, from which the landing place was about six miles distant.* They were to have

1807. November. Loss of the Augustus Cæsar transport, MSS.

* The men were afterwards removed to the fortress of Löwenstein, and the officers placed on their parole at Gorcum. The latter were exchanged, and returned to England in the following spring; but the non-commissioned officers and soldiers, being principally natives of those provinces which formed the new kingdom of Westphalia, were obliged

1807. November. retained their baggage, but the boats being occupied till night-fall with the disembarkation of the men, its removal could not be attempted before morning, and then the vessel was no longer visible; for the wind getting up in the night, her destruction had been completed.

Calamitous as were many of the disasters which befel the legion on the return of this expedition, they were all far exceeded by those which attended the loss of the transport Salisbury.

Narrative of Dr. Rathje, MSS. This vessel, containing the greater part of the second line battalion, had been separated from the fleet on the night of the 22d of October, and reached Yarmouth on the 8th of November, just as the other ships had got under weigh. Her provisions were nearly exhausted, oatmeal being almost the only article of subsistence left; still the master thought it better to follow the fleet, and continuing his course, brought the vessel on the 10th, close under Margate, where several other ships had already anchored. But now he became apprehensive of coming in contact with some of these, and fearing also to approximate an unsheltered coast during such tempestuous weather, stood out to sea.

Between eight and nine o'clock in the evening, the helmsman, mistaking the light ship on a bank called the Kentish Knock, for one of the vessels of

to enter the service of king Jerome. From his rule, however, the greater part took the first opportunity of emancipating themselves.

the fleet, ran the transport direct upon the bank, against which she struck with violence. The passengers, alarmed at the sound, hurried upon deck, from which the breakers were too visible, and the vessel would inevitably have foundered, had not a heavy sea carried her off the bank, and again set her afloat. But the rudder had sprung, and the vessel leaked. Cartridges were now sought for to fire signals of distress, but the powder magazine had filled with water, and a few only were found serviceable. With these, however, some signals were fired, and they were answered by blue lights from several vessels that were near at hand; but the night was too dark and the gale too violent to admit of any boats putting off, and no hope of assistance could be entertained before morning.

1807. November. Narrative of Dr. Rathje, MSS.

The injury to the rudder had rendered the vessel quite unmanageable, and she lay completely at the mercy of the wind and waves. For some time the captain tried, by crowding all his sail, to reach the French coast, but it was found impossible, and about midnight he anchored in twenty-three fathom water. The pumps were at work incessantly, and became often choked, and the soldiers were then obliged to bail out the water from the hold in their caps; in fact the vessel was alone kept afloat by the unceasing and strenuous exertions of the men.

The small supply of ammunition which had been rescued from the water in the magazine having been exhausted, resource was had to the cartridges

1807. November. Narrative of Dr. Rathje, MSS.

of the soldiers for keeping up the firing of signals of distress. For this purpose the men had brought nearly all their pouches upon deck; and two guns were loaded from the supply. Unfortunately, however, on the guns being fired, a portion of the ignited cartridge paper, blown by the wind upon some loose powder, set fire to the whole stock of ammunition, and in a moment from twenty to thirty pouches flew into the air. Lieutenant von Hodenberg and nine men were more or less injured by this explosion.

A ship now appeared in sight, and some of the sailors attempted to put off to her in the skiff, but no sooner had this craft been lowered down, when a sea, dashing it against the ship's side, shivered her to pieces, and those who had entrusted their lives to the frail protection, all went down, filling the air with their cries.

The vessel dragging on her larboard anchor, and being much driven about by the sea, the ballast shifted towards this side, and made it necessary for the larboard gallery and guns to be cut away and thrown overboard. The same would willingly have been done with the masts, had not the weight of their fall been dreaded, as on whichever side they might happen to come, the weight would, in all probability, have brought the vessel under. The cable was now cut, and the ship again abandoned to the fury of the elements. Some empty water-casks and spare planks, which had been lashed to the side, alone kept her above water; whoever let go his hold fell instantly overboard, and many an unfortunate was heard to cry for help, and the next moment seen to sink for ever.

1807. November. Narrative of Dr. Rathje, MSS.

At length day broke, and vessels appearing at a short distance off, hope was rekindled in the minds of the sufferers; but the violent squalls prevented any ship from approaching the Salisbury, and gave all full employment in providing for their own safety. About ten o'clock, however, the weather seemed disposed to moderate, and one vessel came so near that it was resolved to send off the jolly boat, and implore her assistance. Captain Scharnhorst, two soldiers, and two of the crew of the Salisbury embarked in this boat, and reached the vessel; but a violent squall then came on, and no effort to assist their comrades could be made while it lasted. The situation of the Salisbury was now so perilous, that the destruction of those on board appeared inevitable; the sailors, therefore, lowered down the long boat, and all rushed forward to seek refuge in it. Lieutenants von Wenkstern and Magens, forty-three soldiers, one woman and child, and the master and twelve of the crew of the transport succeeded in getting in, after which the rope was cut, and the boat, unprovided with either oars or rudder, drifted off at the mercy of the waves. The other vessel now bore up towards the boat, and as she was driven past her, threw out a rope, but it fell short of the

1807. November. Narrative of Dr. Rathje, MSS.

object; a second and a third time this was attempted, but with equal ill luck, and the last hope of the sufferers appeared to have been extinguished, for the master of the vessel was unwilling to make any further effort for their preservation. A few bold and generous soldiers, however, came to their relief. Major Roberton, who with part of the eighth English infantry was on board the vessel, seeing that the master of the transport declined making any farther exertion to save the people in the boat, energetically appealed to his own men on behalf of their brother soldiers. Several officers and men immediately came forward; from these the best rowers were chosen, and they gallantly put off in the jolly boat, and endeavoured to convey a rope to the boat of the Salisbury. This rope proved too short, and was obliged to be twice lengthened before it would reach the boat, keeping the sufferers in the most painful suspense; at length the brave soldiers succeeded in accomplishing their humane object, and both boats were hauled up to the transport, which now bore away towards the Salisbury.

On nearing the vessel major Roberton sought to cheer the unfortunate people on board, who had despaired of receiving help, by calling out to them, "you will all be saved," which they answered with a grateful hurrah!

Four men of the legion now jumped into the long boat and put off to the Salisbury, but the wind again increased, and rendered their approach dangerous;

the boat reached, however, the stern of the vessel, 1807. November.
and surgeon Rathje, the quarter-master sergeant,
two soldiers, and the mate were enabled to jump Narrative of Dr. Rathje, MSS.
into her; but the transport was fast sinking, and
to have remained longer near her would have endangered the boat, which was obliged immediately to be got away. With the preservation of these five persons, therefore, their gallant comrades were obliged to be satisfied, and scarce had they pulled off, and ensured the safety of the boat, when the Salisbury went down. Nine officers, two hundred and twelve men, thirty women, and five children perished with this transport. The entire casualties of the legion in the expedition amounted to one thousand one hundred and seventy-five, of which thirty-six were officers, and the drowned alone numbered two hundred and twenty-six! Appendix, No. VI.

1807.

December.

CHAPTER IX.

THE effects of the late gale could be traced along the whole south-eastern coast of England, scarce a harbour in the circuit of which but bore some evidence of its fury. The transports that escaped landed their troops at the different ports in which they had found shelter, and the scattered detachments then proceeded to join their respective regiments.

The first and second hussars were re-assembled at Weymouth; the third at Deal; the light infantry at Hastings and Battle, and the first, second, fifth, and seventh line battalions at Bexhill. Of the other four line regiments, but a small part had landed, when they were again ordered to embark, and with the third foot battery of artillery, to join an expedition then about to sail for the Tagus, under the command of major-general Spencer: the rest of the artillery again occupied Porchester.

General Spencer's corps was intended ultimately for the Mediterranean, but in its way out was to support sir Charles Cotton in an attack upon the Russian fleet then in the Tagus, and thus facilitate the emigration of the prince regent of Portugal to the Brazils. About one half of this corps consisted of

German troops; namely, the third, fourth, sixth, and eighth line battalions of the legion under brigadiers du Plat and von Hohnstedt, and the third foot battery of artillery under captain Bussman; captains Appuhn and Berensbach, of the legion engineers, also accompanied the expedition. 1807. December.

On the 20th of December the fleet left Portsmouth for the rock of Lisbon, and on the 31st had reached the Bay of Biscay, when they encountered a gale of wind, which, continuing with little intermission until the fifth of January, obliged the greater part of the fleet to put back to England. About twenty transports, however, among which were the third line battalion, part of the sixth, and the artillery of the legion, had reached their destination on the 13th; but Lisbon was by this time in possession of the French, and these vessels were obliged to cruize about for a week at the mouth of the Tagus, not knowing for what part of the world they were ultimately intended. At length on the 19th the signal was made for Gibraltar, where they anchored on the 23d; from hence, on the 5th of February, they were ordered to proceed to Sicily; but just as their ships were about to get under weigh in compliance with this order, they were all thrown into confusion by a sudden burst of wind in the bay, which drove them about in all directions, forcing the vessels from their moorings, and against each other, to such an extent that much damage was done, and the weather continuing tempestuous,

Journal of 3d line battalion, MSS.

1808. it was some days before they were again ready
February. for sea.

Journal of 3d line battalion, MSS. On the 11th all but five transports got under weigh; these came up on the 15th, and the whole, after having been once more dispersed by a squall in the night of the 24th, anchored in the bay of Palermo on the 1st of March.

But the voyage and its accompanying bad weather had not yet ended. On the 6th the transports were ordered to proceed to Syracuse, and another gale of wind overtaking them, kept the troops at sea for fourteen days more; this was the fourth time these vessels had been dispersed since their departure from England, and now, just as they were about to enter the harbour of Syracuse on the 21st, their destination was changed to Messina. Here, however, they arrived without impediment, and the troops were at length landed on the evening of the 24th.

The transports which had put back to England, having waited a favourable change of weather there, were more fortunate. The fourth, eighth, and remainder of the sixth battalion of the legion sailed from Falmouth on the 21st of February, arrived at Gibraltar on the 10th of March, and landed at Messina on the 6th of April.

Sicily was at this time threatened with invasion by a French force, which, under the command of Murat, occupied the opposite continent of Calabria, and the German regiments were employed in guarding the coast, furnishing the garrisons, and fulfilling the various duties attendant upon the constant state of preparation in which the island was necessarily maintained. 1808. February.

To these monotonous but fatiguing duties we will for the present leave this part of the corps, and proceed to detail the operations of those regiments to whom fortune allotted a more brilliant career.

Another armament for the assistance of Sweden had been fitted out in England, and the third hussars, under colonel von Reden, the light infantry brigade under colonel von Alten, the first and second line brigades under colonels von Langwerth and Drieberg, and the first and fourth foot batteries of artillery of the legion under major Hartmann, were united with seven battalions and four batteries of British; the whole of which, under the command of sir John Moore, were ordered to proceed to Gothenburg. Narrative of major Heise, MSS.

The expedition sailed from Yarmouth on the 10th of May, and after a prosperous voyage anchored in the harbour of Gothenburg on the 18th. But no operation was after all attempted; for a difference of opinion arose between his Swedish majesty and the British commander as to the plan of proceeding, and after a tiresome sojourn of six weeks on ship-board, the troops were ordered to return to England.

During the latter part of this period the heat of the weather was excessive, and the horses of the

1808. June.

Narrative of major Heise, MSS.

hussars being confined to the transports, suffered much;* the officers of the legion, however, endeavoured to lighten the wearisomeness of their stay by every expedient of which their situation admitted, and were not unsuccessful. Lobster fishing, which is to be had here in great perfection, offered a never failing resource to the aquatic sportsmen; and so many betook themselves to the sport, that the army were more than abundantly provided with this delicacy during their stay. Sailing about and exploring the different creeks and inlets on the coast, was also productive of much amusement, and brought many a novel and interesting object to their notice. Nature has been here so little bountiful, that it is with the greatest difficulty the poor inhabitants can find a spot fit for cultivation, and many, in order to provide themselves with

* To those of our readers who may be unacquainted with the manner in which these unfortunate animals are disposed of on board a transport, the subjoined detail will, perhaps, be acceptable.

A horse transport contains, according to its size, from eighteen to forty horses, which are placed close together across the hold, with their heads towards the centre, where is a wooden trough for the reception of forage. Small upright posts are fixed between their heads, which are fastened on each side by short ropes, in order to prevent them from lying down, and their chests and haunches are covered by sheepskins, to save them from being stripped by the rolling of the vessel. This closely packed stable is ventilated by means of sacks, which hang from the deck into the main hatchway; but in still or warm weather this is of little service, and the animals then suffer extremely from the oppression of the atmosphere. If a long voyage be anticipated, the horses are generally slung by tackles, to prevent them from resting on their legs, which expedient enables them to bear the confinement with less inconvenience.

1808. July. Narrative of major Heise, MSS.

gardens, had brought earth from the more fertile places and formed an artificial soil upon the naked rock. Excursions to these curious spots passed away many an evening, and the party being provided with the means of organizing a pick-nick supper, and often accompanied by music, the repast was served between the rocks; the band then struck up, to the wonder and delight of the fishermen and maidens, who cheerfully joined in the dance which followed.

From this tranquil scene the troops departed on the 3d of July, when the fleet sailed for England, and on the 21st all were again at Spithead.

Meantime the English government had determined upon opposing the rapid strides of Napoleon in the Spanish peninsula. Sir Arthur Wellesley, with nine thousand men, had sailed from Cork, and a second expedition was about to sail from England. To this it was intended to add Sir John Moore's army; and the legion transports, without landing either men or horses, were ordered immediately to provision for another voyage: the second foot battery of the corps was also embarked.

The necessary preparations were not completed before the 31st, when the fleet, consisting of a hundred and sixty eight transports, and four ships of war, sailed from St. Helen's, its destination being Vigo Bay.

1808. August. An officer of the third hussars has thus graphically described the progress of the fleet:—

"There is something imposing in the appearance of a large fleet of transports under full sail. The mass of troop-ships in the centre—the accompanying men-of-war ranged in front, rear, and on the flanks, and the whole advancing under the safe guidance of the commodore with all the order of an army marching across a vast plain! Towards evening is heard the signal for re-assembling the ships, and those whose bad sailing has prevented them from keeping up with the rest, come slowly and orderly to their proper stations. Then, should it fall calm, not an unfrequent occurrence at the close of a summer's day, the vessels are seen fixed, as it were, like houses on the glassy surface of the deep. The sun majestically descends into the vast mirror which has reflected his image, and just as the last mild rays of the cheering planet have faded from our view, and a profound stillness reigns, the evening guns burst forth their simultaneous signals from the men-of-war, whose mingled music, wafted in doubtful harmony throughout the fleet, closes this magic scene."

The Bay of Biscay next called forth the wonder of the legion. "Here," writes another officer of the corps, "the waves rolling in slow succession rise mountains high. The approach of one of such waves threatens you with instant destruction, but in a moment the vessel is elevated upon its summit, from whence, as from the top of a high tower, the whole fleet is visible before you. Scarcely is this sight developed, when you sink into a frightful abyss, from whence no traces of the former objects are to be distinguished, and you rise again to witness a repetition of the same scene." 1808. August.

The fleet assembled before Vigo Bay on the 17th; but sir Arthur Wellesley's operations had caused its destination to be changed to the Mondego, for which river it sailed the same evening. Narrative of major Heise, MSS.

The transports coasted along the beautiful Portuguese shore of the Entre Douro e Minho with a favourable wind; but in the night of the 19th a fog arose which caused much inconvenience. The atmosphere became suddenly so dense, that in order to prevent the ships from running foul of each other, it was found necessary to fix lanterns to their mizen masts, and this precaution not proving sufficient, recourse was had to the blowing of horns. This doleful music, by means of which each vessel proclaimed her position, was kept up unceasingly throughout the whole of the night; but notwithstanding its continuance, several vessels were, in the morning, found entangled in each other's rigging, and one transport containing the first foot-battery of the legion artillery was so much injured as to be obliged to return to Portsmouth.*

* This vessel did not land her troops at Lisbon until the 8th of September.

1808. August. Narrative of major Heise, MSS.

On the 21st the fleet reached the mouth of the Mondego river, and the disembarkation of the troops was commenced on the following morning; but meantime the battle of Vimeiro had been gained by sir Arthur Wellesley, and sir J. Moore's army was therefore ordered to land at Maceira Bay. The regiments already on shore were consequently re-shipped, and the whole getting under weigh the same evening, anchored at the embouchure of the little river Maceira on the 23d and 24th.

The landing here, which began on the 25th, was extremely difficult, and attended with considerable danger. The weather was tempestuous, and a tremendous surf broke upon the high shore. Many boats were swamped, and the comparatively few casualties that occurred may be principally ascribed to the intrepid and indefatigable exertions of the navy. The English sailors, stimulated by the example of their officers, were seen wading up to their shoulders in the sea, and hauling in the boats as they were driven ashore by the surf. The horses of the third hussars, which had been seventeen weeks on ship-board, and were now obliged to swim ashore, could with difficulty reach the land. Often was an unfortunate animal, after having been cast upon the beach by one wave and unable immediately to get on his legs, borne back by the next into the sea, and again cast ashore to be driven from it in the same manner. Several horses were thus lost. Forty had already died or had been shot for glanders produced by their confinement on board the transports; the greater part of those which landed were found lame and unfit for immediate service, and when the regiment came to be mustered, scarce half of its original numbers was fit to take the field.

1808. August. Narrative of major Heise, MSS.

These difficulties so much protracted the disembarkation of the troops, that it was not until the evening of the 29th that the whole of the legion regiments had been landed.

In consequence of the exhausted state in which the horses of the hussars reached the shore, that regiment was unable to accomplish an ordinary march, and bivouacked about three miles from the landing place. The spot chosen was a small flat, nearly surrounded by high rocks, through which ran a little rivulet. The weary hussars laid down to sleep with all the satisfaction which the consciousness of being again on *terra firma* after a long voyage invariably creates, and confidently anticipated undisturbed and refreshing slumbers; but scarcely had they passed an hour in this position, when they were suddenly awakened by a violent torrent of rain which burst upon them as if from a water-spout.

Although thus exposed, the weary soldiers would not give up the intention with which they had commenced the night, and covering themselves with their cloaks and blankets, were soon again in a sound sleep.

1808. August. Narrative of major Heise, MSS.

But the enclosed nature of the bivouac formed a reservoir for the rain, and towards midnight it had so accumulated that the most determined sleepers could no longer tolerate their position, all being literally lying in water. A general stir therefore took place, and most fortunately; for by this time articles of every description were floating about the bivouac. Saddles, accoutrements, clothing, &c. mixed up with each other in all directions. Now arose a general anxiety regarding personal effects. The darkness of the night added to the confusion, and to restore order among the unruly articles of equipment became difficult in the extreme. Suddenly, however, the rain ceased, and the accumulated water running off soon after, each man collected his drenched accoutrements, and with the aid of a large fire made them tolerably dry.

Then were the troops first aware that the little rivulet, of whose waters they had drank with so much gratification on the preceding evening, was the last depository of many of those who had fallen at the late battle of Vimeiro.

On the 28th, the hussars marched to Torres Vedras, and the light infantry brigade and second battery of artillery moved the same day into a hut-camp on the other side of Vimeiro, where, on the 29th, they were joined by the four line battalions. The two remaining batteries of artillery also joined the army, and the whole then moved towards, and were stationed in the neighbourhood of Lisbon.

The battle of Vimeiro was followed by the convention of Cintra and the evacuation of Portugal by the French, and the English government now decided upon sending an army into Spain in order to aid the patriotic exertions of the Spaniards against the invaders of their country. Thirty thousand infantry and five thousand cavalry, ten thousand of which were to be sent from England to Corunna under sir David Baird, and the rest drafted from the army in Lisbon, were to be employed in the north of Spain under the command of lieutenant-general sir John Moore.

1808. October.

Napier's History of the War in the Peninsula.

The third hussars and light infantry brigade of the legion formed part of the corps which marched from Lisbon, where the two line brigades and artillery remained, the latter giving up all their serviceable horses to the British artillery.

The army marched from Lisbon towards the latter end of October by four different roads, Burgos being the point of concentration. The main body of the infantry, under the immediate orders of the commander-in-chief, took the direct roads north of the Tagus; that of the cavalry and artillery, under sir John Hope, the more circuitous routes of Badajos and Talavera.

The light brigade of the legion under colonel von Alten (now promoted to the rank of brigadier-general) formed, with general Anstruther's English brigade, the advanced division, which was commanded by the honourable major-general Edward Paget.

Journal of majorRautenberg, MSS.

1808. October. Narrative of major Heise, MSS.

One troop of the third hussars under captain von dem Bussche accompanied this division; the remainder, effective, of the regiment under major von Burgwedel* marched with the 18th English dragoons under brigadier-general Charles Stewart. This brigade formed the entire cavalry of the corps that marched from Lisbon, and did not muster a thousand horses, for many men and horses of both regiments were unable to march; the third in particular had suffered severely from the long confinement on ship board,† and one hundred and forty men and a hundred and twenty-five horses of that regiment were obliged to be left behind at Belem under captain Meyer, who had also the charge of the non-effectives of the eighteenth. Of the legion engineer-corps, captain Meinecke only accompanied this expedition.

Great expectations having been raised among the troops both as to the enthusiasm of the Spaniards in their resistance to the French, and their grateful and friendly feeling towards the British, they were not a little surprised and disappointed at finding, when they had crossed the frontier, no demonstration of either feeling. Hundreds of able-bodied men passed the columns with indifference on their march, or, wrapped in their dark mantles, stood

* Ill health had obliged colonel von Reden to return to England.

† The men were principally affected with dysentery, and the horses in the feet; the latter to such a degree, that many lost their hoofs altogether. *Journal of Dr. Grosskopf, third hussars*, MSS.

stupidly gazing on them in the market-places; and their reception at the houses of the inhabitants shewed an equal absence of any of those noble sentiments for which the "patriots," as they were called, had been so much lauded. 1808. October.

On the 19th, the wreck of Blake's army, which had been completely discomfited at Espinosa on the 11th, and finally disorganized at Reynosa on the 13th, crossed the march of Sir John Hope's division, flying in all directions. Napier.

On the 23d, the centre of the British army, consisting of twelve thousand infantry, and a battery of six guns, was concentrated at Salamanca; detachments of the French had already arrived at Valladolid, and the light brigade of the legion, accompanied by captain von dem Bussche's troop, was sent out to observe the road to that town. Journal of major Rautenberg, MSS.

On the 26th, the head of sir John Hope's column entered the Escurial, but that of sir David Baird, having been delayed in its advance from Corunna by the deception and neglect of the Spanish authorities, had not reached farther than Astorga. Napier.

Sir John Moore was at this time aware that the enemy's force could not be less than eighty thousand men, and that thirty thousand more were expected, and might have arrived;—that the Spanish generals, Blake and Belvidere, had been totally defeated; and that in all probability the little British corps would have to bear singly the combined

1808. November. Napier.

efforts of the whole French force. He would, therefore, have been perfectly justified in not exposing his army to such an unequal combat, and at once commencing his retreat; but he was unwilling to abandon the cause which he had come to support while a shadow of hope remained of his being able to serve it, and believing that the Spanish army of Castanos still kept the field, he proposed to rally it upon his own corps.

But on the 23d Castanos was totally defeated at Tudela, and this design became impracticable. Sir John Moore therefore decided upon withdrawing his troops, and falling back upon Portugal as soon as general Hope's division should have joined him.

Madrid, however, still held out, and promised a vigorous resistance, and Zaragossa and Toledo made equally imposing professions. These encouraging circumstances, together with the plausible representations and assurances of the Spanish authorities, and a generous solicitude for the honour of England, induced sir John Moore to give up his intention of falling back, and to decide upon venturing a forward movement.

He resolved to throw himself upon the communications of the French army, and hoped by thus drawing its whole force upon himself, to relieve the southern provinces of Spain, succour Madrid, and give the Spaniards time to recover courage, and organize their defences.

The capital of Spain held out but one day—still sir John Moore was determined to advance: the movement might, he thought, operate as a diversion, and while a possibility of serving the Spanish cause appeared, he was resolved not to abandon it. 1808. December. Napier.

Preparations for a retreat upon Portugal were, however, continued, and sir David Baird was ordered to form magazines at Benavente, Astorga, Villafranca, and Lugo, by which arrangement two lines of operation were secured: officers were also sent to examine the roads and harbours of Gallicia, and small magazines were established on the line of Orense and Vigo.

After skilfully evading the enemy's watchfulness, general Hope effected his junction with sir John Moore at Salamanca on the 4th, and on the 12th the army commenced its march upon Valladolid.

Previous to leaving Salamanca, the two light battalions of the legion were ordered to form an independent brigade under brigadier-general von Alten, as were the first battalions of the 95th, 43d, and 52d, under colonel Robert Craufurd. Journal of major Rautenberg, MSS.

At Alaejos, where head-quarters arrived on the 13th, an intercepted despatch was brought in, which changed the direction of the march. It was addressed to the duke of Dalmatia, and directed him to drive the Spaniards into Gallicia, to occupy Leon, Benavente, and Zamora, and to keep the flat country in subjection: a chance, therefore, appeared of the British being able to surprise and Napier.

1808. December. Napier.

beat Soult before Napoleon could come to his succour, and in furtherance of this object sir John Hope passed the Douro at Tordesillas, directing his march upon Villepando. Head-quarters were removed to Toro, and Valderas was given as the point of junction to general Baird's division, the head of which was now at Benavente.

On the 18th, head-quarters were at Castro Nuevo, and from hence sir John Moore, having heard that the marquis of Romana, although aware of the advance of the British, was retiring into Gallicia, wrote to inform that general of his intention to fall upon Soult, desired his co-operation, and requested that he would abide by his original plan of reserving the Asturias for his line of communication, and leave the Gallicias open to the British.

On the 20th, the whole of the British forces, consisting of two thousand two hundred and seventy-eight cavalry, nineteen thousand and fifty-three infantry, and sixty pieces of artillery, were united. The cavalry were at Melgar Abaxo, the infantry at Majorga: four batteries of artillery were attached to the infantry, two to the cavalry, and one was kept in reserve.

On this day lord Paget, with four hundred of the 15th hussars, obtained a brilliant triumph over six hundred of the French cavalry at Sahagun, taking one hundred and fifty-four men prisoners, among whom were two lieutenant-colonels, and eleven other officers. Sahagun was on the following day occupied by the British troops, and here they halted, having outmarched their supplies. 1808. December.

The legion regiments, however, which had been acting independently, were pushed forward towards Carrion, and on the 21st, the third hussars occupied the village of Pozurama, about fifteen miles from that place. Journal of 3d hussars, MSS.

Meantime Soult was here concentrating his infantry, and sir John Moore resolved to surprise him. He proposed moving by a night-march, so as to arrive at Carrion by daylight on the 24th, to force the bridge there, ascend the river, and then fall upon the main body of the enemy at Saldañha. Napier.

The surprise was peculiarly entrusted to General Hope's division, which, marching from Villada, was, after forcing the bridge of Carrion, to unite with a second column, coming from Sahagun, under major-general Frazer, and Romana was expected to co-operate on the left.

The light infantry brigade of the legion, under brigadier-general von Alten, was selected to form the advanced guard of general Hope's division,* and at nine o'clock on the night of the 23d of December, the right column left Villada. The air Journal of major Rautenberg, MSS.

* The cheering effect which this notification produced throughout the brigade was conspicuous. The sick and baggage had been ordered to be left behind at Villada; but out of thirty-two men of the brigade who might have taken advantage of this order, twenty-four reported themselves fit to march. *Journal of major Rautenberg*, MSS.

1808. December. was bitter cold: the wide plain over which the line of march lay was covered with snow, and a chilling sleet fell at intervals: the open ground allowing the column to march upon an extended front, it advanced in the greatest order and stillness, and all looked confidently forward to the result of the contest which daylight was expected to bring forth.

CHAPTER X.

It was midnight—the light brigade of the legion had already arrived near Pozurama, and the third hussars were drawn out in front of this village, when suddenly the column was ordered to halt, the advanced guard to occupy the village in its front, and the main body forthwith to countermarch upon Villada.

1808. December. Journal of major Rautenberg, MSS.

This unexpected arrangement for a retrograde movement had been caused by the receipt at head-quarters of a despatch from the marquis of Romana, which stated that the French were in motion on the side of Madrid. This intelligence was confirmed by the British general's spies, and all reports agreed in affirming that the whole French army was in motion to crush the British. The main objects of sir John Moore's advance were, therefore, attained, and it now remained for him to complete his hardy enterprize by a timely retreat. Orders had been, consequently, sent to countermand the advance of the army, and the column which had already commenced its march was directed to retrace its steps.

Napier.

Agreeably to the intentions which had been com-

1808. December. Journal of major Rautenberg, MSS.

municated to general Alten, the light battalions of the legion took up a position at Pozurama before day-break. At ten o'clock these regiments followed the retreat of the main body to Villada, which they found evacuated; for general Hope was already on the road to Majorga.

Napier.

Two divisions of the army marched under general Hope, and were to cross the Esla at the bridge of Castro Gonzalo, opposite Benavente; another column, under sir David Baird, was directed to the ferry of Valencia de San Juan, and the cavalry, reserve, and flank brigades remained behind to cover these movements.

On the 25th, the reserve and light brigades followed the route of general Hope's column to Valderas, the cavalry at the same time pushing forward their patroles towards Carrion: these, consisting principally of the legion hussars, brought in this day about thirty prisoners; towards night-fall, however, the cavalry also withdrew to Villada; but so judiciously, that the enemy did not appear to be aware of the retrograde movement which they had masked.

On the following morning, however, this was fully evident, and the advanced scouts of the French cavalry came up with the rear of the British. The piquets of the fifteenth hussars were attacked; but a reinforcement from the Germans enabled them to repel the enemy, and some prisoners fell into their hands. The British cavalry this day reached Villaldon, but left it again at midnight, and the third hussars of the legion now became the rear-guard of the army. 1808. December. Journal of 3d hussars, MSS.

The hussars left Villaldon on the morning of the 27th, and about three in the afternoon approached the bridge of Castro Gonzalo.

Here the light battalions arrived on the preceding day, and had been transferred to the reserve brigade under sir Edward Paget, which, posted on the high left bank of the Esla, was now employed in protecting the passage of the column across that river. This was happily effected, and the reserve followed the rear divisions to Benavente about four o'clock, general Craufurd's brigade remaining to destroy the bridge. Journal of major Rautenberg, MSS. Napier.

At day-break on the 28th, the German hussars came again in contact with the enemy's advanced horsemen, who about that time attacked their outposts, but were repulsed, and two officers of the imperial chasseurs were taken prisoners. Journal of 3d hussars, MSS.

The third remained as rear-guard on the left bank, under torrents of rain and snow, until the evening of the 28th, when they also passed the Esla, and soon after midnight the bridge was blown up.

The German hussars were here promised a day's rest from the harassing duties of the rear-guard; a party of twenty only, under cornet von der Hellen, was taken to make up the outlying piquet, the rest were ordered to unsaddle and make up Narrative of captain Meyer, 3d hussars, MSS.

1808. December. their horses for the night, holding themselves in readiness to move off to the rear the next morning.

Narrative of captain Meyer, MSS. Fortunately for the British cavalry, major von Linsingen took upon himself to modify this order, and desired that the horses of the third should not be unsaddled. The river might, he thought, be forded, and the rear-guard surprised; he therefore cautioned the men by no means to consider themselves sure of passing the night undisturbed.

Narrative of gen. sir Loftus Otway, MSS. The event verified his precaution; for at daybreak the French cavalry were observed moving down towards the broken bridge. This proving impassable, they made several attempts to find a ford; but the swollen state of the river rendered these ineffectual, and they finally plunged into the stream and swam across.

Colonel Otway, who commanded the outlying piquet, having previously sent to apprize lord Paget of the enemy's apparent intentions, immediately called in his advanced posts, and gave orders that the main body of the picquet should join him without delay.

These orders were not, however, immediately complied with; and the French, amounting to between five and six hundred chasseurs of the imperial guard, had pressed in the detachments to within half-a-mile of Benavente, when colonel Otway, fearing that the British cavalry might be surprised in their quarters, determined to make a stand with the small force (only sixty men) which was at his disposal: he accordingly took up a position on the road where the mud-walls of some gardens of the suburb afforded protection to his flanks, and there awaited the slow approach of the enemy.

1808. December.

Narrative of sir Loftus Otway, MSS.

Sixty men of the inlying piquet (composed of the tenth and seventh hussars,) and a serjeant* and twenty-five men of the eighteenth hussars, now came opportunely to the assistance of the detachments, and colonel Otway, seeing that the enemy had halted one squadron considerably in advance of the rest of his column, resolved to take advantage of this disposition by charging the body thus advanced. The French squadron awaited the charge, and was completely routed, the officer commanding it being killed on the spot; but the remaining squadrons coming up immediately to its support, the piquets were obliged to retire with precipitation to their former position.

Meantime the alarm had been sounded in Benavente, and the third hussars of the legion, prepared by the prudent caution of major Linsingen, quickly repaired to the place of assembly. Without waiting for the general parade of the regiment, captain von Kerssenbruch and lieutenant Jansen hurried all the men they could immediately collect, amounting to nearly three troops, to the scene of contest, and, encreasing the effect of their

Narrative of major von Gruben, 3d hussars MSS.

* Serjeant Jeffs, afterwards adjutant of the seventh hussars.

1808. December. Narrative of sir Loftus Otway, MSS.

numbers by forming them in rank entire, enabled the retreating piquets to rally and prepare to join them in a second charge. This attack, conducted by general Stewart and colonel Otway, was, as the first, also awaited by the enemy, but owing to the deep clayey ground over which the allied cavalry were obliged to pass, did not produce a like impression upon the French column; great havoc, however, was made among the enemy by the British sabre, which lost none of its excellence in the hands of the Hanoverian hussars,* and both sides becoming intermixed, a scene of desperate individual conflict ensued. Thousands of spectators from under the walls of Benavente encouraged their protectors with cries of "Viva los Ingleses," and the brave objects of their acclamation justified the plaudits by redoubled exertions: the contest was, however, too disproportionate to give any hope of ultimate success to the British, and would probably have terminated unfavourably to them, had not the remainder of the third hussar regiment under the command of major Burgwedel, and the main body of the outlying picquet, arrived. Lord Paget, also, who commanded the cavalry, now galloped into the field, and having quickly restored the British squadrons to order, and seeing that he was

* The journal of one of the officers of the third hussars describes the wounds inflicted by the Germans on this occasion as quite extraordinary; arms were cut off—heads split to the neck, and one French horseman is stated to have had his face cut from ear to ear right through the mouth.

supported by the main body of the tenth and eighteenth hussars, then coming down the hill from Benavente, the gallant lord headed a third charge against the enemy. This was completly successful: the imperial chasseurs were driven into the river, and many became easy marks for the carbines of their pursuers. Arrived on the opposite bank, however, the French spiritedly wheeled about, and succeeded in wounding some men by firing across the river; but meantime two pieces of horse artillery had unlimbered close to the bank, and the first shot, falling in the midst of those that had rallied, soon decided their retreat.

1808.

December.

Narrative of sir Loftus Otway, MSS.

In the course of the pursuit a young private of the German hussars, named Bergmann, who had already cut down a French officer, and possessed himself of his sword and pouch, being mounted on a fast English horse, found himself one of the foremost, and came up with a person dressed in a green frock, and cocked hat, who rode in rear of the flying squadrons. The fugitive made a thrust at his pursuer with his sword, which being parried, he demanded "pardon." At this moment one of the English hussars, who was close at hand, seized the bridle of the prisoner's horse, and led him away. Bergmann, then only a lad of eighteen, and little knowing the value of his prize, suffered the more shrewd Englishman to bear it off, and giving himself no farther concern about the matter, rejoined the pursuit: meantime the person

Appendix, No. VII.

1808. December. in the green frock was taken to general Stewart as the prisoner of the English hussar; nor was it until Bergmann's comrades had reproached him for not retaining his prize, that the unsophisticated Hanoverian learned it was the general Lefebvre !*

Journal of 3d hussars, MSS. The third hussars had forty-six killed and wounded in this combat, where the entire loss on the side of the British is stated not to have exceeded fifty;† three only of the above were killed, and major Burgwedel and cornet Brüggemann were among the wounded. The casualties of the regiment in horses amounted to twenty-two killed and forty-seven wounded: the total loss of the enemy was above two hundred men. Napier.

The British cavalry were withdrawn in the evening to La Baneza; but the German hussars were halted at Villabrazura, about six miles from

* The honour of having captured the French general of cavalry at Benavente has been claimed by more than one individual of the several hussar detachments that were there engaged; among the rest by serjeant-major Grisdale, of the tenth, and corporal Lomax of the seventh hussars; the former was made a non-commissioned officer in consequence of his being considered the captor, and was, probably, the person who relieved Bergmann of his prisoner. Bergmann's pretensions were, however, made the subject of an official inquiry at Osterholtz in 1829–30, on the occasion of his petitioning for the Guelphic medal, and the statement in the text is founded upon the depositions which were then made. The medal was awarded him, as well in consequence of his gallant conduct at Benavente as at the Göhrde in 1813, where he was so severely wounded as to be rendered unfit for further service. (See Appendix, No. VII., B. to E.)

† Napier.

Benavente; from hence they retired to Palacios on the following morning, leaving a piquet of twenty-two horses at Villabrazura to cover their retreat. 1808. December.

Lieutenant Heise was entrusted with the command of this party, and placing a non-commissioned officer and six men in front of the place, towards Benavente, he took post with the remainder behind a small rivulet which ran through it. Narrative of major Heise. MSS.

During the night of the 30th they were not disturbed; but scarce had day broke on the following morning, and the piquet were about to fortify themselves with some hot soup, which had been just prepared, when the advanced party came galloping over the bridge, followed by the enemy in considerable force.

The main body of the third hussars was this day on the road to Astorga, and a long day's march from the rear division. Thus out of the reach of immediate assistance, lieutenant Heise was placed in a situation of extreme difficulty. Were he to charge, although with success, the weakness of his detachment would be exposed, and to retreat would naturally be to bring the whole force of the enemy upon him; he was therefore obliged to proceed with caution, and sending off a man with an application for a reinforcement, he slowly retired from the approaching squadrons.

Luckily for his small force a dense fog filled the atmosphere, rendering objects scarcely distinguishable at the distance of twenty paces. The French

1808. December. Narrative of major Heise, MSS.

continued to advance and the piquet to give way; the skirmishers on both sides became engaged, but the enemy made no charge: Benavente, doubtless, had not been yet forgotten.

The skirmishing was thus kept up throughout the whole day, the French appearing to be quite satisfied with this mode of pursuit. At length, towards dusk, they seemed to acquire more confidence, and began to press forward. Most fortunately for lieutenant Heise, an officer and twenty-two men came at this moment to his assistance, and he resolved to try the effect of shewing a bold front and becoming the assailant.

He accordingly spread out his little band in a single rank, and led them stoutly forward at full gallop.

The continued fog, added to the darkness of the night, prevented him from being able to distinguish more of the enemy's force than the retiring skirmishers, until he had arrived within about six paces of their front, when two squadrons met his view. These halted to receive him, and challenged the threatened onset with a tremendous shout.

It would have been madness for the small German detachment to have really charged the French, for those who might chance to escape from their superior force must have taken flight. Heise therefore, after shewing a bold front for a few seconds, put his line about and resumed his march at a steady trot.

This *ruse* had the desired effect. The enemy

did not venture to follow, and the little rear-guard joined the regiment at Tarienzo, a village near Astorga, about eleven o'clock, having sustained no further injury than the loss of one horse which had fallen in the road. 1808. December.

The British columns were united at Astorga on the 30th. Here they found the marquis of Romana, who, having abandoned his position at the bridge of Mancilla, had, contrary to his express promise, now brought his army into sir John Moore's line of retreat. Napier.

Much confusion was the necessary consequence. Large stores had been collected here by sir David Baird, and as they could not be removed, orders were given to destroy all that should remain after the army had been supplied; but neither the distribution nor destruction could be effected with regularity, and the discipline of the troops became materially injured by the tumult and disorder which prevailed in the town.

It was, at this time, sir John Moore's intention to embark the whole of his army at Vigo; and, in order to secure his flanks from the effect of any rapid movement which the enemy might make in that direction, he judged it prudent to send forward the two flank brigades of general von Alten and colonel Robert Craufurd by the shorter road of Orense, while the main body should proceed by the more circuitous route of Villafranca.

Sir John Moore entrusted these brigades, amount- Appendix, No. VIII. A.

1809. January. ing to about three thousand men, to the command of general von Alten. The official order simply directed that general to proceed with the two brigades to Vigo; but at a personal interview with the commander-in-chief, with which he was afterwards honoured, general Alten was enjoined to press quickly forward and secure the bridge over the Minho at Orense; after securing which point, he was to proceed to and occupy Vigo, where the fleet of transports, for the conveyance of the troops, was assembled under the command of sir Samuel Hood.

Appendix, No. VIII. A.

Journal of major Rautenberg, MSS.

Agreeably to these instructions general Alten left Astorga with the flank brigades on the 31st, and that day reached Ravanal.

During the march, he was joined by large bodies of Romana's troops, which, scattered and disorganized, crowded along the road in the most wretched condition.

On the 1st of January, the flank brigades crossing, with difficulty, the St. Salvador mountains, through deep snow and under intense cold, reached Ponferrada. On the following day colonel Craufurd's brigade were at St. Domingo de Flores, and the legion at Sella. This march was nearly twenty English miles, and in many places there was no road to guide the troops; many men were, therefore, unable to keep up with the column, and these not arriving in quarters at night, general Alten directed that an officer from each battalion should remain at St. Domingo to bring them on.

1809. January. Journal of major Rautenberg, MSS.

The division reached la Rua on the 3d, and the following day, Puebla de Sante Tribez. Immediately on arriving here, general Alten ordered a detachment of there hundred volunteers of both brigades, under major Stuart of the 95th, to press forward and occupy Orense; these troops left Puebla the same evening, and after two days' forced marching through a difficult and mountainous country, reached their destination on the 6th.

General Alten arrived at Orense with the column on the following morning; but no appearance of any French force presented itself in that neighbourhood, and he decided upon giving the troops a day's rest. Here he received an official communication from colonel Murray, the quarter-master-general, informing him of sir John Moore's change of plan, and intention to embark the main body of his army at Corunna. General Alten was therefore directed to forward the commander-in-chief's orders to sir Samuel Hood, for the requisite number of vessels to go round immediately to that port. Captain Augustus Heise, the general's aid-de-camp, was accordingly sent off to the admiral by express, and fortunately reached Vigo in time to admit of the fleet getting out of the bay before an unfavourable change of wind which immediately followed their departure, had set in.

On the 8th, general Alten again sent forward major Stuart's detachment for the purpose of taking

1809. January. possession of the forts at Vigo, and having got rid of Romana's fugitives, who remained in Orense, he resumed his march on the following day.

Journal of major Rautenberg, MSS. The stragglers, however, had not yet come up, and major Martin, of the first light battalion, was therefore directed to remain behind, in order that he might take the command of the men and march them after the column.

On the 10th, colonel Craufurd's brigade obtained another halt day at Ribiadavia, and the legion battalions were advanced to Melon. These were, the following day, at Buggarin and colonel Craufurd's at Pontiferro; the latter reached Vigo on the 12th, and were immediately embarked, while the legion brigade remained in the suburb.

Appendix, No. VIII. A. Lest the enemy might reach Vigo before the fleet could get out, general Alten took measures to render unserviceable a battery of heavy guns which commanded the bay, and having lodged a detachment of the legion brigade in the forts, under lieutenant-colonel Halkett, he embarked the rest on the 13th, and waited the arrival of major Martin from Orense.

On the 15th, he was most opportunely joined by brigadier-general Peacock, who was on his way from Lisbon to sir John Moore, with part of the military chest. The supply which this afforded him enabled general Alten to issue a month's subsistence to the troops, as well as to furnish major Martin with money for the conveyance of the sick and stragglers, whose progress the want of funds had much embarrassed. Major Martin came up on the 17th with about six hundred men, which, together with colonel Halkett's detachment, were immediately embarked.

1809. January. Appendix, No. VIII. A.

The men which had been brought up from Orense formed about two-thirds of those that had been left behind, and the wind not yet permitting the fleet to go to sea, many others were enabled to join the fleet before its departure; of the rest, some got back to the army in Portugal, others were never more heard of, and are supposed to have fallen by the hands of the Spaniards, who also had made some violent assaults upon part of major Martin's detachment. The number of the legion brigade which ultimately never rejoined their corps, amounted to about a hundred and thirty-one men; and it could not but be satisfactory to general Alten and the Hanoverians to know that nearly the whole of these were adventurers of various nations, who had been enlisted in Danish Zealand, after the siege of Copenhagen.*

Correspondence of major martin, MSS.

Appendix, No. IX. & No. VIII. A.

* Colonel Napier's observations upon the march of the flank brigades to Vigo, in the second volume of his History of the War in the Peninsula, having led count Alten to address a letter to the editor of the United Service Journal, this letter, with colonel Napier's reply, and a communication from captain Christoph Heise on the same subject, have been placed in the Appendix.

CHAP. XI.

1809. January. Journal of Dr. Grosskopf, MSS.

We left the third hussars at Tarienzo, where, on the night of the 31st of December, lieutenant Heise's party joined the regiment. Before day-break on the morning of the new year they were again in march, and that day reached Ponferrada.

Journal of 3d hussars, MSS.

This line of route to Villafranca turns that by Bembibre, along which the rest of the army proceeded; and so closely did the enemy press the legion regiment that they could not once venture to unsaddle, and were obliged to keep up a continued skirmish to Cacabelos, a small town four miles from Villafranca, where they arrived on the 2d, having had seven horses killed and two men wounded.

Napier.

At Cacabelos the reserve took up a position, in which, about one o'clock on the following day, they were attacked by six or eight squadrons of cavalry under general Colbert. This led to a sharp skirmish, in which the French general was killed, and the advance of the enemy was checked by the English artillery. Two or three hundred men were killed or wounded in this affair, which did not terminate until dark.

The legion hussars which had been posted with the artillery on a high ridge behind Cacabelos during the combat, followed the reserve in the evening to Villafranca, forming the rear-guard with the ninety-fifth riflemen.

Journal of Dr. Grosskopf, MSS. Journal of 3d hussars, MSS.

From Villafranca the road led over a mountainous and rugged country, totally unfitted for the operations of cavalry. The English dragoon regiments were therefore sent on at once to Lugo, and the German hussars alone retained to cover the retreat. These, being at the tail of the column, became the most exposed to the extreme privations and sufferings which, from about this period, attended the march of the army. Want of provisions and forage were severely felt. The inhabitants, locking up their houses and carrying off their effects, fled to the mountains, and their deserted dwellings served only to disappoint the famished soldiers who there sought food. The French cavalry pressed close at their heels, and to the want of sustenance was added that of rest, for little time could be allowed to either men or horses for repose.

Narrative of major Heise, MSS.

The cold and wet of a severe winter season increased the miseries of the march, and completed the wretchedness of a state of trial which few armies have had to endure. "Many a man," writes an officer of the third hussars, "who for four days and as many nights had never been refreshed by one half-hour's sleep, became so indifferent to life, that at the close of a long day of exhausting duty he has thought within himself, and even secretly

1809. January. hoped, that the foreboding might be realized—"To-morrow I shall, probably, be no more!"

Napier. The wine-vaults at Bembibre and the store-houses at Villafranca had proved an irresistible temptation to many of the English soldiers, and the discipline of the army had become seriously affected by the excesses which they had committed at those places. Harassed and debilitated, as well by their own licentiousness as their absolute wants, the soldiers were falling to the rear by hundreds, and the road became covered with stragglers and baggage. Some painful scenes were now witnessed among the more helpless followers of the army. Lord Londonderry's narrative. Napier. New-born infants, with their mothers, were seen perishing from cold; women struggling or falling exhausted in the snow; while broken-down carts, dead or disabled animals, and adandoned articles of equipment, scattered around, bore further evidence of this calamitous retreat.

Among other resources of the army which it was found necessary to abandon, was part of the military chest. This sum, amounting to about £25,000 in dollars, was contained in casks and carried on bullock-carts; but the tired animals were no longer equal to their load, and the casks were ordered to be left behind. Journal of 3d hussars, MSS. Lieutenant Hugo, who commanded the rear-guard of the German hussars, thought, however, that he might be able to save part of the treasure, and halting, made each man of his de-

tachment, which amounted to about five-and-twenty, 1809.
take an equal weight of dollars in his corn-sack; January.
these sums were brought on and safely delivered to the commissariat at Corunna; the remainder was Napier.
rolled down the side of the mountain, and fell into the hands of the enemy and Spanish peasants.

It has been stated that sir John Moore relinquished his intention of marching to Vigo, and ordered the transports which had been assembled there, to go round to Corunna; meantime he decided upon rallying the army at Lugo, and offering battle to the enemy at that place.

After gallantly baffling the repeated efforts of their pursuers to cross the stream at Constantino, the reserve reached the position which had been taken up by sir John Moore in front of Lugo on the night of the 5th, and found the whole army assembled to await the arrival of the enemy. A few of the French cavalry shewed themselves on the 6th, but it was mid-day on the 7th before the columns under marshal Soult formed in order of battle in front of the English, nineteen thousand of whom were brought together here to oppose them.

The German hussars, now mustering only two Journal of 3d hussars, MSS.
hundred and twenty effective horses, occupied the outposts; the British cavalry, much reduced in efficiency from want of shoes and other privations, had been already sent on to Corunna, as well as those horses of the legion which were found unfit

1809. January. Napier.

to take the field, and with these the rescued treasure was forwarded.

The French marshal having satisfied himself by the vigorous manner in which a fire from four pieces of his artillery was answered, that he had more than a rear-guard to contend with, made a feint on the British right, and at the same time sent a column of infantry and five guns against the left. The French were gaining the advantage, when sir John Moore arriving, rallied the light troops, and broke and pursued the adverse columns, whose loss was estimated at between three and four hundred men.

No further hostilities occurred on this day, and the following morning found both sides still arrayed in order of battle; but the French shewed no disposition to renew the attack, and night fell without a shot having been fired.

The British general, therefore, decided upon taking advantage of the impression which he had made, and resuming his retreat, and large fires having been lighted on the heights, the troops were drawn off in silence at ten o'clock.

The weather set in wet and tempestuous as the army broke up from the position; marks which had been placed to point out their line of march were destroyed, and much confusion ensued. One division having been imprudently permitted to leave their ranks and take shelter from the weather, disorganization and plunder followed, and the main body arrived at Betanzos on the evening of the 9th, in a state of extreme disorder. 1809. January. Napier.

The loss of men in this last march was greater than that in all the former part of the retreat; nevertheless fourteen thousand infantry were still in column, and these moved on in good order to Corunna on the following day.

The nearer the troops approached the coast, the greater was the exertion of each individual to reach the desired point, and discipline returned as the prospect opened of their sufferings being soon at an end. Joy was eloquent in the countenances of all, when the towers of Corunna first appeared in sight; but this expression was exchanged for one of despair, when not a single transport could be discovered in the harbour! Journal of of major Heise, MSS.

Sir John Moore made immediate dispositions to receive the enemy, who were not able completely to assemble on the Mero before the 12th. On the 14th, the first transports arrived, and were succeeded by the rest on the following day, when the embarkation of the cavalry was commenced. Napier.

The condition of this force on its arrival at Corunna was truly lamentable; many horses had died, or been destroyed on the march, and the greater part of those which were brought up alive, were foundered. The embarkation of these in the face of an enemy would have been attended with diffi-

1809. January. culty and delay, and, therefore, in order to prevent them from falling into the hands of the French, where their sufferings would have been protracted, they were ordered to be shot. Two hundred and ninety horses of the legion were thus disposed of; about half only of this number could be considered effective, the rest being either lame or wounded.

Journal of 3d hussars, MSS.

To a German hussar, whose interests are so identified with those of his horse, the execution of this order could not but prove highly painful. Many of the third had shared their scanty portion of bread with the noble animals which they were now ordered to destroy, and many a tear fell as they reluctantly complied with the apparently hard sentence.

Narrative of major Heise, MSS.

While some officers of the legion were dressing on the morning of the 14th, the house in which they were quartered shook so violently that the windows broke, and they hurried into the street in the full belief that they had experienced the shock of an earthquake. Here they found hundreds of half naked inhabitants who had jumped from their beds, under the same impression, and were in fearful expectation of another shock; the alarm, however, proved to have been caused by the explosion of a magazine, containing some thousand barrels of gunpowder, which had been collected in a storehouse near the town, for the use of the English, and was set on fire by them in order to prevent it from falling into the hands of the enemy. 1809. January.

A general engagement took place at Corunna on the 16th, which, ending in the complete defeat of the French, gave a glorious termination to a retreat which had hitherto been attended with so many disasters. The loss of the gallant chief by whom it had been so ably conducted, clouded the splendour of a victory which deprived England of one of her most valuable soldiers; but the honour of the British arms was upheld, and the pre-eminence of British infantry made conspicuously manifest. The public press in England afterwards heaped base aspersions upon the military character of the fallen hero, and triumphed for a time in their illiberal persecution. But justice has been at length rendered to the virtuous Moore, and the calumnies which ignorance and malignity had heaped upon his fame, have been dispelled by the pen of truth in the eloquent pages of a brilliant historian.*

Immediately after the action, sir John Moore's intention of embarking the troops was proceeded with by general Hope, upon whom the command had devolved. The night was dark, and expedition being the main object, the men were hurried off to the ships with little regard to regiments or vessels, and many transports were overloaded, while others Narrative of major Heise, MSS.

* Colonel W. F. P. Napier.

1809. January. had not half their compliment: the baggage, also, could not be entirely brought off, and the German hussars were among the other sufferers in this particular. The cries of the wounded as they were moved about in the ships, mingling with the noise of the boats as they passed to and fro to the shore, continued through the night, and before morning the greater part of the troops had been got on board. About ten o'clock on the 19th, the French managed to establish a battery of light guns on the heights which commanded the harbour, and opening a fire upon the shipping, caused much consternation among the masters of transports. Many of these cut their cables, and suffered the vessels to drive about, by which they became intermixed in disorder, and some ran ashore. A British man-of-war, however, soon silenced the battery, and the fleet got to sea.

Journal of Dr. Grosskopf, MSS.

During the 18th and 19th, the wind setting right into the bay, they were obliged to cruize about in the offing; but on the 20th, a favourable breeze sprung up, and all sail was made for England.

Journal of major Rautenberg, MSS.

The same day on which the main body of the army left Corunna, the flank brigades, under general Alten, sailed from Vigo; the wind was, however, so violent that the vessels were unable to clear the narrow entrance of the harbour, and attempted to anchor; but the bottom proved rocky, and few anchors would hold; four vessels broke away, of which two were lucky enough to reach the channel between the rocks; but the others were nowhere to be seen, and great alarm for their safety was entertained in the fleet. 1809. January.

On the morning of the 21st, some more vessels were driven from their moorings, upon which the fleet put back to the harbour, and the loss in cables was made good at Vigo.

At length on the afternoon of the 23d, the flank brigades got to sea with a favourable wind, and on the 25th had arrived off Cape Finisterre. Here further orders were expected from sir Samuel Hood, and the vessels lay to, to await them; but general Alten, having been informed by captain Seymour of the Pallas, of the events which had taken place at Corunna, and seeing that symptoms of infectious fever had broken out among the troops, thought it advisable not to lose the advantage of a favourable passage, which the fair wind offered, and took upon himself the responsibility of proceeding with the division to England. Accordingly, after lying to, for about eighteen hours, without any instructions arriving, and the wind being adverse to Vigo, whither they were supposed to have gone, the fleet made sail for the British shores. Appendix, No. VIII. C.

After having been again assailed by stormy weather, on the night of the 29th, they reached Spithead on the 31st, and had the satisfaction to find there one of the two transports which had been lost sight of at Vigo; but no account could be had Journal of major Rautenberg, MSS.

1809. January. of the other, and it was afterwards ascertained that she had gone down.

The master of this transport, which was called the Smallbridge, had, it appeared, during the gale of the 29th, mistaken Brest light for that of Scilly, and ran the vessel upon a rock near Ushant. She was immediately stove in; the high sea prevented any assistance reaching her from the coast; and at day-break on the following morning she went down. Five officers, two hundred and nine non-commissioned officers and soldiers, seven women, and nine children of the German light brigade, together with the master and crew of the transport, perished on this melancholy occasion.* (Appendix, No. X.)

The legion cavalry were more fortunate than the infantry; one vessel narrowly escaped shipwreck off the Isle of Wight, but the whole of the regiment were safely landed at Plymouth, Falmouth, and Portsmouth, towards the end of the month, and from these ports they marched to Chichester. (Narrative of major Heise, MSS.)

Landing without horses or baggage, the third hussars did not, it may be supposed, make a very brilliant figure on their re-appearance in England; they were not, however, the less well received.

* So violent was the gale on the night of the 29th, that ten vessels doubly anchored at Spithead were driven out and stranded; among these was a transport with part of the 1st light battalion, under major von dem Bussche, from which, however, notwithstanding the difficulties of their situation, the men were all saved.

" D—n all the horses," said a thorough John Bull in reply to the dispiriting observations of a by-stander on the state of the regiment, " Yorkshire has horses enough to mount them again—thank God that the lives of the brave men are saved."

1809. January. Narrative of major Heise, MSS.

Great exertion was now made to recruit and re-mount the regiment, which, removed to Ipswich, enjoyed uninterrupted repose until the " war of freedom" in the north of Germany called them again into active service.

CHAPTER XII.

1809. January. Napier.

The return of sir John Moore's army from Spain was followed by a series of successes on the part of the French. That general's daring advance from Sahagun had for a short time diverted the torrent of war in the Peninsula; but now that these troops were withdrawn, the French generals could co-operate for the subjugation of Portugal, and three armies were soon assembled around her frontiers for that purpose. Soult was marching upon Oporto, General Lapisse was at Salamanca, and marshal Victor on the banks of the Tagus. The small British force, under the command of sir John Cradock, in Portugal, was insufficient for any offensive operation; the population of Lisbon were in open hostility to the British authorities; anarchy reigned in Oporto; and the English government had absolutely come to the resolution of abandoning Portugal if the enemy advanced, when, suddenly, vigorous measures emanated from their counsels, and they decided upon reinforcing the army, and placing it under the command of sir Arthur Wellesley.

In furtherance of this object, five thousand men, who had been sent from England under general

Sherbrooke to aid the Spaniards in the south, and were just about to enter the port of Cadiz, were now directed to land in the Tagus; other bodies of troops were collected along the English coast, and sent off under able officers to Lisbon, and every preparation for an active campaign was immediately commenced. 1809. March. Lord Londerry's narrative.

The four line battalions, and three batteries of artillery of the legion, which, as has been stated, were left behind in Portugal on the march of the light brigade and third hussars into Spain, were employed during the winter months in various duties and detached commands, at and in the neighbourhood of Lisbon. Frequent marching in rain through the inundated country of the Tagus caused some sickness among the men, and in the month of January several were in hospital; but though temporarily weakened in this respect, their numbers received a considerable accession; for many of their countrymen in the French service came over to the more honourable cause under the British standard. Journals of line battalions, MSS.*

The fourth battery of artillery formed part of a corps, which, in the beginning of February, was sent under major-general Mackenzie to Cadiz, but which, without having landed, returned to Lis- Narrative of general Hartmann, MSS.

* The journals which are referred to under this title, were kept by captain Schnath of the first, lieutenant Fienck of the second, major Heinemann of the fifth, and captain Stutzer of the seventh regiments, late king's German legion.

1809. March. bon on the 12th of March. Major Hartmann was entrusted with the dismantling of the forts between Belem and Cascaes, and both this officer and captain von Arentschild of the same corps were frequently employed on reconnoitring parties; the latter was permitted to enter the Portuguese service with the rank of major, and rendered valuable assistance to the bishop of Oporto in the defence of that place against Soult.

Napier. The French generals continued to overcome all resistance. Romana, who had again collected an army, fled before Soult, and the Portuguese general Silveira vainly endeavoured to oppose his progress. Another army which had been brought into the field under Cuesta, and part of which had at first gained considerable advantages, was completely defeated near Medellin by marshal Victor on the 28th of March, and on the following day Soult entered Oporto.

Sir Arthur Wellesley landed at Lisbon on the 22d of April, and the regency of Portugal immediately nominated him marshal-general of their armies. Previous to this general Beresford had been entrusted with the organization of the Portuguese troops; an independent corps called the Lusitanian legion had been raised by sir Robert Wilson; a considerable body of native troops and volunteers were on the Vouga under colonel Trant, and Cuesta had again brought an army into the field.

Sir Arthur decided upon attacking Soult without

delay, intending, if successful, to establish a good system of defence in the northern provinces, and then, in conjunction with Cuesta, to turn his arms against Victor. 1809. May. Napier.

On the 2d of May the British general reached Coimbra, where, on the 5th, were concentrated about twenty-five thousand sabres and bayonets. Of these the king's German legion formed about three thousand, which were thus brigaded.

INFANTRY.

MAJOR-GENERAL JOHN MURRAY.

FIRST LINE BRIGADE, BRIGADIER-GEN. VON LANGWERTH.

1st line battalion .... lieut.-colonel von Ompteda.

2d line battalion .... colonel von Barsse.

SECOND LINE BRIGADE, COLONEL VON LÖW.

5th line battalion .... colonel von Drieberg.

7th line battalion .... colonel von Drechsell.

ARTILLERY.

MAJOR G. J. HARTMANN.

2d foot battery six six-pounders ...... captain von Rettberg.

4th foot battery six six-pounders ...... captain Heise.

RIFLEMEN.

MAJOR VON WURMB.

Skirmishers* of the four line battalions.

Detachments of the 1st and 2d light battalions.

Captain Meyer's detachment of the 3d hussars was attached to the 14th English light dragoons, commanded by Colonel Talbot.

A grand review of the allied forces took place

* To each company of the German line regiments were attached ten men armed with rifles, who uniting in action, formed a corps of skirmishers, and were called *scharfschützen* (sharp shooters.)

1809. May. here, the observations on which, in the pages of a contemporary historian, offer too liberal a tribute of praise to the legion regiments, to be left unnoticed in this work:—

"On the 5th of May," says lord Londonderry, "the army being at length assembled, a grand review took place, and a most imposing and magnificent spectacle it presented. To some of the troops which stood that day under arms, it is not going too far to affirm that the whole world can produce none superior. Of this description were the brigade of guards, the twenty-ninth, the eighty-third, and the four battalions of the king's German legion; and the rest, if in a few minor points they fell short, were such as any general might be proud to command. The whole were indeed in the highest state of discipline and efficiency, and all appeared animated by one spirit—an ardent desire to meet the enemy."*

Napier. The French army was extended by detachments from the Vouga to the Tamega, and the wings, separated by the Douro, had no mode of communication but by the boat-bridge at Oporto.

Sir Arthur Wellesley decided upon making his principal attack by the high road to Oporto, while a smaller corps under general Beresford should march by Vizeu, and having left on the right bank of the Tagus, under general Mackenzie, a body of troops sufficient to secure Lisbon from any attack

* Narrative of the Peninsular War, by the Marquis of Londonderry, vol 1, p. 325, 8vo. edition.

by which that capital might be threatened by Victor, he prepared to advance upon the Vouga. 1809. May.

The army formed one division of cavalry and three of infantry, exclusive of Marshal Beresford's corps, which consisted principally of Portuguese. The cavalry were commanded by lieutenant-general Payne, the first division by lieutenant-general Paget, the second by lieutenant-general Sherbrooke, and the third by major-general Hill, and the whole amounted to about fifteen hundred cavalry, fourteen thousand five hundred infantry, and twenty-four guns. Napier.

General Beresford marched for Vizeu on the 6th, and the following morning the advanced guard consisting of one British brigade, the four line regiments of the legion, general Cotton's division of cavalry, and two batteries of artillery, the whole under the command of lieutenant-general Paget, took the high road to Oporto by Vouga bridge.

On the 9th, general Hill's division marched for Aveiro, and that evening the whole reached the line of the Vouga river.

The French general Franceschi, with all his cavalry, a regiment of Mermet's division, and six guns were at Albergaria Nova, eight miles beyond Vouga bridge, and the remainder of Mermet's division was at Grijon on the main road to Oporto.

Sir Arthur Wellesley determined upon surprising Franceschi, and turning the enemy's right by the lake of Ovar, to effect which object general Hill

1809. May. Napier. embarked on the evening of the 9th with one brigade, which was landed at Ovar at sunrise on the following morning. The same day marshal Beresford having repulsed Loison, reached Pezo de Ragoa.

Both flanks of the French army were now turned; but the corresponding movements of the centre columns of the British on the night of the 9th, were unfortunately baffled by accidental and unexpected difficulties which the troops encountered on crossing the Vouga; for although driven from his position by Paget's infantry, and the corps of colonel Trant, Franceschi was enabled to make good his retreat to Oliveira without any serious loss, and continuing his march throughout the night, he joined Mermet at Grijon on the following morning. The legion bivouacked, the night of the 10th, in a pine-wood near Oliveira, at which town the advanced guard halted; a light gun, which had been abandoned by the enemy, fell into the hands of the first line battalion on the march.

Journals of line battalions, MSS.

Early on the morning of the 11th the advanced guard resumed their march, and about eight o'clock came up with the enemy at the village of Grijon.

Napier. The French were drawn up on a range of heights behind the village, having a wood, occupied with infantry, on their right; but their left was ill protected, and sir Arthur Wellesley determined upon attempting to turn it. Without once halting the column, the head of which became instantly engaged, he ordered general Murray's division of the king's German legion, which was in rear of the rear-guard, to bring their left shoulders forward, and attack the enemy's flank, while the 16th Portuguese were directed to occupy his attention in the wood. The legion brigades immediately set forward in double quick time, and after continuing at this pace for a considerable distance, at length came up to the enemy's left. The skirmishers of the four line battalions, and the detachment of the light brigade under major von Wurmb, became instantly engaged with the enemy's tirailleurs, whom they drove back, and the French advanced upon them in line; but after firing a volley, the line also faced about and retired, pursued by the skirmishers. Lieutenant Lodders of the fifth battalion, and five men were wounded in this skirmish, the former severely.

1809. May.

Lord Londonderry's narrative.

Notes of major von Hölle, first line battalions, MSS.

While the light troops of the legion were thus engaged, two companies of the first line battalion, under the command of captains Detmering and von Marshalk, and one company of the second line battalion under captain Langrehr, which had been sent up to support the skirmishers, became also engaged with the French light infantry, whom they in like manner drove back, but not without some sacrifice; for captain Detmering was killed, captain Langrehr received a shot through the arm, and eight men were wounded.

Journal of captain Schnath.

Notes of major von Hölle, MSS.

1809. May. Lord Londonderry's narrative. Napier.

The French, seeing their left turned, abandoned the position, and having been sharply followed by brigadier-general Stewart, with a few troops of cavalry, lost upwards of one hundred men in prisoners. At Carvalhos, however, they halted, and forming up their infantry upon the heights, checked the pursuit of the cavalry, who, wheeling off to the right, now threatened their flank.

This movement had the desired effect, and the heights of Carvalhos were also abandoned by the enemy. Thus marching and fighting, the British column continued to move on until five o'clock, when the advanced guard bivouacked for the night, and the head-quarters halted at Grijon.

The French passed the Douro during the night, and removing all the boats to the right bank, completed their measures of security by destroying the bridge. About ten o'clock the advanced guard under general Paget arrived at the opposite suburb of Villa-Nova, where it was joined by general Hill's corps from Ovar. Sir Arthur Wellesley now planned and executed the passage of a river, which for boldness of design and skilfulness of execution stands unrivalled in the history of ancient or modern warfare.

Soult, expecting the English from the sea, had left the right bank of the river insufficiently guarded, and sir Arthur seeing a large building on that side which would contain at least two battalions, and the direct passage to which was hidden from the town, he resolved, if he could find but one boat, to attempt to cross, and colonel Waters of the staff was immediately despatched in search of the mode of conveyance. 1809. May.

This officer accidentally discovered among the bushes a small skiff, which had been brought over in the night by a poor barber of Oporto, and, having been aided by the exhortations of a friar, who stood on the bank, he persuaded some peasants to accompany him in the skiff to the opposite side. Here they found, lying in the mud, four large barges, and with these colonel Waters returned in half-an-hour, having effected his daring enterprize unperceived by the enemy. Napier. Lord Londonderry's narrative.

Meantime, eighteen or twenty guns were planted at the neighbouring convent of Sarea, which commanded the large building or seminary on the opposite bank, and major-general Murray with two light guns, two squadrons of the fourteenth dragoons, the first line battalion, and major von Wurmb's riflemen of the legion, were sent to the ferry of Avintas, about three miles higher up the river, with orders to effect a passage there also. Napier. Journal of captain Schnath.

One boat having been brought up to the point of embarkation under the convent, an officer and twenty-five men of the buffs got on board, and in a quarter of an hour were lodged in the seminary without having created any alarm; a second, and then a third boat followed; in the last was lieutenant-general Paget; but scarcely had the men Napier.

1809. May. Napier. from this boat landed, when a tumultuous noise arose in Oporto, and the French came furiously down upon the seminary.

General Paget was struck down, and severely wounded, and the enemy's fire augmenting fast, the combat became fierce and unequal; but the English artillery from Sarea, sweeping the left of the wall round the seminary, the French attack was confined to the side of the building towards the Valonga road, and on this side the troops under general Murray were expected to appear.

Several large boats were now brought over to Villa-Nova, and general Sherbrooke's division began to cross in strong bodies. These were followed by the remaining three battalions of the legion. Murray's troops were now seen descending the right bank from the ferry, and joyful demonstrations from the lower part of the town denoted that it had been abandoned by the enemy.

Journals of line battalions, MSS.

Napier. The French were seen in full retreat on the road to Valonga, the British infantry from the seminary, and the guns from the opposite bank pouring a destructive fire into the flying columns. Had the Germans on the right been now ordered to fall upon this disorganized crowd by general Murray, the enemy's difficulties would have been much encreased; but the skirmishers of the first line under lieutenant von Hölle, and two companies of the same regiment, the first under ensign Hodenberg, were alone brought into fire; the skirmishers made

Notes of major von Hölle, MSS.

several prisoners, and one rifleman, named Henry Hauer, was lucky enough to capture a French lieutenant-colonel: seven of the legion were wounded. 1809. May.

Although the infantry of general Murray's corps were not pressed forward in pursuit, the two squadrons of the fourteenth, led on by brigadier-general Stewart and major Harvey, followed after the retreating columns with much spirit, and by repeatedly charging the disorganized masses as they crowded along the road, committed great slaughter among them. The gallant major Harvey lost an arm in the pursuit. Lord Londonderry's narrative.

The casualties of the French on this day were about five hundred men in killed and wounded. Five pieces of artillery, a considerable quantity of ammunition, and fifty dismounted guns also fell into the hands of the conquerors, and several hundred men were taken prisoners in the hospitals. The British had only twenty killed, and a general and ninety-five men wounded. Napier.

The German brigades bivouacked near Oporto for the night, and in the afternoon of the following day were sent to Valonga, about six miles on the Amarante road, in pursuit of the enemy; but Soult having destroyed his artillery and abandoned his military chest and baggage, had already crossed the Sierra de Catalina to Guimaraens, and here luckily falling in with Loison, who had retired before Beresford from Amarante, and being joined by the dragoons of Journals of line battalions, MSS. Napier.

1809. May. Lorge from Braga, this able commander concentrated his whole army.

Journals of line battalions, MSS. At five o'clock on the morning of the 14th, the legion battalions were again in march, and passing the wreck of Soult's artillery and stores, reached Penafiel at seven in the evening. This day the main body of the army marched from Oporto upon Braga.

The Germans were allowed but little rest at Penafiel, for general Murray, thinking to surprise the French at Guimaraens, ordered the pursuit to be resumed the same night. The division left Penafiel about one o'clock by torch-light; but when at eight in the evening they reached Guimaraens, Soult was at Napier. Salamonde, and this night the French marshal, surprising the Portuguese who were sent to destroy the Ponte Nova, passed the Cavado river there, and was in full march for Montalegre.

Meantime sir Arthur Wellesley had reached Braga, and leaving this place on the morning of the 16th, he came upon Soult's rear-guard at Salamonde about four o'clock. The French made but one discharge and fled in confusion to the Ponte Nova. Some guns were brought to bear upon them here, which, strewing the place with slain, closed the work of destruction on the part of the British.

When the direction of Soult's retreat had been ascertained, the legion battalions were ordered to fall into the line of march of the principal column, and they bivouacked within two leagues of Montalegre on the 18th; but Soult having drawn up in force behind the Sulas, the pursuit was on this day discontinued, and the battalions returned to Guimaraens. For eight days they had been marching under constant rain and over dreadful roads: the baggage had been left behind the Vouga; and when they arrived at Guimaraens on the 21st, there was a general want of shoes in the division, as was indeed the case throughout the army. Here, however, the Germans were given a few days' rest, the officers received their baggage, and a partial supply of shoes was obtained for the men. On the 25th, the retrograde movement upon Oporto was resumed, and proceeding from this capital to Coimbra by the lake of Ovar, they followed the rest of the army through Abrantes to the left bank of the Tagus, where, on the 27th of June, the troops were encamped.

1809.
May.
Journals of line battalions, MSS.

CHAPTER XIII.

1809. June. WITH a reinforcement of five thousand men which joined the British army on its return from the campaign of the Douro, came the first hussars of the king's German legion, under the command of lieutenant-colonel von Arentschild. This regiment, about six hundred strong, joined the army at Castello Branco on the 25th of June, and were united with the twenty-third English light dragoons into a brigade under major-general Anson.

Journal of colonel von Linsingen, MSS.

Captain Meyer's detachment of the third hussars were now ordered to return to England. Their effective horses were distributed among the fourteenth British dragoons and waggon-train, and, thus dismounted, the troop joined the regiment at Ipswich about the end of July.

Napier. The army had suffered much from sickness; four thousand men were in hospital, and those present under arms, which did not exceed twenty-two thousand, were nearly barefooted and totally without pay.

These and other difficulties kept the troops in a state of inactivity until the end of June, when sir Arthur Wellesley, having learned that a reinforcement of eight thousand men were off the rock of

Lisbon, that the first French corps had retreated from Torremocha, and that Cuesta had consequently advanced, determined upon commencing his march into Spain. 1809. July. Napier.

The head-quarters broke up from Castello Branco on the 1st of July, and moved in one column by Moralejo and Coria.

On the 10th the army reached Plasencia, and on the 18th, crossing the Tietar river and taking the route of Miajadas, reached Talayuela.

On the 20th they arrived at Oropesa, where the army halted the 21st, on which day Cuesta united his whole force at Velada, except a small detachment which threatened the bridge of Talavera.

The German hussars were with the advanced guard in the division of general Mackenzie, and this day a patrole of the regiment under lieutenant Ernest Poten came in contact with the enemy, from whom they took some prisoners, with the loss of only two horses wounded. Journal of colonel von Linsingen, MSS.

On the 22d the allies moved in two columns to drive the French posts from Talavera; Cuesta marching by the high road came first up with the enemy near the village of Gamonal, where general Latour Maubourg, with two thousand dragoons, not only checked the head of the Spanish leading column, but obliged general Zayas, who commanded it, to display his whole line, consisting of fifteen thousand infantry and three thousand cavalry; nor did the French retire until the English troops Napier.

1809. July. appeared on their right. Supported by some infantry they then retreated behind the Alberche. The first hussars were ordered to move upon the enemy's right flank, but having gained the opposite bank of the river, they could effect nothing, and suffered a little from cannon fire, having had three horses killed and three wounded.

Journal of colonel von Linsingen, MSS.

Napier.

A general attack was agreed upon for the next morning, and the British troops were under arms at three o'clock in the forenoon; but Cuesta, after keeping them waiting until seven, objected to fighting at all upon that day, alledging, among other absurd reasons, that it was Sunday; but the English quarter-master-general de Lancy, who had been sent on a reconnaisance, accompanied by thirty of the German hussars under captain von Linsingen, having reported in the afternoon that the enemy were retiring, Cuesta changed his mind, and came in a coach and six horses to sir Arthur Wellesley, for the purpose of examining Victor's position in concert with the British general. On the following day he crossed the Alberche, and regardless of sir Arthur Wellesley's expressed determination not to move the British army further until its wants were supplied, pressed forward singly in pursuit of the French. Meantime colonel de Lancy had repeated his reconnaisance with captain von Linsingen's detachment, and crossing the Alberche on the evening of the 23d, saw the French outposts drawing off about midnight; he

Journal of colonel von Linsingen, MSS.

then cautiously followed the column by cross roads, and at day-break could perceive the whole French army in retreat. Their rear-guard was, however, too strong to admit of any attack being made upon it with effect by the hussar detachment, which was accordingly ordered to return. On its way back, a French staff-officer and several men, who had remained behind, fell into the hands of the hussars, and captain von Linsingen joined the advanced guard of the English army in a camp which had just been abandoned by the French at Cazalegas, on the left bank of the Alberche, and to which point sir Arthur Wellesley, fearing the consequences of Cuesta's imprudence, had sent forward general Sherbrooke with two divisions of infantry and all his cavalry.

1809. July. Journal of colonel von Linsingen, MSS. Napier.

This morning brigadier-general Stewart, with two squadrons of the first hussars under major von Grote, went forward in front of Cuesta's army, and came up with the French rear-guard at St. Olalla. A smart skirmish ensued as the enemy were quitting the town; but the French being supported by infantry, the hussars could make but little impression on them; general Stewart, however, was enabled to ascertain that the enemy's main body had fallen back to Torrijos, on the Toledo road, and that sir Robert Wilson's corps had reached Escalona. The two squadrons returned on the following day.

Journal of colonel von Linsingen. MSS. Lord Londonderry's Narrative.

At length Cuesta had some perception of his

1809. July. Napier.

danger, and he ordered a retreat for the 26th; but the French passing the Guadarama at two o'clock in the morning, drove the Spanish cavalry out of Torrijos, and pursued them to Alcabon. Here general Zayas offered battle; but the moment the French infantry appeared in sight, the Spaniards broke and fled. Luckily for Cuesta, the duke of Albuquerque came up with a division of three thousand fresh cavalry, and held the enemy in play, while Cuesta retreated towards the Alberche in the greatest disorder.

Although the French made no attempt to profit by the unconnected position of the allies, the disorder among the Spaniards continued to increase, until general Sherbroke, marching out of Cazalegas, placed his division between them and the enemy. Sir Arthur Wellesley now endeavoured to persuade Cuesta to withdraw to Talavera, but the old man was obstinate, and said he would fight where he stood: however, on the following morning, when the French cavalry appeared in sight, and general Sherbrooke was about to retire, he at length yielded to sir Arthur's entreaties. The British chief now assumed the command of both armies, and leaving general Mackenzie's division and general Anson's brigade of cavalry to cover the retrograde movement, he put the rest of the allied troops in march for the position, where he had resolved to offer battle to the enemy.

Sir Arthur Wellesley placed the Spaniards on

his extreme right, close to the town of Talavera, 1809.
where their front was covered, and they could not July:
be seriously attacked. General Campbell's divi- Napier.
sion, formed in two lines, touched the Spanish left; general Sherbrooke's stood next in one line, general Mackenzie's being intended to form a second; and the left was closed by a round steep hill, which formed one of a chain of heights that bounded the woody plain between Talavera and the Alberche; still further on the left, the lofty Sierra Gredos ran nearly parallel with these heights, and from the valley between, opened the bed of a mountain rivulet, which ran in front of this flank of the position. Part of the British cavalry was with general Mackenzie's division, and in the plain in front of the left; the remainder was posted behind a great redoubt which stood at the junction of the Spanish and English flanks. The Spanish cavalry were posted behind their infantry on the right.

The British and Germans under arms this day amounted to somewhat more than nineteen thousand sabres and bayonets, with thirty guns, and the Spaniards to from thirty-three to thirty-four thousand, with seventy guns; but the French having been reinforced at Torrijos on the 25th, were advancing with nearly fifty thousand men, of which above seven thousand were cavalry, and they had at least eighty pieces of cannon.

It has been stated that general Mackenzie's division of infantry and general Anson's brigade of

1809. July. Napier. cavalry were left behind on the Alberche to cover the march of the rest of the allied army into the position at Talavera. About noon the French cavalry appearing, these troops also withdrew, and the infantry proceeded to take post at the *Casa des Salinas* in the wood on the right bank of the river, while two squadrons of the first hussars of the legion, under captains von Linsingen and Krauchenberg, covered their retreat. Of these squadrons one was to cross the Alberche by the bridge, the other by a ford about two miles higher up the river; and this squadron, commanded by captain von Linsingen, got into an awkward predicament; for close by the ford was the French hut camp which has been before mentioned, and this had been set on fire by the rear of the English division, as it marched through. The flaming huts scared the horses, and so impeded the march of the squadron, that the rear-guard were obliged to engage the enemy's advanced cavalry in the river, and these, coming on in superior numbers, rendered the contest most unequal. The enemy would not, however, venture to the right bank until their infantry had come up, and the squadron retired behind general Mackenzie's division, having lost two men and nine horses killed, and one officer (cornet von Heimbruch), and three horses wounded. But general Mackenzie's division was not prepared for this rapid advance of the enemy, and, being mostly young troops,

Narrative of colonel von Linsingen, MSS.

got into confusion and were driven into the plain; the old regiments of the division, however, restored order, and the fight was afterwards so steadily maintained, that the enemy were checked. Another brigade of cavalry was ready in the rear for their support, and covered by this brigade and that of general Anson, they retreated in good order across the plain, and gained the left and centre of the British position, one brigade forming in second line behind general Sherbrooke's division, the other (that of colonel Donkin) taking post on the hill on the left; the two cavalry brigades joined the rest of that force in rear of the right wing. Captain Heise's battery of German artillery was planted on the right of this hill, and that of captain von Rettberg between the first and third divisions. The infantry brigades of the legion, by some mistake of the staff-officer who was appointed to conduct them to their ground, had been led away an hour's march behind Talavera, where they were preparing to bivouac, when another order arrived, correcting the error, and requiring them to hurry forthwith to the left of the position. Victor had already brought up one division and all his artillery to a height in front of colonel Donkin's brigade; and on Donkin's right, about eight in the evening, the two line brigades of the legion were ordered to deploy.

1809. July. Napier.

Journal of captain Schnath, MSS.

Meanwhile the French light cavalry advancing

Napier.

1809. July. Napier.

on the right, had, after a slight skirmish, caused ten thousand Spanish infantry and all their artillery to fly to the rear, and Victor conceived the design of profiting by the disorder thus created, and the approach of twilight, to seize the hill on which colonel Donkin's brigade was posted, and which was the key of the British position; he, accordingly, directed Ruffin's division to attack the troops on the hill, Villattes to follow in support, and Lapisse to create a diversion by falling upon the two brigades of the legion. The attack upon the hill was vigorous, and Donkin's force being too weak to defend every part, many of the French turned his left, and gained the summit in his rear; but general Hill soon arriving with a re-inforcement, this point was re-covered, and the enemy driven back. Lapisse now advanced upon the legion. It was dark, and captain von Ompteda, of the first light battalion, had been sent up the hill with a party of riflemen to plant outposts: upon part of this detachment, consisting of the skirmishers of the first line battalion under lieutenant von Hölle, the enemy's column fell, and charging, obliged them to retire, and lieutenant von Hölle was severely wounded. In re-treating, the skirmishers received the fire of the seventh line battalion, which regiment and part of the fifth being thrown into confusion by the suddenness of the attack, were charged by the French column, and gave way; they were, however, rallied

Notes of Major von Hölle, MSS.

Journal of captain Stutzer, MSS.

by major Berger and adjutant Delius, the latter of whom received a severe wound in the arm. 1809. July.

Meantime the French column which had been driven back by general Hill, again advanced, and the contest, renewed on both sides with vigour, appeared for a time doubtful; but the French were finally driven down the hill, and Lapisse abandoning his false attack upon the legion, the combat ceased. Notes of major von Hölle, MSS. Napier.

The line was, however, frequently disturbed by false alarms during the night, and several men and officers were killed by the desultory firing of both the British and Spanish troops.

The British lost about eight hundred men, and the French about a thousand on this day; the casualties of the legion were principally confined to the seventh battalion, which had eighteen rank and file killed, two officers and nine rank and file wounded, and seventy-seven rank and file missing; lieutenant Delius was obliged to have his arm amputated. Journal of captain Stutzer, MSS.

At day-break the French again renewed the attack. Ruffin's troops marched in columns of battalions against the left of the British, embracing two sides of the hill; these were followed by Villatte's division, and a roar of artillery preceded their advance. The German regiments, in consequence of some of the guns having been brought up directly in their front, became much exposed to this fire, and were ordered to throw back their left; this movement, which was performed with the Napier

1809. July. greatest order and precision, but not without considerable loss from the constant discharges of grape, brought the retired flank of the brigades close under captain Heise's battery of artillery, immediately on the right of the hill, against which the advancing columns were directed. The French closed with general Hill's division. The fifth line battalion of the legion which formed the left of the German brigades, was ordered to ascend the height, and the corps of riflemen became hotly engaged. The struggle was furious and obstinate. The inequalities of the ground not permitting the troops to retain their compact formation, separate contests of small bodies ensued. Major von Wurmb, gallantly leading on the German riflemen, was followed by captain Langrehr bearing the regimental colours, at the head of the fifth battalion; the skirmishers fell upon the enemy's left flank, while the battalion attacked him in front, and furiously assailing one of the French columns with the bayonet and butt-end of the musket, caused tremendous destruction around them. Near four hundred of the twenty-eighth French regiment are stated to have fallen before the German battalion alone. Meantime the English regiments had been also victorious, and the enemy's broken columns flying down the hill, returned to their position, having in the space of forty minutes lost above fifteen hundred men.

Notes of major von Hölle, MSS.

Napier.

These repeated efforts of the French against the hill, and the appearance of some of their light troops on the mountain beyond the left, caused sir Arthur Wellesley to prolong his flank across the valley, and he placed the principal mass of his cavalry in rear of the left of general Hill's division. General Anson's brigade had been removed early in the morning to this point, and was now formed in two lines with the leading squadrons looking into the valley, the twenty-third dragoons on the right, and the first hussars of the legion on the left; a division of Spanish infantry was posted in the mountain to observe the enemy's light troops, and this flank was further strengthened by the Spanish division of the duke of Albuquerque, which was placed in rear of the British. 1809. July. Journal of colonel von Linsingen, MSS.

After the failure of Ruffin's attack, the French generals held a council on the policy of risking a general action, and while they were thus engaged, the troops on both sides took some rest; the wounded were taken to the rear, and the British availed themselves of the only refreshment they could procure—the water of a brook which divided the positions. The troops were suffering much from hunger; since the 22d they had had no bread; a few ounces of raw wheat was the only subsistence issued to the army, and the Germans had more than once been obliged to seek nourishment from a sort of pea called *corovanzen*, which they found in the fields. Thus physically debilitated, these gallant soldiers had driven back their opponents; but the victory was yet unfinished, and about one o'clock Napier. Journals of line battalions, MSS.

1809. July. they were again called upon to meet the furious onset of the enemy.

Napier. A general attack was made upon the position. General Sebastiani, with the fourth corps of the French army, fell upon the right of the allies, Villatte and Ruffin moved upon the left, and Lapisse attacked the centre. The first was gallantly repulsed by the British and Spaniards, and the enemy driven back with the loss of ten guns; but while the victory was secured here, a charge fatal to part of general Anson's brigade took place in the valley on the left.

Here, threatening the contested height, marched the division of Villatte, supported by two regiments of light cavalry, while, on his right, that of Ruffin, covered by the light troops on the mountain, advanced to turn the British left. To check these movements, general Anson's brigade of cavalry was ordered forward, and it advanced at a trot in the same order in which it had been previously formed; the twenty-third dragoons on the right, and the first hussars of the legion on the left; the whole in two lines. The leading columns of the French, seeing that they were threatened by a charge of cavalry, formed three squares, behind the intervals of which their light horsemen took post, and thus they awaited the advance of the brigade. After the first order to trot, no further word of command was made known to the squadron officers; but as soon as the leading squadrons of the twenty-third

Narrative of lieut.-col. von der Decken, 1st hussars, MSS.

1809. July.

came within range of the French artillery, the horses crowded to the left and began to canter. The hussars were now galled by the enemy's riflemen from the mountain, and several from the serre-file ranks of this regiment were killed and wounded. Arrived under the hill, the brigade was loudly cheered by general Hill's division, and the encouraging shout met with a corresponding answer from the fearless horsemen who gallantly advanced upon the bayonets, the twenty-third taking the larger square which was in front of that regiment, while the hussars moved upon the two smaller squares on the left. But just when the pace had been increased and the charge had commenced, a hollow cleft, till now hidden by the long grass, presented itself in front of the leading squadrons. Too late to pull up, the foremost horsemen rode headlong at the hollow, and a frightful scene ensued. Some tumbled in and over the ravine, some scrambled through it, while others leaped boldly across the chasm, and gained the other side; but great disorder was the consequence. In front of the hussars the ravine was from six to eight feet deep, and from twelve to eighteen feet in breadth; while widening in front of the twenty-third, it was there also more shallow, and the greater part of that regiment were able to get across, but so dispersed and in such confusion that they could make no impression upon the square, and the French artillery sweeping their ranks, and fresh troops arriving to the already over-

Narrative of lieutenant-colonel von der Decken, MSS.

Narrative of colonel von Linsingen, MSS.

1809. July. Narrative of colonel von Linsingen, MSS.

powering mass of the enemy, they were obliged to give way, and leaving nearly half their number in the field, escaped from the unequal contest. The hussars suffered less, their flank not having been exposed to the fire of the artillery, and the rear squadrons crossing the ravine more cautiously on seeing the fate of the front;* but the unlooked-for impediment having thrown the first line into disorder, few of them arrived before the bayonets of the enemy, and no impression was made upon the squares; the rear squadrons halted after crossing the ravine, and the twenty-third being now dispersed, the attempt was abandoned, and the whole retired behind the heavy cavalry brigade of general Fane.

Napier. Appendix No. XI.

The twenty-third left on the field two hundred and seven men and officers; the casualties of the hussars amounted to thirty-seven men and sixty-four horses. Among the wounded were lieutenant Ernest Poten and cornet Teuto.

Although this charge, in consequence of the unlooked-for impediment by which it was baffled,

* Colonel Napier gives Arentschild, who commanded the German hussars, the credit of having reined up at the edge of the ravine in consideration of the lives of his men. This act of prudence cannot, however, be justly imputed to the veteran, who, perilous as was his course, did not hesitate to follow the orders which he had received. It is singular that general Ponsonby, who was present as major of the twenty-third on this day, should also be under the impression that the hussars did not cross the ravine. See letter from general Ponsonby appended to the third volume of Napier's "History of the War in the Peninsula."

failed in its intended effect, the French troops in the valley were paralyzed by the boldness of the attempt, and they remained stationary; but the left and centre of the British position were furiously assailed, and general Sherbrooke's division became involved in a critical struggle. The second line brigade of the legion under colonel Löw co-operated in repulsing the attack of the French on the hill, while the guards and first brigade met the attack on the centre. Reserving their fire until the French had crossed the ravine, these regiments received the enemy with a volley, and then rushing forward with the bayonet, drove their assailants in disorder to the other side; from hence the fire of a second line opening upon them, and being also exposed to a murderous discharge of grape, the legion brigade was ordered to retire, and it fell back with little disorder, leaving general von Langwerth among the slain. The guards, however, accompanied by a detachment of the first line battalion skirmishers under lieutenant von Rettberg, had inconsiderately quitted the line and passed beyond the German brigade, and thus insulated, they became enveloped in the fire of the enemy's musquetry and artillery, and the French swarmed in the centre of the position. At this critical moment, when the British centre was broken, and victory seemed about to decide for the French, the forty-eighth regiment, timely sent down from the hill by the vigilant British chief, advanced through the disordered mass and checked

1809. July.

Napier.

Journal of line battalions, MSS.

Notes of colonel von derDecken, MSS.

Journal of captain Schnath, MSS.

Napier.

1809. July. Napier. the pursuing columns. The guards immediately rallied; the Germans again advanced; a brigade of light cavalry trotted up from the second line; the artillery battered the enemy's flanks; the French relaxed their efforts; and soon the British shouts proclaimed the victory.

The casualties of the British in this action amounted to upwards of five thousand; those of the French exceeded seven thousand: the enemy also lost seventeen guns.

Appendix No. XI. The entire loss of the legion in both days' fighting, was six officers, eight sergeants, and a hundred and seventy-six men killed, forty-one officers, fifty-eight sergeants, and eight hundred and forty-three men wounded, and two hundred and seventy-five men missing. Of these, upwards of eleven hundred and fifty fell on the 28th. Their casualties in horses amounted to eighty-eight. The admirable manner in which the German artillery under major Hartmann was served on this day contributed much to the glorious result, and drew forth the personal commendation of sir Arthur Wellesley. Guelphic archives, MSS. Captain von Rettberg's battery being stationed on the hill, came more immediately under the observation of the commander-in-chief, who condescended particularly to notice the precision with which a bombadier named Dierking directed the fire of one of the guns of the battery.* An instance of zeal

* Dierking, in his memorial for the Guelphic medal, states that lord Wellington, having suggested throwing shells into the French columns

and presence of mind in a sergeant of the same battery deserves also to be recorded. 1809. July.

The sergeant in question, named Bostelmann, with four gunners and four workmen, was entrusted with the supply of the battery from the ammunition waggons in its rear. The enemy's bombs had set fire to the dry heath, with which this part of the field was covered, and the flames spreading, Bostelmann was constantly obliged to change the position of the waggons, in order to keep them away from the burning heath. Just as four full limbers had been sent off to the battery, the enemy directing their fire upon the ammunition park, set the whole space between and around the waggons in flames. Two waggons, the limbers of which had not been yet sent off, could be immediately removed, and they reached the high road, which was at some distance, in safety; but the empty limbers of the remaining four not having yet returned from the battery, the danger became imminent, and the quick explosion of these waggons appeared inevitable. Guelphic archives, MSS.

Bostelmann, well aware of what was to be apprehended, but at the same time considering that the loss of the ammunition might have a material effect on the result of the battle, as the battery to which it belonged was posted on the key of the allied position,

against which the cavalry charge was directed, and orders having been given by captain Rettberg to that effect, was so pleased at the precision with which the German bombadier executed his task, that his lordship clapped him on the back, and said, "Very well, my boy."

1809. July. Guelphic archives, MSS.

against which the enemy's main efforts were directed, determined to attempt the preservation of the waggons, regardless of the personal danger with which the effort would evidently be attended. Of his assistants, the four gunners only were available, the workmen, expecting every moment an explosion, having run away; and with the aid of these four men, Luttermann, Zingreve, Warnecke, and Lind, the gallant sergeant succeeded in removing the heavily loaded ammunition waggons through the burning heath, and placing them on a spot in the rear, which a little trench had yet preserved from the flames. Here they awaited the empty limbers, which, at length arriving, enabled them to remove the waggons to the high road in safety. This important service of the sergeant and gunners met with a deserved acknowledgement from major Hartmann, who, after the action had ceased on the evening of the 28th, called them forward and publicly expressed to them that approbation which their spirited conduct so well merited. Bostelmann was afterwards rewarded with a commission.

The fifth battalion of the legion had, in their contest with the twenty-eighth French regiment on the hill, gained more honours than at the period of the fight they were at all sensible of. Some men of the battalion having gone in the evening from their bivouac towards the spot where the glorious struggle of the morning had taken place, in search of materials to make a fire, brought back, among other

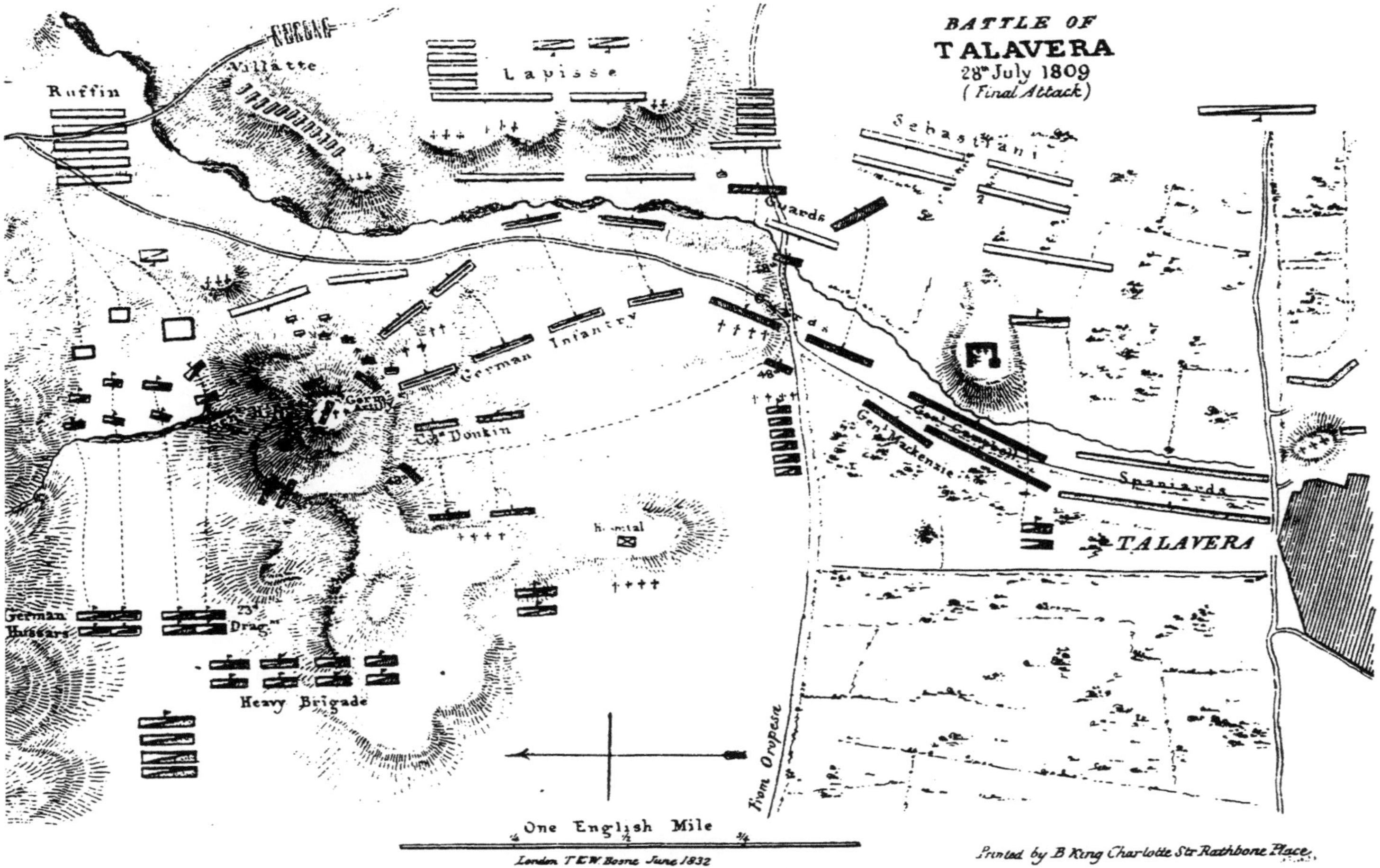
BATTLE OF
TALAVERA
28th July 1809
(Final Attack)
Ruffin
Villatte
Lapisse
Sebastiani
Guards
German Infantry
Col. Donkin
Genl. Campbell
Genl. Mackenzie
Spaniards
TALAVERA
Hospital
German Hussars
23d Drag.
Heavy Brigade
From Oropesa
One English Mile
London T.&W. Boone June 1832
Printed by B King Charlotte Str Rathbone Place

articles, three poles, which the officers soon recognized to be such as bear the French eagles. A strict search among the slain was consequently made for the parts deficient. This was successful, and captain George von Düring had the next day the honour of personally presenting these trophies of the gallant regiment to which he belonged, to the commander-in-chief.

1809. July.

CHAPTER XIV.

1809. July. WHILE the first hussars, four of the line battalions, and two batteries of artillery of the German legion were thus participating in the first successes of the British arms in Spain, the light infantry brigade, second hussars, and those battalions of the line that were stationed in Sicily, were simultaneously engaged in conjunction with two other British armies; the two first in an expedition to the Scheldt, the Sicilian corps in an invasion of Italy.

Bissett's reign of George III. The expedition to the Scheldt consisted of an army of forty thousand men, under the command of lieutenant-general lord Chatham, accompanied by a powerful fleet under admiral sir Richard Strachan, and had for its object the capture or destruction of the French ships which might be either building at Antwerp and Flushing, or afloat in the Scheldt; the destruction of the arsenals and dock-yards at Antwerp, Terneuse, and Flushing; the reduction of the island of Walcheren, and the rendering the Scheldt no longer navigable for ships of war. Should all these objects not be found attainable, as many as possible were to be secured, and the army was to be then re-embarked, leaving behind a force sufficient to maintain possession of the island of Walcheren. 1809. July.

Lieutenant-general sir Eyre Coote was second in command; lieutenant-general sir John Hope commanded the reserve; and the cavalry of the army were under the orders of major-general von Linsingen, of the king's German legion. Journal of major Rautenberg, MSS.

The expedition sailed from the Downs in three successive divisions on the 28th and two following days of July, and the whole had reached the Scheldt in safety by the 31st of August. Two troops of the second German hussars, under major von Müller and captain Clamor von dem Bussche, were attached to the first division, which, commanded by sir John Hope, was directed to land on South Beveland; the second division under sir Eyre Coote, which was particularly destined for the conquest of Walcheren, was to disembark on the north part of the island; while the remaining division under lord Rosslyn to which the rest of the legion hussars were attached, should await the operations of the two first divisions.

In the afternoon of the 30th, the fleet having effected the difficult passage of the Veer-Gat, hitherto considered impracticable for large ships, sir Eyre Coote, with six brigades and a few light artillery and riflemen, landed on the Bree sands, about a mile to the westward of fort der Haak, without opposition. The fort was abandoned by the enemy on the advance of the British, and the Dutch general Osten, who commanded on this part

1809. July. of the coast, drew off his troops towards the principal fortress of Flushing; at the same time the Dutch general Bruce, with about two thousand men, passed over to South Beveland.

Journal of major Rautenberg, MSS.

After the fort had been abandoned by the enemy, the disembarkation proceeded without further opposition, and before night-fall the whole of the second division was on shore.

Sir Eyre Coote immediately took up a position on the sands, and sent forward the division of general Frazer to invest Terveer and fort Rammekens.

Letters from Flushing.*

Ter-Veer was summoned, but the governor refused to surrender, and preparations for a bombardment were accordingly commenced. Meantime the gun-boats and bomb-vessels under sir Home Popham arrived before the town in the Veer-Gat, and on the following morning commenced the cannonade.

The garrison received the attack bravely, and returned the fire of the ships with spirit; but the effects of the British guns were soon conspicuous. Houses fell; bricks, mortar, and timber were hurled over the heads of the besieging army on the other side of the town, and large fragments of chimneys were driven into the adjacent country. The falling lumber began at length to fill every space, and the garrison being no longer able to work their guns,

* Letters from Flushing, containing an account of the Expedition to Walcheren, Beveland, and the mouth of the Scheldt, under the command of the Earl of Chatham, with a topographical and statistical account of the Islands of Walcheren and Beveland, &c. By an officer of the eighty-first regiment, London, 1809.

it became evident that the town would not hold out much longer. Night now coming on, the humanity of the British commanders interposed, and the fire was slackened; but the enemy seemed to consider this forbearance a reflection on their courage, and having cleared away some of the rubbish from the guns, re-commenced firing. In this manner, tempered by the rain and darkness, the operations continued during a good part of the night; but this resistance proved fatal to the town, which, the next morning, presented the melancholy spectacle of a smoking pile of bricks, through which the flames seemed struggling for an outlet.

1809. August. Letters from Flushing.

The garrison now offered to capitulate, and the offer was accepted by the British commanders, who allowed the brave defenders to march out with all the honours of war. Their numbers proved to be not more than about four hundred men, consisting of four companies of infantry and one of artillery, commanded by lieutenant-colonel Bogart, whose gallant defence was a just subject of admiration in the besieging army. The British had about eighty men and officers killed, and double that number wounded.

Sir John Hope landed near Ter-Goes, in South Beveland, on the 1st of August, and met with no opposition; the enemy's general Bruce withdrawing his troops into Bergen-op-Zoom. Fort Bathz was evacuated on the night of the 2d, and thus the whole island of Soult Beveland fell into quiet possession of

1809. August. Letters from Flushing. the British. The enemy's ships then retired up the Scheldt, beyond fort Lillo, and some even above Antwerp, where they lay quite out of the reach of the British fleet.

After the surrender of Ter-Veer, sir Eyre Coote's corps moved on to Middleburg, which town, although without guns or garrison, was permitted to enter into capitulation, and the troops followed the retiring army towards Flushing, where the enemy had determined to make a stand.

Two British regiments, the 14th and 71st, pursued the enemy up to the gates of the fortress, and endeavoured to force an entrance with them by a direct assault. The attempt caused a great panic in the place; but the British commander deemed it advisable to call off the troops, and to commence operations in the more regular form of a siege.

Narrative of the Campaign* The defences of Flushing on the land side were but indifferent. The town was inclosed within a single line of bastions, whose flanks were perpendicular to the curtains; these works were of earth, and their construction was in other respects extremely defective. The rampart was low and commanded by the sea dyke; except on the flanks of the position, it was in great want of repair, and had neither traverses nor bomb-proof cover for the garrison. In front was a respectable ditch, though

* A short Narrative of the late Campaign of the British army under the orders of the Right Honourable the Earl of Chatham, K.G. with preliminary remarks on the topography and channels of Zealand. London, 1810.

without any sort of glacis. The bastions on the flanks, where the sea-dyke met the works, were of brick, but in a very weak and neglected state, and they were liable to be breached at the distance of a thousand yards from the place. In front of each flank on the sea-dyke, the French had constructed a sort of outwork with a low parapet, on which a few guns were mounted; and, they had also added a ravelin before each of the gates communicating with the country. Throughout the land front there were distributed about fifty pieces of artillery, fourteen only of which were twenty-four pounders, the rest being principally field-pieces and howitzers, and almost all of them were mounted *en barbette*, without merlons or traverses.

1809. August.

Narrative of the Campaign.

Towards the sea the town was enclosed by a wall of brick, behind which was a rampart, which in many places presented powerful batteries both of guns and mortars towards the Deurloo channel, and the anchorage in front of the town; a battery called the Dykeshook protected the entrance to the harbour on the west, while fort Rammekens, commanding the channel which separates the island of Walcheren from South Beveland, defended the entrance on the east: a sea bombardment appeared, therefore, to have been more apprehended than a regular siege.

Journal of major Rautenberg. MSS.

More extensive projects of defence had been made by the French, the basis of which was

1809. August. founded on a proposed inundation, with respectable casemated works on either flank, for the security of the dykes leading to the body of the place, and excavations had already been commenced about two thousand yards in front. The town was defended in all by one hundred and seven pieces of artillery, but out of fifty guns in battery on the land side, where the work was above a mile in extent, only fourteen were twenty-four pounders, the rest, including mortars, being all of small calibre; however, by opening the sluices, and cutting the dykes, the surrounding country could be inundated, and the assault of a besieging army that might give time for the water to flow, (about ten days,) altogether prevented.

Narrative of the Campaign.

Journal of major Rautenberg, MSS.

Previous to opening the trenches before the fortress, it was necessary to get possession of the batteries, which, it has been stated, commanded the south coast of the island on its eastern and western sides, and these were not abandoned without opposition. Major-general Graham had a sharp contest with the enemy on the morning of the first, when he obtained possession of the Dykeshook, and two small batteries; brigadier-general Houston's brigade at the same time forced the troops that were stationed on the Middleburg road, to retire with the loss of four guns, and several killed and wounded. Lord Paget's division took up a position at West Soubourg, and lieutenant-general Fraser's,

Lord Chatham's Despatch.

1809. August. Narrative of the Campaign.

marching in the evening upon Ruttern, detached a corps for the reduction of fort Rammekens, to complete the investment. Rammekens capitulated on the 3d of August with a garrison of one hundred and twenty-seven officers and men, and the passage of the West Scheldt was thus opened; but the fleet could not yet take advantage of the surrender, being prevented by contrary winds from entering the channel.

Letters from Flushing.

The taking of Flushing was lord Chatham's first object; after this should have been accomplished, his plan of operation was understood to be, to assemble the land forces at fort Bathz, in South Beveland, and then passing over to the east bank of the eastern branch of the Scheldt, to continue along that line until he should reach the main river; sir Richard Strachan in the mean time was to proceed down the Scheldt with the fleet, and clear the channel. In this manner the combined forces were to advance to Fort Lillo, where some strong opposition was expected.

The number of the enemy's troops at this time in the island of Walcheren was about four thousand men, consisting chiefly of Prussians, Spaniards, Dutch, and Irishmen; they had few artillery-soldiers, and were wholly unprepared for the defence of such a place as Flushing. The investing army under sir Eyre Coote exceeded fifteen thousand men; one battalion remained at Ter-Veere, another garrisoned Middleburg, and about thirty

1809. August. thousand men were under sir John Hope in Beveland.

Letters from Flushing. The necessary preparations for commencing the siege on the land side went on; artillery, ammunition, and stores were brought up to the vicinity of the fortress, and the construction of batteries was begun; but the approach of the flotilla to the sea front was still delayed by contrary winds, and the communication thus laying open with Cadzand, which island was left unoccupied by the British, the enemy soon took advantage of the neglect, and on the 4th, and two following days of August, about three thousand men passed over from Cadzand to Flushing. This reinforcement enabled them to keep up an active and enterprising opposition to the operations of the besiegers, and it was found necessary to land additional troops. Journal of major Rautenberg, MSS. General Grosvenor's division and general von Alten's brigade of the legion were therefore ordered to disembark. The German brigade landed in the afternoon of the 5th, and marched to Middleburg, and the following day joined the outposts of the besieging army at Ost-Zobourg.

Letters from Flushing. About four o'clock in the afternoon of the 7th, two thousand of the garrison of Flushing, under the command of general Osten, sallied out from the place by two different roads, with the intention of dislodging the advanced party of general Graham's brigade, amounting to about six hundred men, which was posted on the right wing of the position. The enemy, gallantly led on by their officers, advanced with a great shew of resolution, and their charge was vigorous, but the deliberate courage of the besiegers repelled the attack, and after a contest of about two hours they were driven back with loss and completely routed, their officers in vain endeavouring to rally them. The main brunt of the combat fell upon the English regiments, but a detachment of the first German light battalion was also engaged, and their conduct drew forth the special approbation of the British commander, in the general orders of the following day. Four rank and file of the battalion were killed, and lieutenant du Fay, ensign Hedemann, and twelve rank and file wounded; the two officers severely. The French colonel du Bois, several officers, and a considerable number of the assailants were made prisoners.

1809. August.

Journal of major Rautenberg, MSS.

The trenches were completed on the 9th, and two six-gun batteries ready for action, but the fleet was still detained by contrary winds, and the bombardment was delayed until their arrival. On this day the divisions of lord Rosslyn and the marquis of Huntly landed on South Beveland. The construction of a strong mortar battery was commenced within three hundred yards of the north-east part of the fortress, and the enemy made no attempt to interrupt the work, which led to the general opinion that the garrison were instructed to run no risks, but to keep the place as long as possible,

Letters from Flushing.

1809. August. thus giving the French marshals time to assemble their armies at Antwerp.

Letters from Flushing. The heavy artillery was landed at Terveer from the ships, and dragged across the island to Flushing by the British seamen, a body of whom, amounting to nearly five hundred men, had been formed into a marine brigade, and, under the command of captain Richardson of the navy, rendered most effective assistance to the besieging army. The difficulty and time required to drag these guns a distance of eight miles, caused much delay in the progress of the siege, and meantime the garrison of Flushing were receiving reinforcements from the opposite island of Cadzand; on the 9th, however, the gun-boats took up a station which prevented any further communication with this coast, and on the 11th, the wind having become favourable, ten British frigates, under lord William Stuart, passed the two batteries of Cadzand and Flushing in gallant style, and, after being exposed for nearly two hours to the enemy's fire, anchored off the sea front of the fortress.

Meanwhile general Monnet caused the sluices to be opened, and the dyke on the right of the town to be cut, and the water began to flow; but the tide not being at the highest, and the wind blowing off shore, his expectations were not fully answered, and although the besiegers were much incommoded, their operations were not delayed. A

1809. August. Lord Chatham's Despatch.

large portion of the British flotilla, under sir Richard Keats and sir Home Popham, reached Bathz on the 11th, and secured the navigation of the river as far as Lillo, to which place the enemy's flotilla retired, abandoning six of their gun-boats, which had grounded.

Letters from Flushing.

The investing army was most unpleasantly lodged; the men built themselves huts, but the rain penetrated them, and rendered these dwellings of little service; positive orders having been given against landing more than a certain weight of baggage, many of the soldiers were without blankets, and there was scarcely a change of linen throughout the army. The position of the troops, close to the most unhealthy town in the island, caused these wants to be the more severely felt; for even the inhabitants of Middleburg, which is only five miles distant, speak of Flushing with horror, and it is a proverb in the island that "no one but a sailor can live there."

The troops were already knee-deep in water, which now began to flow so fast that scarcely an inch of dry ground was to be seen, and all the fresh water in the island was tainted;* it rained much, and the army began to suffer in health; the sentries were frequently obliged to be relieved in consequence of sudden indisposition, and the men were

* Throughout Zealand there are no springs or fresh water rivers. The rains alone supply the inhabitants with water.—*Narrative of the Campaign.*

1809. August. Letters from Flushing.

frequently carried from parade, being attacked by dysentery and intermittent fever. For the last week the climate had been variable in the extreme. In the morning it rained heavily; at noon there was a burning sun, which produced intense perspiration, and the nights again became extremely cold; but the cold and hot damps were the most perilous, as the first caused rheumatism, and the other was absolutely pestilential. The men were now dying hourly: the troops stood for hours together up to their knees in water, and things began to wear a most gloomy appearance.

The batteries were not finished until the night of the 12th, and by noon on the following day the ships had taken their stations, and all preparations for the bombardment were completed. Previous to its commencement a flag of truce was sent to general Monnet, intimating that, as the fire would be very heavy, the British commander-in-chief would wish him to remove the women and children, who were promised free egress through the lines. General Monnet, assuming a lofty tone, and little regarding the dictates of humanity, sent for answer that he must decline the proposal, as he felt fully competent to defend the women and children himself, a presumption which the event proved he was by no means prepared to justify.

Orders were therefore issued for the bombardment to commence, and about two o'clock on Sunday, the 13th of August, both ships and batteries opened upon

1809. August. Letters from Flushing.

the town. The effect was tremendous. The island shook as if under an earthquake, and every report of the cannon was followed by a crash which loudly spoke destruction. The batteries being all near the place, the guns had their full force, and they appeared as if absolutely tearing the city up from the roots. The cannonnade was at first answered with spirit and several Dutch burghers were seen gallantly pointing the cannon on the ramparts; but the fire soon became too hot for these sober citizens, and even for the garrison. The opposing harbour batteries were demolished, the walls fell in large fragments, the churches took fire, the houses fell in, the town was fast sinking into a heap of ruins, and every thing became so enveloped in smoke that the British guns were aimed at random.

Lord Chatham's Despatch.

This evening a detachment, consisting of the 14th regiment and part of the light infantry brigade of the legion, under lieutenant-colonel Nicolls, forced an intrenchment in front of general Graham's position in most gallant style, making a lodgement within musket-shot of the town, and taking one gun and thirty prisoners.

The devastating cannonade was continued during the whole of Sunday afternoon and night, and although the town was repeatedly in flames, the enemy bravely kept up their fire. Gradually, however, it became less frequent; instead of volleys it was reduced to single shots, and instead of the guns being fired at regular intervals, they were let

1809. August. Lord Chatham's Despatch.

off at random. About ten o'clock on Monday morning sir Richard Strachan got under weigh, and passing immediately under the sea line of defence, poured in repeated broadsides for some hours into the place, and brought down the town in masses. Lord Gardner followed, and both vessels anchored close under the walls. The garrison still stood to their guns, but the ruins fell so thickly around them that even the guns became buried in the mass, and the fire of the brave defenders necessarily ceased. Still no appearance of surrender was evinced, and they obstinately kept up their colours when they could no longer fire a gun.

Letters from Flushing.

This frightful slaughter continued till about five o'clock in the afternoon of the 14th, when the fire of the enemy entirely ceasing, it was also stopped on the side of the British. A summons was immediately sent in to general Monnet, who answered that he would reply to it as soon as he had consulted a council of war. An hour was given him for this purpose, but three hours having elapsed without an answer arriving, the bombardment was resumed, and once more the ships and batteries began to play upon the devoted town. The cannonade was now more tremendous than at first. Congreve rockets blazed about in terrific splendour, and Flushing was soon in flames. The fire raged unchecked amidst the darkness of the night, the cannon still thundering, and the walls, chimneys, and roofs falling under the stroke of the balls.

The interior of almost every house was laid bare, and when there was an interval of cannon roar, it was filled up by the howling of dogs and the shrieks of the distracted women in the fortress; owls and bats flew affrighted around the light, and the whole scene presented a sublime but horrific picture of a successful siege.

1809. August. Letters from Flushing.

It having been discovered that a battery of three twenty-four pounders, which was erected on the left of the British line, was so far from the place as to be not only unable to injure the works of the town, but even to silence a *barbette* battery of two guns, which was advanced upon the dyke about five hundred and sixty yards in front of the fortifications, the dyke was ordered to be occupied one thousand yards in front of the existing batteries, and the enemy's advanced battery to be carried by assault, and the guns spiked, if it were not possible to keep possession of them, and put the battery in a state of defence. Lieutenant-colonel Pack was charged with the execution of these orders, and this gallant officer, at the head of detachments from the 36th, 71st, and the two light battalions of the legion, set out about midnight to carry them into effect.

Narrative of the Campaign.

All access to the battery from the low ground being cut off by deep ditches, the troops were obliged to march along the confined breadth of the dyke, and this approach was rendered still more perilous in consequence of the cut which had been

1809. August. made in the dyke to produce the inundation, being exactly in front of the battery to be attacked. The night was dark and tempestuous, the cannonade was yet raging, and rockets were hissing through the air, when the storming party set out. In consequence of the extreme darkness, the men could only perceive the mouths of the guns upon which they were marching, when the fire of the town or the rockets threw the light in that direction. Under these discouraging circumstances they boldly dashed forward, and although met by a great superiority in numbers, carried the battery at the point of the bayonet, taking forty prisoners, and killing and wounding many of the enemy. Lieutenant Sprecher and three men of the second light battalion were killed, and seventeen men of both battalions wounded.* The entire loss of the detachments in killed, wounded, and missing, was thirty-eight officers and men.

Letters from Flushing.

Lord Chatham's Despatch.

Journal of major Rautenberg, MSS.

The bombardment continued until two o'clock

* The author of "Letters from Flushing," after describing the capture of this battery by the troops under lieutenant-colonel Pack, adds the following tribute to the gallantry of general von Alten's brigade.

"I know not whether I have ever before mentioned the extraordinary gallantry of the German legion; there is not a regiment in our service which can excel these foreigners. In every service of peril they have been the first to volunteer; and it is equal justice to add that in the most dangerous services they have always conducted themselves with the most brilliant valour. I hope that their repeated proofs of the most heroic bravery will extinguish those remains of prejudice which the common people of England are but too apt to indulge against foreigners," &c. page 160.

in the morning of the 16th, when general Monnet requested a suspension of arms for forty-eight hours. Two hours only were granted him, the bombardment ceased, and colonel Long, of the staff, and captain Cockburn, of the navy, were sent to negotiate terms. In an hour the business was concluded by these officers, and the fortress was immediately put in possession of the British; the garrison, to the number of about five thousand eight hundred officers and men, surrendering as prisoners of war. Besides the number killed, which was considerable, upwards of one thousand wounded men had been transported to Cadzand previous to the complete investment of the town. The entire British loss in killed and wounded, from the 8th of August to the surrender of Flushing, amounted to only one hundred and thirty-six officers and men. The islands of Schauwen and Duiveland capitulated without opposition on the same day.

1809. August. Lord Chatham's Despatch.

CHAPTER XV.

1809. August. Letters from Flushing.

Flushing presented an awful spectacle in the morning light. The buildings of the town having stood considerably above the walls, and the artillery having been pointed with the sole view of destroying them, had almost all been battered in, and the interior of the houses exposed to view; large chimneys, which, according to the Dutch fashion, had been built up in masses on the partition walls, having been struck down by the balls and shells, were precipitated on the roofs of the houses, which had fallen in under their weight. Congreve rockets had obtained admission through the openings thus made in the roofs, and the destruction which these missiles caused was frightful. More than two hundred and forty-seven private houses, two churches, and the town-house, containing many important documents, were destroyed; and about three hundred and thirty-five inoffensive persons, men, women, and children, had lost their lives; besides a far greater number who were wounded. The burghers of every rank were now seen digging the smoking heaps to search for the mangled bodies of their relations, and

Narrative of the Campaign.

Letters from Flushing.

every moment some of these disfigured objects might be seen raised on biers, in order that they might be claimed by their relatives. The French had contrived to post the citizens in all the most exposed and dangerous places, and the destruction of life among them had consequently been considerable.

1809. August. Letters from Flushing.

Arrangements were now commenced for putting the town in a state of defence, as the enemy were assembling in great force on the opposite coast of Cadzand, where they had already established a regular encampment. But disease had begun to make frightful ravages among the British troops, and the army became every day less able to retain its conquest. The medical men in vain exerted all their ability to check the progress of the fatal disorder, which raged among them, but the root of it could not be successfully reached. It appeared to be contained in the atmosphere, every inhalation of which was poisonous. The nerves became relaxed and the blood corrupted. The disease commenced with every symptom of an ague; from thence it passed into a fever, and when the fever had subsided, the blood was putrified. Livid spots broke out on the arms, legs, and other parts of the body; and the unhappy sufferer, when in the absence of the fever some hopes were entertained of his recovery—died. It was observable that the foreigners in the English army did not at all suffer

1809. August. from this disease in the same proportion as the British, to whom the mortality appeared to be almost exclusively confined.

Journal of major Rautenberg, MSS.

A strong garrison having been left in Flushing under general Picton, the rest of the investing army moved by successive divisions into South Beveland.

Narrative of the Campaign.

General von Alten's brigade marched on the 17th, and crossing over at Sloo, were cantoned at and in the neighbourhood of Gravenpolder. The head-quarters, however, did not leave Middleburg until the 21st, on which day lord Chatham removed to Ter-Goes, a distance of fourteen miles. On the 23d the commander-in-chief reached the village of Aralbendyk, thirteen miles on the road to fort Bathz; and, on the following day he accomplished the remaining six miles; so that not until eight days and a half after the surrender of Flushing were head-quarters established at Bathz.

This languid mode of following up the capture of Flushing, and the time which had already been consumed before that fortress, enabled the French to collect large reinforcements both on the left bank of the Scheldt, and in the neighbourhood of Antwerp; and lord Chatham soon found himself beset with difficulties which might have embarrassed a more able commander. Measures had been taken to cut the dykes of Tholen, and thus overflow the country between that place and Bergen-op-zoom, as also to lay the low ground in the neighbourhood of

Lillo and Liefkenshock, and the whole of the Polders* between Hulst and the *Tête de Flandres* under water; a boom chain had been fixed across the Scheldt, and arrangements made for sinking vessels in that channel and obstructing its navigation.

1809. August. Letters from Flushing.

Bernadotte was reported to be at Cadzand with twenty thousand men; Dumonceau at Brussels with about the same number; and another corps under Kellermann was stated to be advancing from the Weser. Three hundred gun-boats had been brought from Boulogne to Cadzand by the canals, and it was evident that the enemy intended the reconquest of Walcheren. It was now also discovered that the French fleet could, if necessary, retire beyond Antwerp; the reduction of which place became, therefore, indispensable to the accomplishment of the main objects of the expedition.

Meantime the epidemic was raging in the British army; the men were dying at the rate of two hundred and fifty per week, and three thousand were already on the sick list. The supplies were nearly exhausted. Scarcely a week's provisions remained for the army, and the navy were but furnished for a month. The soldiers had neither flannels nor blankets, and their shoes were so worthless, that, after a few wettings, the soles came off.

Lord Cathcart's Despatch.

Bissett's reign of Geo. III.

Letters from Flushing.

* Tracts of land recovered from the sea, and surrounded by dykes.

1809. August. Letters from Flushing. Water was obliged to be sent for to England. Even the medicine chests were deficient. Bark, the medicine which was considered of most service in the prevailing disease, had been brought out but in small quantities; the supply was expended, and none was to be procured in the country; in short there was a miserable deficiency of every thing that could protect the soldier from the dangers of the climate; the condition of the army had become frightful in the extreme; every day diminished its numbers, and heightened its distresses.

Journal of major Rautenberg, MSS. Under these circumstances the commander-in-chief judged it prudent to take the opinions of the generals of his army on the course which he should pursue, and a council of war was assembled at Bathz on the 27th. The lieutenant-generals were required to state "how far it appeared to them advisable that the siege of Antwerp should be engaged in, it being believed that this operation could alone ensure the destruction of the naval arsenals, and the possession of their ships, and to which operations the reduction of forts Lillo and Liefkenschock was an indispensable preliminary measure." The total French force at Bergen-op-Zoom, Antwerp, Breda, on the left bank of the Scheldt, and at Tholen, was estimated at thirty-five thousand men. The effective British force was thirty thousand; but of these six thousand were required in Walcheren, two thousand in South

Beveland, and eight thousand to observe Bergen-op-Zoom and Breda, guard the depôts of stores and provisions, and perform the duty of escorts. Fourteen thousand, therefore, only remained for the siege of Antwerp, and reduction of forts Lillo and Liefkenschock; and the lieutenant-generals were required to consider "whether it was advisable to undertake operations so serious and extensive, with so small a force." 1809. August.

The lieutenant-generals declared themselves to be of opinion, that under the circumstances which had been laid before them, the siege of Antwerp was impracticable, and, as the reduction of that place could alone effect the ultimate object of the expedition, that no possible advantage could result from attempting to reduce forts Lillo and Liefkenschock, or from undertaking any minor operation.

Letter from lord Castlereagh to lord Chatham.

The opinion of the council of war having been communicated to the English ministry, lord Chatham was directed, "after providing effectively for the security of Walcheren, to return with the remainder of the army to England; at the same time he was required to give effect to any measures which sir Richard Strachan might think fit to adopt for obstructing the navigation of the Scheldt, and also to confer with that officer on the practicability of destroying any works which the enemy might have constructed at Terneuse, should they be found of

1809. August. sufficient importance to justify operations against them."

Journal of major Rautenberg, MSS. Fort Bathz was now demolished, and the troops in South Beveland were ordered to return to Walcheren. The first division marched on the 1st of September; head-quarters were re-established at Middleburg on the 2d, and the last division marched into the island on the following day. South Beveland was immediately occupied by the French division of general Dumonceau.

Lord Chatham embarked for England on the 11th of September, and was followed by the greater part of the army, including the second hussars of the legion, only two squadrons of which regiment had been landed. Letters from Flushing. About sixteen thousand men, not more than about ten thousand four hundred of whom were effective, were left behind for the protection of Walcheren, and of this force sir Eyre Coote was given the command.

Sir Eyre Coote's despatch. The Polder of St. Joostland being, from its proximity to South Beveland, that part which was most exposed to an attack, it was necessary to send two battalions there, and general von Alten's light infantry were selected for that purpose. Journal of major Rautenberg, MSS. This brigade had neither barracks nor quarters, and sickness was much more to be dreaded in St. Joostland than in the other part of Walcheren. The German troops, however, appeared much better able to stand the climate than the British, for although a detachment of the legion brigade was stationed in this island during the whole time that the army remained in Walcheren, comparatively but few men either died or were rendered non-effective by the disorder.

1809. September

Letters from Flushing.

Notwithstanding the appalling calamity with which the army was visited, reducing every day their numbers and efficiency, and the little prospect that appeared of their being able to keep possession of Walcheren, the British government still hesitated whether they should retain or abandon that island; indeed, their first intention was to retain it, and this, as has been supposed, to favour the negotiations of Austria with Napoleon. About the middle of September, preparations were made to renew and strengthen the works. Bricks and lime were sent out in large quantities from England, and about the end of October one hundred artificers arrived. Lieutenant-general Don now relieved sir Eyre Coote in his distressing command, which sir Eyre gave into his hands on the 29th.

Bissett's reign of Geo. III.

The medical department at length received a liberal supply of port wine and bark, but the inroads of the pestilence were not to be checked, and the mortality increased daily. In the beginning of November many battalions were reduced to fifty effective men, the average number of deaths being at this time thirty-five men daily.

Journal of major Rautenberg, MSS.

Seeing the troops thus perishing before his eyes, general Don called a council of war, and the result

1809. November. of their deliberations at length brought an order from England for the army to evacuate Walcheren. Effective measures were also directed to be taken for destroying the basin and naval defences of the island, but these directions were neutralized by the expression of a hope that events might render their execution unnecessary, and the defences were slowly and but partially destroyed. Nearly a hundred transports arrived on the 20th and following days, bringing with them four fresh battalions to cover the embarkation in case of necessity. The sick, heavy baggage, guns, and stores were got on board without delay, and arrangements commenced for evacuating the island.

Bissett's reign of Geo. III.

Journal of major Rautenberg, MSS.

The French, however, were apprised of the intended embarkation of the troops, and made active preparations for an attack, which, it was expected, would be attempted at the time of embarkation. The generals in command of divisions and the commanding officers of artillery were therefore ordered, as soon as the troops should have embarked, to make immediate arrangements for disembarking and taking the field.

General orders of sir George Don.

The legion battalions were embarked on the 9th of December, but the weather being boisterous, and general Don conceiving it probable, from the active and continual preparations of the enemy, that they might hazard an attack, judged it expedient still to hold the towns of Flushing, Middleburg, Terveer, and fort Rammekens. No opposition, however, was

1809. December. General Don's despatch. Journal of major Rautenberg, MSS.

made, and the rear-guards being withdrawn on the morning of the 23d, the fleet then got under weigh. A few shots were fired from the enemy's batteries at Bresken, on the Cadzand coast; but although the guns were doubly loaded, the distance of the ships from the land was too great to allow of their being much affected by the fire, and one man only was killed, and two men were wounded. On the 25th, the fleet anchored in the Downs; general von Alten's brigade disembarked at Deal and Dover on the following day, and from thence marched to Bexhill barracks, which they reached at the end of the year. Nearly one half of the brigade were ill with the exterminating disease which had carried off so many of their companions in arms, and which had now received from the army the distinguishing but too moderate appellation of the "Walcheren fever."

Thus terminated the expedition to the Scheldt—an expedition in which nearly one-half of one of the finest armies that ever left the British shores either perished from sickness, or returned home sinking under a pestilential disorder—by which the treasury of England was uselessly deprived of twenty millions of money, and one million of annual taxes was added to the burthens of the country.* Projected in ignorance, planned without judge-

* Annual Register for 1809.

1809. December. ment, and directed with a degree of languor which would have been alone sufficient to prevent its success, this fatal expedition stands ingloriously prominent in the annals of a glorious reign, strikingly exhibiting rashness on the part of a government, and inefficiency on that of a commander.

CHAPTER XVI.

WE shall now return to those regiments of the king's German legion, which, in the spring of 1808, had been removed to Sicily, and which, while one part of the corps was co-operating with lord Chatham's army at the northern extremity of Napoleon's territory, were aiding the operations of another British force at the southern limits of that emperor's dominions. 1808. September

These regiments were, it is to be remembered, the third, fourth, sixth, and eighth battalions of the line, under the command of brigadiers du Plat and von Honstedt, and the third foot battery of artillery under captain Bussmann.

Up to the beginning of September the troops in Sicily experienced little other changes than those incidental to the frequent removal of the regiments from one part of the island to another. On the 2d of this month, however, the skirmishers of the eighth battalion, under lieutenant Marburg, and a detachment of the artillery of the legion under lieutenant Ueberfeldt, were suddenly ordered to embark at Melazzo, with an equal number of the English artillery and a hundred and fifty of the fifty-eighth regiment, the whole amounting to two hundred and Narrative of captain Bussmann, MSS.

1808. September. thirty men, with an howitzer and two three-pounders; and these detachments, together with the royal Malta fencibles, were, it was understood, to proceed on a secret expedition, under the command of lieutenant-colonel Brysse of the engineers.

Journal of 8th line battalion, MSS.

The troops sailed from Melazzo on the 3d of September, but were so long detained by calms, that a part only reached the gulph of Policastro, which proved to be their destination, on the afternoon of the 7th. The transports which then arrived contained the artillery, the detachment of the fifty-eighth, and from two to three hundred of the Malta regiment, and these anchored before the town of Damietta the same evening. A fire was now opened upon the place from two sloops of war, an armed transport, and a Neapolitan galliot, which was continued throughout the night, and at day-break on the following morning, under cover of the fire of the sloops of war, the troops landed without opposition.

Narrative of captain Bussmann, MSS.

As soon as the guns were mounted, the detachments advanced, and dragging the two three-pounders through the town after them, with the assistance of the sailors, placed the howitzer at its entrance, while the skirmishers drove the enemy from the hedges and vineyards which bounded the place.

The two guns having been brought up to a height on the other side of the town, the enemy retired out of fire, and took post on an adjacent hill.

Here they were kept in check by the main body of the infantry, while the remainder, together with the artillery and sailors, proceeded to dig out and set afloat thirty coasters loaded with oil, wine, silk, and other merchandize, which had been drawn on shore by windlasses, and covered with a breast-work of sand. Several casks filled with oil and wine were also found hidden in the sand, and ten twenty-four pound English caronnades, eight Neapolitan guns, two six-inch howitzers, and a considerable quantity of ammunition, were taken. The troops embarked the same evening at nine o'clock, on their return to Melazzo, where they arrived in safety on the 14th, having suffered no loss, and being amply repaid by their capture for the little labour with which it had been accomplished.*

1808. October.

Narrative of captain Bussmann, MSS.

On the 9th of October the skirmishers of the third and fourth battalions were embarked as reinforcements for the troops in Capri, where the French had landed three thousand men; but Capri had capitulated before the reinforcements arrived, and the skirmishers returned to Sicily on the 23d.

Journal of 3d line battalion, MSS.

During the winter months the troops were not disturbed; but in the following year, when the successes of Napoleon's arms on the Danube had checked the progress of the archduke John in

* The German artillerymen, fifteen in number, received each sixteen dollars, twenty-four groschens prize money, or about £2 : 15 sterling.

1809. June. Sir J. Stuart's despatch.

the north of Italy, a project to create a diversion in favour of Austria was formed by lieutenant-general sir John Stuart, then commanding in Sicily, in concert with rear-admiral Martin, and an expedition against the kingdom and capital of Naples was planned and undertaken by these commanders.

The British and German troops that were employed on this expedition amounted to about fifteen thousand men, to which was added a division of the Sicilian army under prince Leopold. The troops of the legion were the third, fourth, and sixth line battalions, and the third foot battery of artillery; the eighth line battalion alone remaining behind. Forty gun-boats accompanied the fleet; three line-of-battle ships, some frigates and smaller vessels formed the convoy, and the whole sailed from Melazzo on the 11th of June.

The fleet reached the coast of Calabria on the morning of the 13th, and its appearance induced the enemy immediately to abandon the greater part of their posts along the shore; at the same time lieutenant-colonel Smith, who had been detached to the coast opposite Messina immediately after the sailing of the fleet, with three battalions of infantry and the German battery of artillery, seized and disarmed the posts upon that line also.

After experiencing many calms and contrary winds, that part of the fleet which contained the British troops and German infantry anchored off Cape

Miseno, in the vicinity of Baia, on the 24th, and preparations were immediately made for a descent upon the island of Ischia.

1809. June. Sir J. Stuart's despatch.

The command of the troops which were selected for this operation, amounting to two thousand three hundred and eighty men, with four six-pounders and two howitzers, was entrusted to major-general Macfarlane, who, under the fire of two of the British ships of war, and aided by the British and Sicilian gun-boats, forced a descent upon the island on the morning of the 25th, in the face of a formidable chain of batteries, with which every accessible part of the shore was perfectly fortified, and which were turned and successively abandoned as the troops gained a footing. About two hundred and fifty, or three hundred men fell into the hands of the British, and general Colonna, who commanded the enemy's troops, retired with his prinpal force into the castle.

Journal of 6th line battalion, MSS.

On the morning of the 26th, the skirmishers of the sixth line battalion of the legion, under lieutenant von Hohnstedt, and a detachment of captain Harling's company of the same battalion, were landed at Cape Miseno, and, in conjunction with some marines and sailors from the fleet, gallantly stormed and took possession of a battery which was defended by a superior force of the enemy, whom they drove back, killing and wounding many, and taking twenty prisoners. The capture of this battery enabled the

1809. July. navy to seize a division of gun-boats which had taken shelter under its guns. The detachment of the sixth battalion had only one man killed, and six or eight men wounded.

Sir J. Stuart's despatch. The castle of Ischia was summoned by major-general Macfarlane; but general Colonna refused to surrender, and held out until the 30th. On this day, however, a breaching battery having been erected against the works of the place, he surrendered the castle on terms of capitulation.

Sir John Stuart and admiral Martin, conjecturing that the success and promptitude with which the landing on Ischia had been effected might influence the adjacent garrison of Procida, sent immediately a summons to the governor of that island, who, in the course of the day, submitted to the terms proposed. This surrender contributed to the almost entire capture or destruction of a flotilla consisting of about forty heavy gun-boats, which, expecting to find protection and co-operation from the artillery of the fortress, in the narrow strait that separates the island from the main, had, during the night and following morning, attempted to pass from Gaeta to Naples, and were there seized upon by the British ships.

Exclusive of the killed and wounded of the enemy in these different encounters, which was believed to be considerable, more than fifteen hundred regular troops were made prisoners; among whom were a general of brigade, two colonels, and upwards of seventy-five officers of progressive ranks. Nearly 1809. one hundred pieces of ordnance, with their corresponding stores, were also captured. July.

Lieutenant-colonel Smith's operations in Lower Calabria were not followed by such successes as those which attended the main body of the army in the gulf of Naples. Just as the garrison of the castle of Scylla had hoisted the white flag, a preponderating force of the enemy coming suddenly down to relieve the place, obliged colonel Smith to raise the siege, leaving his besieging train in possession of the enemy. This proved, however, but a temporary sacrifice, for on the night of the 2d of July, the enemy, struck by some sudden panic, again retreated from the coast, blowing up the works of the fortress, and leaving behind not only the British captured stores, but an immense quantity of ordnance and stores of their own, which had been placed here in depôt. The British loss was trifling, and of the Germans only a few of the artillery-men were wounded.

Narrative of captain Bussmann, MSS.

Although the appearance of this expedition on the coast of Calabria had the immediate effect of causing a considerable body of troops, which had been detached from Naples as a reinforcement to the army of Upper Italy, to be precipitately withdrawn, as well as the whole of those troops which had been sent to aid Napoleon's usurpation of the papal dominions, the projected attempt on the city

Sir J. Stuart's despatch.

1809. November. Sir J. Stuart's despatch.

and kingdom of Naples was obliged to be abandoned; for besides a preponderating regular force which Murat had assembled in the vicinity of his capital, he was also aided by a large body of national guards, and no hope could be entertained of a successful attack upon his kingdom.

Sir John Stuart therefore decided upon returning to Sicily, and all means of defence in the captured islands having been destroyed, the fleet left the gulf of Naples on the 26th, and the troops were again at Melazzo on the 31st.

Journal of captain von Hohnstedt, MSS.

The south-west coast of the island being disturbed by the incursions of privateers from the opposite coast of Tunis, which, taking advantage of the absence of the British cruizers, used to come over and interfere with the navigation, the sixth battalion of the legion were, on the 30th of November, removed to the fortress of Trapani, which, as well as the forts on the neighbouring islands, was garrisoned by the battalion. A number of gunboats were also built here and manned by the regiment; telegraphs were established, the fortifications strengthened, and thus an ample demand made upon the services of the corps. During the remainder of the year no movements of any importance took place in Sicily; in the following June, however, Murat threatened the island with an invasion, and now commenced a period of most wearisome duty for the British and German troops.

1809. June. Journal of 3d line battalion, MSS.

A large force, supposed to amount to nearly thirty thousand men, were collected on the opposite coast of Calabria, where, spread out in several distinct camps on the mountains, they were clearly visible from Sicily with the naked eye. A number of vessels, capable of conveying at least ten thousand men, were in readiness on the coast, and every appearance indicated an intention on the part of the enemy to force a landing on the east shore of the island.

To meet these demonstrations, all necessary precautions were taken by the general commanding in Sicily; the works on the Faro and coast north of Messina were put in a state of defence, while the south side of the island was placed under the protection of the British ships and gun-boats; the land force amounted to about fourteen thousand men, and occupied an extent of more than twelve English miles. Almost daily affairs took place between the ships and gun-boats; but the enemy's vessels were too well protected by batteries to risk their suffering any serious injury from such attacks, which served little purpose but to amuse the soldiers on shore. Frequent embarkations of troops were also made in the evening from the opposite coast. About this time a flotilla would get under weigh from the Calabrian side, and oblige the troops that guarded the opposite shore to turn out, and make preparations to oppose a landing. In this state of

Narrative of captain Bussmann, MSS.

1810. September

watchfulness they were generally kept until the next morning at day-break, when the mockery ended, and the French returned to their tents: in short, although no serious operation was attempted by the enemy, their maintenance of a threatening attitude rendered constant vigilance indispensable on the part of the troops in Sicily.

This state of demonstration on the one side, and expectation and watchfulness on the other, lasted for nearly four months; at length on the 16th of September Murat attempted a landing in good earnest.

Narrative of captain George Appuhn, 3d line battalion, MSS.

It was customary for the troops that were stationed on the coast opposite Calabria to be under arms every morning before day-break, and on the morning of the 18th before the moon had yet set, some movements upon the water indicated the approach of the enemy.

A thick fog covered the approach of their boats, which seemed to take the direction of St. Stephano, and a cavalry piquet, which had been stationed here, soon gave notice that the enemy had landed on the Marino in considerable force.

The alarm having been spread along the coast, the skirmishers of the third and fourth battalions of the legion, who were stationed at Mili, quickly pushed up to the beach, and became immediately engaged with the enemy's advanced troops, who had taken possession of a height near the place where they

1810. September

had landed; the second light infantry* at the same time moved up towards the same point from St. Placido; the twenty-first regiment, third battalion of the legion, and two light six-pounders, soon afterwards joined; so that, before it was fully day, about two thousand men were in readiness to oppose the invaders.

General Campbell's despatch.

Major-general Campbell had been apprized of the approach of the enemy's boats about a quarter after four o'clock, and quickly repairing to Mili, took the command of the troops, which had been very judiciously posted by lieutenant-colonel Adam. The left wing (four companies) of the third battalion of the legion occupied the heights behind Mili, to oppose the advance of the enemy upon Rometta; the remaining four companies, together with the twenty-first regiment, were posted in the Fiurama before that place, while the skirmishers occupied the vineyards in front.

Narrative of captain George Appuhn, MSS.

The light troops on both sides became sharply engaged; but the British ships and gun-boats being detained in the harbour of Messina by the wind and current, the enemy continued to land troops on the coast, and the debarkation was persevered in without intermission until about eight o'clock. Their boats came over in perfect order, covered by Scampavias and gun-boats from the Calabrian

* Two battalions of light infantry were formed in Sicily, the first out of the light companies of the English regiments; the second out of those of the foreign battalions in British pay.

1810. September coast, and after having landed their men, with all precision, between St. Stephano and Galati, returned with equal regularity to the Capo d'Arno.

General Campbell's despatch. As these troops gained the shore, they ascended the heights, and occupied the whole crest of a ridge of rising ground, extending from the place of their debarkation to the front and ridge of the Mili Fiurama; meantime the mountain passes adjacent to this position were secured by the British and German regiments; the second light infantry hung upon the enemy's left and rear, and every precaution was taken for arresting their further progress.

The promptness of these arrangements appeared to have caused a panic among the invaders; for they were yet being executed, and general Campbell was engaged in eagerly looking for the enemy's further movements, when a sudden hesitation was perceptible in their ranks; the advance upon the heights was discontinued, and the troops nearest the shore began hastily to re-embark.

Major-general Campbell, having satisfied himself that they were in retreat, directed the twenty-first regiment with the guns to move briskly forward by the great road and beach from Mili, preceded by the legion skirmishers, and flankers of the twenty-first, while the right wing of the third German battalion remained in front of Mili, to cut off the retreat of the troops on the hill. These dispositions were completely successful; the troops that were about to embark hurried with precipitation to the boats; several fell into the water, and the commanding general Cavignac was said to have only escaped by swimming. The guns were now brought to bear upon the boats, which induced some to return and surrender; but the principal object was the troops on the heights. These, seeing themselves surrounded on all sides, as well by the troops as by the country people, who had now joined them armed with guns, forks, and other weapons, and that their retreat to the boats was effectually cut off, laid down their arms, and surrendered as prisoners of war at discretion. They consisted for the most part of Murat's favourite corps, the royal Corsicans, amounting to upwards of eight hundred men, which with a stand of colours, a colonel and chief of the staff, a lieutenant-colonel commanding, with forty inferior officers including the aid-de-camp of general Cavignac, were conducted in triumph to Messina.

1810. September

Journal of 3d line battalion, MSS.

Narrative of captain George Appuhn, MSS.

Except this affair on the 18th, no absolute landing in Sicily was attempted by the enemy, and in the beginning of October their boats being altogether withdrawn from the opposite coast, the British troops were relieved from their wearisome duty, and were no longer required to turn out before day-break.

Journal of 3d line battalion, MSS.

CHAPTER XVII.

1809. July. THE gallantry of the British and German troops, and the able dispositions of the general by whom they were commanded—now raised to the peerage under the title of viscount Wellington—had, as we have seen, gained a brilliant victory at Talavera, defeated the efforts of the intrusive king, and caused the French veterans to retire from the field of contest—but the victors were unable to follow up their successes.

Napier. Privations, fatigue, and their late losses had weakened the numbers of the English army to such a degree, that a forward movement was quite impracticable; in vain were Cuesta and the Spaniards applied to for provisions; the necessary assistance to prevent the wounded from perishing could not even be procured, and the army was reduced to a state absolutely bordering on starvation.

A light brigade of about three thousand men, which, under general Robert Craufurd, had come up by severe forced marches, joined the army the day after the battle, and now took charge of the outposts.

On the 30th information was recieved at Talavera that marshal Soult was in march for the pass of Baños, and lord Wellington requested that a Spanish corps might be sent to oppose his progress. After twice refusing to comply with this request, Cuesta at length detached general Bassecour on the 2d of August; but Soult had by that time entered Plasencia. 1809. July. Napier.

This night also letters from sir Robert Wilson announced the appearance of the French at Nombella; Cuesta was now roused, and it was agreed to between him and lord Wellington, that the British should march to meet Soult, while the Spaniards should remain at Talavera and secure the rear; lord Wellington, however, supposing that Victor would endeavour to join Soult, and that the Spaniards would therefore be driven from Talavera, obtained Cuesta's promise that he would collect carts for the purpose of transporting as many of the English sick and wounded as would be removed; but this promise he shamefully violated.

On the 3d of August Lord Wellington marched to Oropesa with seventeen thousand men. In the evening, patroles of the first hussars of the legion fell in with Soult's outposts near Naval Moral, which shewed that the French were between the allies and the bridge of Almaraz. The same evening Cuesta informed his lordship that Joseph was again advancing, and on the following morning Journal of of colonel von Linsingen, MSS.

1809. August. Napier. the old Spaniard, under the pretence of aiding the English against Soult, followed lord Wellington to Oropesa; thus inhumanly abandoning the British sick and wounded to the enemy.

The situation of the allies now became critical: their progress in front was completely stopped; the Tagus was on their left; impassable mountains on the right, and Joseph and Victor were in their rear. Lord Wellington had no alternative but to cross the Tagus by the bridge of Arzobispo, and take up a line of defence behind that river; Cuesta opposed this movement, and said he would fight at Oropesa; but there was no time for humouring the Spanish general, and lord Wellington, leaving him to do as he pleased, marched the British columns at noon to the bridge of Arzobispo, and at two o'clock the whole army was in position on the other side of the Tagus.

General Craufurd's brigade and six guns were now pushed forward to the bridge of Almaraz, which, after being obliged to drag the guns by the force of men up the Meza d'Ibor, they reached on the evening of the 5th. The same day the head-quarters reached Toraleda among the mountains, where they remained for the night, and resting at Meza d'Ibor on the 6th, reached Deleytosa on the 7th.

Lord Londonderry's narrative.

Cuesta did not long persevere in his intention of making a stand at Oropesa, but crossed the bridge of Arzobispo the day after the British, and leaving a strong rear-guard there, protected by an entrenchment with twenty guns in battery, he moved the rest of his force towards Meza d'Ibor. 1809. August.

Marshal Victor entered Talavera on the 6th, and the wounded fell into his hands; but his treatment of them was in the highest degree creditable to that general's humanity; they were well fed and taken care of, and the reports addressed to lord Wellington, after Victor had given over his charge to marshal Mortier, stated that the wants of the British were attended to even in preference to those of the French. Lord Wellington's despatch.

On the 8th, the Spanish rear-guard, which consisted of two divisions of infantry and one of cavalry, was surprized and completely routed by general Mortier, and Soult prepared to effect the total destruction of the Spanish army, when king Joseph recalled the corps of marshal Victor to oppose Venegas, and the impending fate of the peninsula was again averted. The allies were now enabled to re-establish their line of defence; the British head-quarters were removed to Jaraicejo, the Spanish to Deleytosa, and the cavalry were pushed on to Truxillo, on the high road to Badajos. Napier. Lord Londonderry's narrative.

The troops were still suffering from want of provisions; from the commencement to the close of the march to Deleytosa no bread had been issued, and the men had tasted none for three whole days. In the first day's march from Oropesa, the forcible Napier.

1809. August. Lord Londonderry's narrative seizure of a drove of pigs afforded a temporary and partial relief to the famished soldiers, and during the first few days of their sojourn at Jaraicejo, they were tolerably supplied; but the rations were soon exhausted, and they were again reduced to a scanty and uncertain allowance. The conduct of the Spaniards was most disgraceful; not only did their authorities make no exertion to meet the necessities of the British army, but the Spanish cavalry absolutely interrupted the provisions and forage which was destined for its use. The effect upon the cavalry regiments was soon manifest. Before the Napier. middle of August a thousand men were completely dismounted, and the horses of seven hundred others were unserviceable.

The Spanish general Venegas was completely routed by Sebastiani on the 11th of August at Almonacid, and King Joseph returned in triumph to his capital.

The British were now threatened by a force of at least seventy thousand men; and lord Wellington, convinced that he could not operate with any effort in Spain, decided upon retiring into Portugal: he had already sacrificed a part of his ammunition to obtain conveyances for the wounded men in the first march from Oropesa; and to continue the retreat without leaving his sick behind, he was now obliged to abandon all his parc of ammunition and stores, and, thus bereft, to commence his march for Portugal. On the 20th the main body of the army quitted Jaraicejo, and marched by Truxillo upon Merida, the light brigade taking the road to Valentia de Alcantara. On the 24th head-quarters reached Merida, and here Sir Arthur being able to obtain provisions, and wishing to allay the excitement which had been caused among the Spanish junta by his retreat, halted for some days; he, however, positively refused to co-operate again with the Spaniards. 1809. August. Napier.

The retreat was continued, the German hussars protecting the flanks and keeping up the communications of the army; and on the 4th of September the head-quarters were established at Badajos. The troops were disposed in cantonments along the Guadiana, where they were furnished abundantly with provisions and forage; but here a pestilential disease assailed them. The fogs, which in the dry season hang over the vicinity of the Guadiana, produce fever and dysentery, which, acting upon bodies weakened by fatigue and want of nourishment, carried off numbers. Not fewer than eight or nine thousand men were computed to be in hospital, and in a little time above five thousand had died there. Lord Londonderry's narrative. Napier.

Of the German battalions which were at first hutted near Talavera Real, but afterwards, in consequence of the extreme wet, were quartered in that place, the seventh line battalion appears to have suffered most from the Guadiana fever: out of Journal of captain Stutzer MSS.

1809. November. twenty officers present seven were ill, and the companies frequently marched to parade not more than from three to six files strong. The hussars and artillery lost also several men.

Napier. The Spaniards, now left to themselves, met with a series of signal disasters. An army of more than fifty thousand men was defeated with tremendous loss at Ocaña on the 19th of November; and a few days afterwards, thirty thousand, under the duke del Parque, were routed and dispersed at Alba de Tormes. Gerona also, in the following month, was driven to surrender, and fortune seemed every where to favour the progress of the French.

Ciudad Rodrigo being endangered by the defeat of del Parque, and the Spanish force that remained after their late losses being sufficient for the moment to defend the passes of the Morena, and cover Seville, lord Wellington decided upon no longer exposing his troops to the destructive climate of the Guadiana, and leaving general Hill with five thousand British and the same number of Portuguese at Abrantes, he commenced his march for the north of Portugal. The army were put in motion on the 15th of December, and in the beginning of the new year were established on a new line in the valley of the Mondego, where the health of the troops was soon restored. Head-quarters were at Viseu, the cavalry by single regiments at Golegao, Punhete, Torres Vedras, Celerico, and Santarem;

and the infantry (except one regiment which was left to garrison Lisbon) were distributed along the valley of the Mondego. 1809. November.

The German hussars were cantoned in Celerico, Trancoso, Guarda, and Pinhel, one troop under captain Aly being pushed forward to Escarijo, towards the Agueda; the line battalions were distributed at Toyal, Pedoza, Castende, and Incuberto; the light troops, under major von Wurmb, at Noritz and St. Olaya; captain von Rettberg's battery of artillery remained with general Hill, while that of captain Heise followed the fourth division; the first foot battery, under captain Gesenius, continued at Lisbon, and served as a depôt, from whence the deficiencies of the other batteries were supplied. From this battery, in consequence of the remarkable steadiness and vigilance of the men, detachments for the convoy of stores to the army were specially selected, and to its captain was entrusted the responsible duty of inspecting the guns and artillery stores in the chain of forts from Lisbon to Peniche, as well as those of the three important lines of Torres Vedras. To these defences lord Wellington's attention was now particularly directed; for the greatness of the French reinforcements forbade him to venture on any offensive operation, and conceiving the bold design of turning these vast mountains into an impregnable citadel, wherewith to defend Lisbon and provide for the retreat of his troops, he proceeded to make such dispositions on

Journal of colonel von Linsingen, MSS.

Journals of line battalions, MSS.

Narrative of general Hartmann, MSS.

Napier.

1810. February. Napier. the frontier as would procure time to complete these works, to secure the resources of the country, and to give full effect to the other able arrangements which he had made for the defence of Portugal.

In the month of February, Ciudad Rodrigo was threatened by marshal Ney, and Badajos by Mortier; general Hill, therefore, advanced from Abrantes to Portalegre, and lord Wellington, desirous to succour Rodrigo, advanced his head-quarters to Celerico, sent a brigade of heavy cavalry to Belmonte, brought up the third division to Pinhel, and sent the light division across the Coa. This division, augmented in the following month by the addition of two Portuguese light battalions, a battery of horse artillery, and the first hussars of the legion, to four thousand men, became engaged in a series of remarkable operations under general Robert Craufurd, to whom lord Wellington entrusted the command of all the outposts.

Journal of colonel v. Linsingen, MSS. The German hussars joined the light division on the 18th of March, and were immediately spread along the left bank of the Agueda, occupying a chain of posts which extended from Barba de Puerco to Fuente Guinaldo; the infantry were distributed in small parties in the villages between Almeida and the lower Agueda, and the guns were stationed at fort Conception.

The Agueda is subject to sudden floods, but when not flooded, it is fordable in many parts, and runs in an extremely serpentine direction, with banks in some places nearly inaccessible. These circumstances rendered the greatest vigilance and activity necessary on the part of the light division, for the French were collecting by tens of thousands in their front, and already the enemy's cavalry, to the number of eight regiments, occupied a distance of not more than fifteen miles on the opposite side of the river, which they often crossed, and drove in the outposts; thus constantly calling forth the quickness and intelligence of general Craufurd's troops. 1810. March. Napier.

The light division was further strengthened by a corps of Spaniards under Carrera, which joined the English during the siege of Astorga. This fortress surrendered to marshal Junot on the 21st of April.

In the beginning of June, marshal Ney, at the head of fifteen thousand men, invested Ciudad Rodrigo, throwing two bridges over the Agueda, the one above, the other below the fortress. On the 8th, four thousand French cavalry crossed the river, and general Craufurd's situation became critical; he, however, daringly maintained his position on the unprotected plain, concentrating his troops at Gallegos and Espeja, and drawing in the hussar posts to the Azava, thus encouraging the garrison of Rodrigo, and protecting the villages between the Azava and the Coa from the enemy's foraging parties.

In proportion as the siege of Rodrigo advanced, the enemy increased their pressure on the British

1810. June. outposts, and the hussars were engaged in constant skirmishing. They were also employed in escorting convoys to the fortress, and in consequence of the immense preponderating force of cavalry which was opposed to them, (at least six thousand men,) experienced little rest.

Correspondence of colonel v. Linsingen, MSS. On the 21st the French proceeded to forage with a few squadrons in front of the British piquets; but general Craufurd causing a gun to be fired, they withdrew. In about an hour afterwards, however, they returned to the same place with fifteen squadrons and several regiments of infantry, and captain Bergmann of the hussars, with about thirty horses, was engaged with double his force for upwards of four hours. The enemy had from ten to twelve men and horses severely wounded, without causing any loss to the hussars, and simply displaying their force, they did not venture to pass the stream. In the evening they withdrew.

Napier. The following night, Julian Sanchez having sallied out from Rodrigo at the head of two hundred horsemen, and joined the light division, marshal Ney was led to reinforce his troops on the left bank of the Agueda, and to make a movement against Craufurd in considerable force on the 25th.

On this day the batteries were opened against the fortress, and four regiments of cavalry, as many of infantry, and some guns advanced upon the piquets, and after a skirmish of several hours drove them across the Azava. The hussars lost but two horses, both of which were shot under an old soldier named Rangenier. A general attack was this day expected; but the enemy contented themselves with keeping possession of the Azava, and placing strong outposts along the left bank of the stream. Carrera now retired to the dos Casas; but lord Wellington, hoping that the enemy, by detaching troops, would furnish an opportunity of relieving Rodrigo, advanced his head-quarters to Alverca.

1810. June.

Journal of colonel von Linsingen, MSS.

Napier.

On the 26th two squadrons of the sixteenth light dragoons came to the relief of the hussars, none of whom, however, was general Craufurd willing to part with; but lord Wellington, who visited Gallegos the same day, and saw how much the Germans wanted rest, expressly ordered that the relief should take place. One squadron, therefore, marched the same day to Minneal, and another, the day following, to Mazal de Chao. The fourteenth light dragoons were also brought up to Val de la Mula. The cavalry outposts were now doubled, and the duty became very severe. Within the last few days the enemy had occupied the stream with strong detachments of infantry, and to a corporal's piquet of hussars, consisting of five or six horses, full a hundred of the enemy were often opposed; but the vigilance of the small British posts amply compensated for their deficiency in number, and so much was the enemy's jealousy excited on this occasion by the alertness of the German cavalry, that a hundred

Correspondence of colonel von Linsingen, MSS.

1810. June. doubloons are stated to have been offered by the general who commanded their outposts, to any party that would cut down one of the small British piquets !*

Correspondence of colonel von Linsingen, MSS.

An attempt was soon made. On the night of the 29th, all the infantry of the light division, except two companies of the ninety-fifth, fell back to about four miles from Gallegos, leaving two squadrons of the sixteenth dragoons, one squadron of the first hussars, and two guns in that place under the orders of lieutenant-colonel von Arentschild. The outlying picquet of the sixteenth was posted at the village of Marialva, about two miles in front of Gallegos, and this party the French attempted to surprise on the morning of the 4th July.

Journal of major Cordemann, MSS.

On this day nearly an hour before day-break,

* The many rencontres which took place at the outposts during this period, led to frequent exhibitions of individual bravery, and among the most conspicuous on the side of the British, was a private of the German hussars named SCHROEDER.

Schroeder was an excellent horseman and swordsman, and gifted with a degree of daring seldom equalled. He was regularly the first in the attack, and the last in retreat, and so often distinguished himself on these occasions, that he became at length known by name to the French. *Ah ! vous voila monsieur Schroeder !* was often heard from their ranks, as the German was descried in advance, ready to signalize himself by some new exploit. A French officer, who, one day, came over to the British posts with a flag of truce, begged that he might be presented to the famous *monsieur Schroeder*, of whom he had heard so much, and having been formally introduced, paid him some high compliments on his gallantry. It has been ascertained that between the years 1810 and 1812, this man individually cut down twelve different persons, wounded many, and took twenty-seven prisoners.

the piquet at Marialva was attacked by so superior a force of the enemy's cavalry, that it was obliged to retire with precipitation upon Gallegos, and so quickly did the enemy follow, that both the retiring piquet and the pursuing squadrons appeared in front of the troops at Gallegos at the same moment.

1810.

July.

Journal of major Cordemann, MSS.

Here the high state of efficiency and alertness in which the veteran Arentschild ever kept the troops under his command, was conspicuous. The reserve were found drawn out ready to take up the piquet; one squadron of the hussars under captain Krauchenberg was in front, having the sixteenth in line in its rear, and the guns were planted in the church-yard of the village.

Krauchenberg, seeing the importance of immediately checking the enemy's progress, led his squadron forward at a gallop to within about fifteen paces of the French line, and then spreading it out into a chain of skirmishers, engaged in a sharp fire with the advanced horsemen, upon whom the two guns also opened. This unexpected reception had the desired effect; the intended surprise was completely foiled, and daylight shewed nearly three regiments of French cavalry hesitating before the squadron of hussars.

Strict orders having been given by general Craufurd that no engagement should be unnecessarily entered into with a superior force of the enemy, the sixteenth commenced their retreat, covered by

1810. July. the squadron of hussars under Krauchenberg, and two guns of the English horse artillery under lieutenant Alexander Macdonald.

Journal of major Cordemann, MSS.

The village of Gallegos was defended by this little force for a considerable time; a party of dismounted men, under cornet Cordemann, maintaining a small bridge in front, while two other parties of hussars under lieutenants George von der Decken and Schaumann observed two fords on the flanks. One of these fords was at length passed by the enemy in considerable force, while the hussars were at the same time pressed hard in the village. Captain Krauchenberg, therefore, ordered the guns to the rear with directions to unlimber on the other side of the town at a bridge which led from Gallegos to Alameda, and from whence the retreat of his squadron could be protected. This movement was well executed by lieutenant Macdonald; and Krauchenberg, as soon as he saw that the guns were nearly in position, led his squadron off at a gallop to gain the bridge. The enemy followed with their utmost rapidity, and in column; but the Germans had the speed of the French, and Krauchenberg was enabled to draw up his squadron at the other side of the bridge before they reached it. The head of the enemy's column, however, came close after the rear skirmishers of the hussars, and the leading divisions had passed the bridge, when Krauchenberg, taking advantage of a little disorder which the hasty pursuit had caused in the enemy's ranks, suddenly charged the divisions which had passed. Full three times the strength of the hussars were, at this moment, opposed to them; but the well-timed charge succeeded, and the French were driven back in disorder. Again they advanced, confiding in their numerical superiority, and again the Germans charged and dispersed them. Three officers and from ten to fifteen men were cut down by the hussars, whose only loss was one horse killed, and four men and two horses wounded.

1810. July.

Journal of major Cordemann, MSS.

Correspondence of colonel von Linsingen, MSS.

Krauchenberg maintained his position for some time, nor resumed his retreat until an order arrived from lord Wellington directing him to give up the bridge and retire on the infantry support, which had been judiciously posted by general Craufurd in some corn-fields in the rear. This, opening a fire upon the French cavalry as they cautiously followed the hussars, caused them some loss, and they gave up the pursuit, leaving the squadron to continue its retreat undisturbed.

Journal of major Cordemann, MSS.

The conspicuous bravery of the German hussars in this little affair was a just subject of admiration and praise at the head-quarters of the light division. General Craufurd complimented the gallant squadrons in a speech which he addressed to them in their own language, and on the ensuing day thus noticed them in the division orders.

Correspondence of colonel von Linsingen, MSS.

Val de la Mula, July 5th, 1810.

" Brigadier-general Craufurd, in making his

1810. July. report to lord Wellington of the affair that took place yesterday, did not fail to mention in terms of merited praise, the gallant manner in which captain Krauchenberg and cornet Cordemann of the first German hussars, with only part of a squadron, charged about three times the number of the enemy's cavalry close in front of a column, and he begs that captain Krauchenberg, cornet Cordemann, and the non-commissioned officers and privates that were engaged in this action, will be assured that it caused the admiration of the brigadier-general, and all who saw it."

The following extract of a letter from lord Wellington to general Craufurd was also read to the hussars.

Journal of major Cordemann, MSS.

"I have received your letter of the 4th instant, and am highly satisfied with the conduct of captain Krauchenberg, cornet Cordemann, and the squadron of hussars. I request you will inform lieutenant-colonel von Arentschild that I shall take the first opportunity of laying before his majesty my opinion of the conduct of his excellent regiment during the long and fatiguing period that it has been upon outpost duty with you."

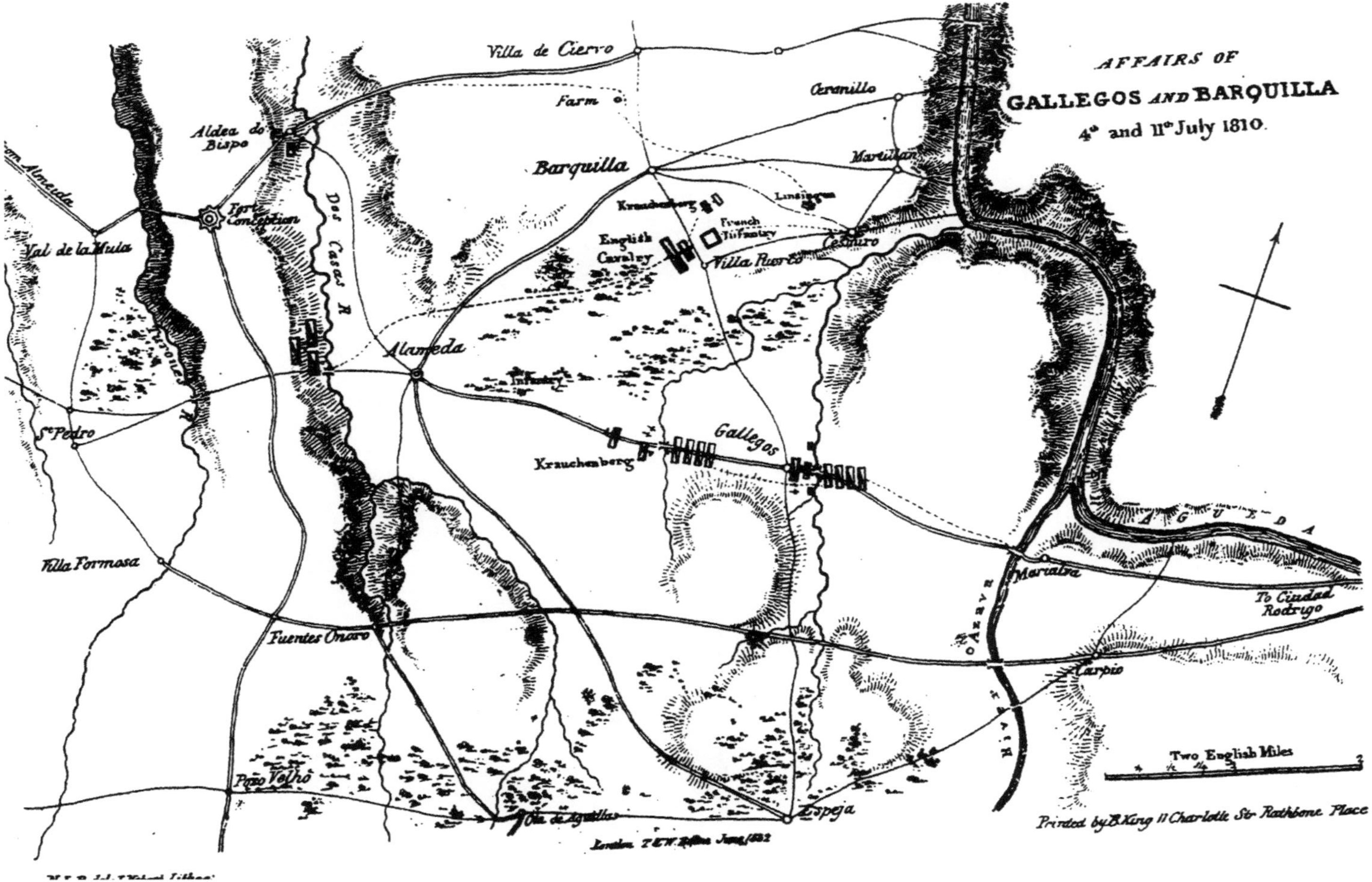
AFFAIRS OF
GALLEGOS AND BARQUILLA
4th and 11th July 1810.
Villa de Ciervo
Farm
Ceranillo
Aldea do Bispo
Barquilla
Martillan
Linsingen
Krauchenberg
French Infantry
English Cavalry
Villa Puerco
Cesuro
Fort Conception
Val de la Mula
Des Casas R
Turones R
Alameda
Infantry
St. Pedro
Gallegos
Krauchenberg
AGUEDA
Marialva
To Ciudad Rodrigo
Villa Formosa
Fuentes Onoro
RIVER AZAVA
Carpio
Two English Miles
Pozo Velho
Espeja
Printed by B. King 11 Charlotte Str. Rathbone Place

CHAPTER XVIII.

THE skirmish at Gallegos not having been followed up by the enemy, general Craufurd took up a new position, placing his infantry and guns in a wood near fort Conception, and his cavalry, now reinforced by Julian Sanchez and Carrera, on the dos Casas. The French withdrew behind the Azava, leaving only a piquet at Gallegos; but their marauding parties infested the villages in front of the British position, and general Craufurd, desirous to put a stop to the excesses which they committed, formed a plan to surprise and cut them off, which he purposed putting in execution on the morning of the 11th. Taking with him four squadrons of English dragoons and captain Krauchenberg's squadron of the German hussars, the general marched, on the night of the 10th, towards Villa de Puerco, and placed the troops in ambuscade near that place. The squadron under captain von Linsingen was, at the same time, ordered to proceed from its station at Aldea da Bispo, and taking up its quarters for the night, at a farm between Barquilla and Ciervo, be prepared to cut off any of the enemy's cavalry that might endeavour to escape in that direction.

1810. July. Napier.

Narrative of lord Londonderry.

Correspondence of colonel von Linsingen, MSS.

1810. July. Correspondence of colonel von Linsingen, MSS.

According to expectation, about four o'clock on the morning of the 11th, a party of between thirty and forty horsemen were seen moving through a defile between Cesmiro and Martillan, taking the road to Barquilla. Another of the same strength followed, but did not venture beyond Martillan. As soon as general Craufurd saw the advanced party enter Barquilla, he set forward at the head of the five squadrons to effect his object, captain Krauchenberg's squadron leading the column. The hussars made straight for the enemy's cavalry, but before they had yet come within charging distance, Krauchenberg, perceiving the glimmer of bayonets in the corn, through which he rode, immediately apprized general Craufurd that they had infantry to contend with. The general briefly replied "charge them," and hurried on with the squadron, whose progress was much impeded by a stony road over which it had to pass, and the files became consequently extended; Krauchenberg, however, formed them up in as good order as the general's impatience would permit, and led his men towards the bayonets, which quickly disappeared, the infantry lying down as the hussars approached. When, however, the squadron had arrived within about fifty paces of the French, they jumped up, shewing a square of about two hundred men, and fired. Two horses were killed, and eleven men and eight horses were wounded; but only one wing of the squadron having received the fire of the square, the rest remained effective, and Krauchenberg was about to charge with these while the French were yet reloading, when general Craufurd ordered him to leave the infantry to the other squadrons and attack the cavalry; he, therefore, galloped on. The French horsemen, seeing the hussars approach so strongly supported, judged it advisable to surrender, and the whole party, consisting of two officers and thirty-three men, became Krauchenberg's prisoners. Meantime a squadron of the sixteenth had been led against the square, but opening round it, they produced no effect, and passing on, got into confusion. The fourteenth now came up, and colonel Talbot, leading a squadron of this regiment, rushed upon the bayonets with daring intrepidity; but this charge was also unsuccessful. The brave fourteenth were received with a deadly fire, and their gallant colonel, with eight of his men, was killed upon the spot. Fifteen men and several horses were wounded, and the rest, crowding forward upon the sixteenth, increased the disorder. At this instant, enveloped in clouds of dust, appeared the squadron of captain von Linsingen, who, according to his instructions, had galloped up from the farm on hearing the first shot. These were, in the confusion of the moment, taken for French cavalry, and some of the enemy's horsemen really appearing on the other flank, the scattered squadrons were called in, and the French infantry made good their retreat to Cesmiro without losing a man.

1810. July.

Correspondence of colonel von Linsingen, MSS.

1810. July. Napier.

On this day Ciudad Rodrigo surrendered after a noble defence, and the Spanish troops departed from the light division and joined Romana at Badajos. General Craufurd, still anxious to hold his ground, took up a new position a mile and a half from Almeida, and applied to lord Wellington for reinforcements; but his lordship knowing that it was not to be maintained, did not comply with his request, and repeated his former orders "not to fight beyond the Coa."

Craufurd, however, was resolved to fight on the right bank of that river, and the enemy's cavalry advancing on the 21st, he fell back to Almeida, under the protection of whose guns he placed his left flank; his right lay on some broken ground; but in his rear was a deep ravine forming the channel of the Coa, and the bridge which led across it was more than a mile distant, and in the bottom of the chasm.

His force was only four thousand infantry, eleven hundred cavalry, and six guns. Pouring down on these came nearly six times the number of cavalry and infantry, with thirty pieces of cannon, on the morning of the 24th, and a retreat upon the bridge was necessarily commenced. The French cavalry sweeping over the plain, forced the British horse to make with speed for the pass, which, owing to the interposition of the enemy's cavalry, some were not able to reach, and part of captain Krauchenberg's squadron of hussars were obliged to swim across the river, exposed to the enemy's fire, and narrowly escaping capture. The guns and the Portuguese battalions next crossed, and the three British regiments alone remained to meet the furious onset of the enemy; but, notwithstanding several ill-judged dispositions of general Craufurd, the quickness and intelligence of the battalion officers, and the gallantry and discipline of their men, extricated the division from its perilous situation. Falling back slowly, yet disputing the ground whenever opportunity afforded, they made their way over a rugged country tangled with vineyards, passed the bridge in succession and gained the other side, and here, supported by the artillery, the whole drew up, and defeated three several attempts of the enemy to force the passage. Heavy rains caused the combat to cease about four o'clock, and the division retired behind the Pinhel river, having lost in killed, wounded, and prisoners, three hundred and eighteen officers and men, two hundred and seventy-four of whom were British. The hussars had only a few horses killed and wounded. The French lost above a thousand men.

1810.
July.
Napier.

The enemy's posts began to thicken on the Pinhel river; but Massena's design was not yet apparent, and from the 25th to the 27th lord Wellington remained quiet. On the 28th, however, he withdrew the main body of his infantry behind the Mondego, leaving one division at Guarda, and advancing the

1810. September cavalry to Frenadas, and thus awaited Massena's further movements.

Napier. On the 15th of August, Almeida was formally invested, and lord Wellington expecting that the garrison would make a vigorous resistance, and that he might still further delay the enemy's advance, re-crossed the Mondego, and occupied his old position; but the unexpected surrender of that fortress on the 27th caused the army to be again withdrawn.

On the 1st of September Regnier entered Sabugal, the British piquets at Pinhel were attacked on the following day, and lord Wellington, transferring his head-quarters to Louvea, withdrew his infantry behind Celerico. Regnier, however, suddenly returned to Zarza Mayor, and the French projects became again obscured.

At length Massena prepared in good earnest to invade Portugal, and strange to relate, selected the very worst line of march that offered itself, namely, the road by Viseu and Coimbra. This line, he had been credibly informed, was easy; no important position, he believed, covered Coimbra, and he was absolutely ignorant of the lines of Torres Vedras. He, therefore, resolved to assemble all his forces, amounting to about fifty-five thousand infantry and eight thousand cavalry, and pour in one solid mass down the right bank of the Mondego, not doubting to reach Coimbra before general Hill could join Lord Wellington.

Wishing, however, to keep his intended line of

march concealed, he disposed his columns so as to threaten three different roads, and it was for some days uncertain by which route his main body was to be expected. When the infantry retired behind Celerico, the cavalry remained in that place, the hussars keeping the outposts; on the 4th, the latter were reinforced by a brigade of heavy dragoons, which divided the duty with them, a hussar officer always taking the command. Until the 15th, the enemy's movements did not call for any more active operations than occasional skirmishing; on this day, however, the British posts at Guarda, Celerico, and Trancoso, were driven in, and the latter chased towards Monqualde; generals Hill and Leith, under the latter of which officers a reserve had been formed at Thomar, were therefore ordered to concentrate on the Alva, for Massena's intentions were no longer doubtful.

1810. September

Journal of colonel von Linsingen, MSS.

Early on the morning of the 16th the enemy's cavalry again pushed forward, and closely following the German hussars through Celerico, got considerably in advance of their infantry. Captain Aly, who had the rear squadron, profiting by this circumstance, quickly formed up about thirty of his men, and charged the French advanced horsemen, several of whom were cut down, and some were made prisoners. This caused the enemy to keep for a time at a more respectful distance; but in the afternoon they again pressed on, and lieutenant George von der Decken, who commanded the rear skirmishers, spi-

1810. September. Journal of colonel von Linsingen, MSS.

ritedly made front as they were debouching from the village of Cortiçao, and dashing against the head of their column with a few files, brought several of his pursuers to the ground. The brave skirmishers, however, paid dearly for their success; for cornet Teuto was killed, lieutenant Decken and four men were wounded, besides two horses killed and one wounded. The hussars then retired to Sampayo without molestation, and were relieved by the fourteenth; but an officer of this regiment having been taken prisoner while visiting his posts in the night, they resumed the duty on the following morning.

Napier.

The enemy now ceased to press forward on this road, sending only small patroles to Sampayo, and it was soon ascertained that Massena had turned off to the bridge of Fornos. Lord Wellington, therefore, directed his main body upon the Alva, withdrew the heavy cavalry from the front, and placed the light division at St. Romao, to cover his head-quarters, which were that night transferred to Cea.

Journals of line batalions, MSS.

On the 18th the French advanced guard entered Viseu; general Pack's Portuguese brigade was immediately pushed across the Mondego, and posted behind the Criz; and on the following day the German brigades of the first division entered Coimbra. On the 20th colonel Waters of the staff having been sent forward from head-quarters with four hussars to reconnoitre the enemy's movements, returned with the baggage of a French general officer, and it was now known that Massena was marching in one mass on the road to Viseu. 1810. September

Journal of colonel von Linsingen MSS.

The following day the hussars passed the Mondego at Barca de Cova, following the 3d, 4th, and light divisions, which were now brought to the right bank; the light division was posted at Mortagao in support of Pack, and the other two divisions in the villages between the Sierra de Busaco and Mortagao, the cavalry occupying a plain in front of the latter place. Napier.

But it was still doubtful whether Massena would not endeavour to reach the main road leading from Oporto to Coimbra; for one of his army corps still pointed towards the Vouga; the first division was, therefore, marched upon Mealhada, and colonel Trant was directed to join it with his Portuguese. Meanwhile generals Hill and Leith had arrived on the Alva; thus, on the day that the main body of the enemy entered Viseu, both corps of the allied army were united, and Massena's project of surprising Coimbra was completely baffled.

The main body of the army now ceased to press forward on this line of march, but turning towards the British left, directed their steps upon Viseu. Lord Wellington, having ascertained this change, altered accordingly his line of retreat. He threw the light and fourth divisions to the north bank of the Mondego, and advanced the first division from Coimbra, where it had latterly been stationed, to

1810. September. Napier. Mealhada, leaving on the south side of the Mondego the third division and the cavalry, to keep open the communications with generals Hill and Leith, as soon as which generals had effected a junction, these corps were to follow the rest of the army across the river. It was now manifest that Lord Wellington was preparing to offer the enemy battle, and not many days elapsed before the general expectation was fulfilled.

Journal of colonel von Linsingen, MSS. The hussars of the legion arrived on the 21st behind Mortagao, about seven leagues from Coimbra, where the light division and several Portuguese regiments were already stationed. The following day the Germans were again on the outposts, and on the 24th captain Aly had another opportunity of attacking the French chasseurs, from whom he took seven prisoners. The whole Lord Londonderry's narrative of that part of the army which was under the immediate orders of the commander-in-chief, had crossed the Mondego by the 26th, on which day the corps of generals Hill and Leith reached that river; the light division and the cavalry were then pushed forward as far as Santa Comba Dao to meet the enemy's advance, and the fourth division occupied the left of the mountain of Busaco, where lord Wellington had now determined to take up a position.

The light division retired, according to instruction, before the enemy's advance, coming into occasional contact with them; but with little loss on either side; it was then placed upon some commanding heights above the great road to Viseu, so as to communicate with the first and fourth divisions. Generals Hill and Leith had now arrived, and took post with their divisions on the right, while the line brigades of the legion were placed as reserve in rear of general Craufurd. The cavalry, not being available on the heights, were sent to the plain in front of Mialhada.

1810. September

Lord Londonderry's narrative.

The enemy shewed a strong force in front of the third and light divisions on the 26th, and it became evident that Massena was preparing to attack the almost impregnable position of the British. Before day-break on the following morning, the riflemen of the legion under major von Wurmb were sent forward to meet the enemy's tirailleurs, and a sharp skirmish ensued. Three sergeants and five of the legion were killed, and major von Wurmb, Captain Stolte, Lieutenant von Düring, three sergeants, and thirty-six men wounded. The enemy's skirmishers were, however, driven back through the village of Busaco; but here the German detachment was near being cut off; for two heavy columns of French infantry appeared in full advance upon the British position.

Journal of major Heidemann, MSS.

One of these columns moved against the division of general Craufurd, the other against that of general Picton (the third), which stood on the right of the first division. They pressed forward with

Lord Londonderry's narrative.

1810. September. Lord Londonderry's narrative.

great spirit and determination, that which was opposed to the third division being evidently the one that was intended to produce the greatest effect. Grape and round shot were poured upon them as they ascended the heights; but, undismayed, they continued to mount, and, gaining the summit, actually formed. But there was no support in their rear, and the British and Portuguese vigorously meeting them with the bayonet, they were hurled over the cliffs and crags, after a short contest, and borne back into the plain with tremendous slaughter.

The other column attacked general Craufurd with equal intrepidity; but one volley from the English regiments of the light division, followed by a charge of bayonets, sent the hardy assailants down the hill in fearful disorder.

Journal of captain Stutzer, MSS.

The German line battalions now pressed forward, and throwing off their knapsacks, prepared to join the light division in its work of destruction; but the victory had been already decided; the British remained masters of the field, and the legion riflemen were alone sent forward to gall the retiring masses as they hurried from the heights.

Lord Londonderry's narrative.

As one of Massena's corps had not been engaged, a repetition of the attack was expected by the British on the following day; but the French general was prudent enough not to risk another discomfiture, and soon after day-light he was seen moving with his entire force upon the Mialhada road, with the evident intention of turning the British left. Lord Wellington, therefore, abandoned the heights, leaving the light division, and captain von Linsingen's squadron of the German hussars, as rear-guard, and in the dusk of the evening resumed his retreat on the line of the Mondego. 1810. September

The loss of the French in this battle was estimated at between five and six thousand; that of the British fell considerably short of one thousand. Lord Londonderry's narrative.

CHAPTER XIX.

1810.
September

Journal of colonel von Linsingen, MSS.

The light division and one squadron of the legion hussars remained, it has been stated, on the heights of Busaco, while the main body of the army resumed its retreat. Early on the morning of the 29th, large bodies of men were discernible from the heights, and general Craufurd not being able to ascertain at that distance of what description of persons they were composed, sent down captain von Linsingen with his squadron to ascertain the point. After scrambling with difficulty over the numerous dead bodies by which their path was blocked up, the hussars reached the crowd, and found it to consist of Portuguese peasants, who were assembled round from three to four hundred wounded men who had been abandoned by the enemy.

These unfortunate creatures had been so disabled that they were unable to move, and they now lay in momentary expectation of being murdered by the peasants. On seeing the hussars, they implored their protection, which was readily given; some litters that were found in the field afforded means of transport, and driving off the peasants, the Germans succeeded in getting the unfortunate fellows conveyed to the neighbouring convent, where they were taken in charge by the monks. 1810. September

The squadron followed the march of the army in the evening, and on the following night reached Fornos, where they found the remainder of the regiment. Here the outposts, under captain Krauchenberg, were attacked the next day, and had to sustain a long skirmish, in order to admit of the rest of the cavalry getting through a defile which led from the place into a large plain that opened towards the Mondego. Several men fell, and captain Krauchenberg was wounded. Arrived in the plain, the hussars were taken up by three regiments of English cavalry and a battery of horse artillery, which were there drawn out, but without any intention of making a stand; and after a few effective cannon shots had been fired upon the enemy's advance as it defiled from the village, the British cavalry and guns resumed their retreat, and for some hours during the middle of the day were suffered to proceed unmolested. They retired, however, much too leisurely, and the rear-guard became consequently involved in rather a serious skirmish at the passage of the Mondego. This river was to be crossed by a ford below Coimbra, from whence the road led through a defile of nearly three miles in length, and the head of the British column had scarcely entered this defile, when the French cavalry, discontinuing the forbearance which they

Journal of colonel von Linsingen, MSS.

1810. October. Journal of colonel von Linsingen, MSS.

had hitherto assumed, rushed towards the ford in considerable force, and swarmed in front and flank of the German hussars, who brought up the rear of the column. Infantry were also seen running up in their rear. Seeing that the safety of the column demanded that a stand should be made here, Arentschild immediately sent two squadrons of the hussars across the river and posted them in front of the defile, keeping the other two squadrons on the right bank to check the enemy's advance, and these had now to sustain the whole weight of the French cavalry, who rushed forward and endeavoured to cut them off from the ford.

But the little rear-guard preserved a bold front, and when the enemy's advanced horsemen plunged after them into the stream, they wheeled about, and stoutly opposed their progress. Several horses fell, and the riders were drowned; but some of the Germans, dismounting on the opposite bank, poured in a sharp fire upon the French, and covered the passage of the rear files. To meet these the enemy also dismounted some men, and their fire proved most destructive; the hussars, however, held their ground until the French infantry came up, and then followed the column, whose retreat through the defile had been now secured.

Captain Krauchenberg and lieutenant Schaumann were both wounded in this encounter, the former severely; four men and six horses were killed, thirteen men and eight horses wounded, and three men and four horses missing.*

Lord Londonderry's narrative.

It was the left of the army, under general Spencer, that crossed the Mondego by the ford, the main body having marched straight upon Leiria by the high road; general Spencer's corps, however, came into this line of march near Pombal, and the head-quarters were at Leiria on the 2d. Here the army rested until the morning of the 5th, when the retreat was resumed, and the same evening head-quarters were established at Alcobaça.

The crowds of men, women, and children, who, in obedience to the proclamation which had been issued to the Portuguese inhabitants, had abandoned their dwellings, and were now following the fortunes of the British army, without scarcely a hope of being again restored to their homes, rendered this day's march most distressing to all who witnessed it. The old and infirm, as well as the robust and young, carrying with them all their most valuable effects, covered the roads and fields in every direction, and often were the weary fugitives, unable to carry further the articles which they had endeavoured to save, forced to leave them on the way side, and then to struggle onward bereft of all their little property. This apparently harsh mea-

* It is recorded in one of the MS. accounts of this skirmish, that, during the fight, a large dog, which had for some time attached itself to the hussars, seeing one of them in the water, plunged in, and brought the man out through the midst of the combatants.

1810. October. sure was adopted by lord Wellington to increase the difficulties of the invading army, by depriving them of all the resources in their front; and although its immediate effects were revolting to humanity, its ultimate consequences led to the evacuation of Portugal by the French, and, perhaps, saved that country from subjugation.

Journal of colonel von Linsingen, MSS. A piquet of the German hussars which had been posted as rear-guard in front of Leiria, was attacked by the enemy soon after the departure of the main body of the army from that place. The French advanced with a considerable force of cavalry and six guns, and drove the hussars through the town with the loss of six men and three horses in wounded and prisoners.

Napier. The road was crossed by a succession of ravines, and captain Cox, of the sixteenth, took advantage of one of these to charge the enemy, whom he succeeded in keeping back until the British light cavalry brigade and a troop of horse artillery came up. The French were now vigorously opposed, and their progress delayed, but with the loss of three officers and fifty men to the British; the enemy lost a considerable number more; among the rest were some officers, one of whom was the prize of corporal Bergmann of the hussars. Journal of colonel von Linsingen, MSS.

Napier. During this delay Leiria was cleared, and the army retreated, the right by Thomar, the centre by Rio Mayor, and the left by Obidos: Massena followed in one column by Rio Mayor.

On the 7th colonel Trant daringly penetrated into Coimbra, at the head of his Portuguese, and took possession of the French marshal's depots and hospitals, containing five thousand men; but Massena continued his march, and in the afternoon of the 8th, his advanced guard came so unexpectedly upon the piquets of the sixteenth, at Alcoentre, that a battery of artillery and all the baggage were near falling into the enemy's hands; the piquet, however, rallied on their reserves, and re-entering the town, drove back the French, and took from them ten or twelve prisoners.

1810. October.

Journal of colonel von Linsingen, MSS.

On the 8th the main body of the cavalry retired from Alcoentre to Quinta de Torre, about six miles to the rear, leaving captain von Linsingen's squadron of the German hussars on piquet, near Alcoentre. Between this piquet and Quinta de Torre a squadron of the sixteenth was posted as reserve, and captain von Linsingen was directed to keep back the enemy's advanced guard as long as possible.

Correspondence of colonel von Linsingen, MSS.

About noon on the following day, the third regiment of French hussars appeared in march, followed by a regiment of chasseurs in close column. To these captain Linsingen could oppose but eighty horses; but the ground on which he stood being higher than that occupied by the enemy, from which it was divided by a stream and defile leading to a little bridge, a small force could here be rendered very efficient, and he prepared to dispute the passage of the bridge.

1810. October. Correspondence of colonel von Linsingen, MSS.

Ordering his skirmishers, who were posted on the other side of the stream, to join the squadron immediately on the approach of the enemy, he placed a small body of dismounted men in ambuscade, on the height above the bridge, upon which they had a direct fire. This party, being hidden by the trees on the height, the enemy were ignorant with what force they had to contend, and hesitated for some time before they ventured to pass the bridge, sending several squadrons up the stream to look out for a ford. Torrents of rain, however, obliged the hussars, after a time, to give up firing, and one squadron of the enemy then crossed, followed by the rest of the column at a little distance. The piquet was posted at about a hundred yards from the end of the defile, and as the enemy deployed from thence, Linsingen attacked their advance, and after an obstinate contest, drove the leading divisions back into the pass, which became completely filled, the column meeting the divisions as they faced about. An officer and about thirty men were made prisoners by the hussars, who might have impeded the progress of the enemy for a considerable time, had not the squadrons which had been sent up the stream found a ford, and were, by that means, enabled to threaten the piquet in rear. This obliged Linsingen to make a hasty retreat, which was much embarrassed by the number of his prisoners, and the greater part of these were consequently enabled to escape. The enemy pressed after

1810. October. Correspondence of colonel von Linsingen, MSS.

the squadron in close order, as fast as their horses could gallop; and although a few of the best mounted of the hussars, who were sent forward under cornet von der Wisch, checked their progress for a few minutes, by charging them as they crossed a moor over a narrow road, the other French squadrons got round the obstacle, and again put the Germans to their speed. The reserve were not yet in sight, and no hope of a successful stand was offered to the hussars for nearly two miles, when a bridge presented itself. By this time the two leading divisions of the enemy were some distance in advance of their column, and as soon as about thirty had passed the bridge and formed, Linsingen again led his exhausted squadron to the charge, which the enemy did not await, but went about, and were driven with rapidity back upon the column, whose advance they completely stopped, crowding the bridge in the greatest confusion. But again one of their squadrons threatened the rear of the hussars, and again Linsingen was obliged to retreat, losing seven or eight prisoners which he had just taken. And now another long defile was to be passed, the enemy close at his heels, and going at such a pace that the hussars could with difficulty keep a head of them. Many brave fellows fell wounded from their exhausted horses, without a possibility of any assistance being afforded them; and it was a matter of surprise how men who had had no provisions for two days, and horses that were without forage for twenty-four hours,

1810. October. Correspondence of colonel von Linsingen, MSS.

could have held out with so much energy. At length they cleared the defile, and were cheered by the sight of the reserve, about half a mile before them. Upon these they rallied, and charging with them, checked the pursuit of the enemy. In this affair the hussar squadron had two men and two horses killed, and one sergeant, eight men, and seven horses wounded; captain von Linsingen also received four sabre cuts, but none of sufficient importance to oblige him to leave the field. To the great distance from the piquet, at which its support was placed, the loss is to be mainly attributed, as also the escape of more than thirty prisoners; two officers, one man, and a few horses only were brought away; but the enemy had suffered considerably in killed and wounded, whose number, according to the statements of some prisoners that were afterwards taken, amounted to one officer and five men killed, and thirty-two severely wounded.

The check given by the squadron of the sixteenth kept the enemy back long enough to admit of the British cavalry and artillery, at Quinta de Torre, turning out, and the French awaited the arrival of their infantry, which coming up in about an hour, the British resumed their retreat, covered by captain Aly's squadrôn of the hussars, and two squadrons of the royals. In following these, the French advanced guard of chasseurs were inprudent enough to march, unsupported, a considerable distance in

1810. October. Correspondence of colonel von Linsingen, MSS.

front of their infantry, and Aly, taking advantage of the circumstance, charged them so unexpectedly with his squadron, that they broke, leaving one officer, nineteen men, and eighteen horses in the hands of the hussars, who, with the exception of a slight wound received by captain Aly, remained uninjured.

This night three squadrons of the Germans were encamped behind Castanheira, and one at Alemquer, near which latter place, on the following day, they had another skirmish with the enemy. On this day the British cavalry were drawn within the lines of Torres Vedras, and the French marshal had, for the first time, a view of those formidable works, before which his army was destined to suffer such privations, and from whence they were ultimately obliged to reti e in mortification and disappointment.

Correspondence of gen. Löw, MSS.

A party of the legion light detachment, under captain von dem Bussche, had some smart skirmishing with the enemy's tirailleurs on the 12th, in front of Sobral, and checked their advance; and on the 14th, in conjunction with the piquets of the seventy-first, and another detachment of the legion, under captain Langrehr, were again engaged. Lieutenant Müller, of the fifth line battalion, and nine rank and file of the fifth and seventh battalions, were wounded on these occasions; lieutenant Müller's wound proved mortal.

The infantry of the legion entered the lines with the first division of the army on the

1810. October. 15th, and were cantoned in three villages on the right of the centre redoubt; the hussars went to Mafra; captain von Rettberg's battery of artillery to Zibreira; that of captain Heise, now under the command of captain Andrew Cleeves, with the fourth division, to La Runa, and the disposable men of the first battery, under captain Gesenius, were withdrawn from Lisbon to fort Santa Graca.

Narrative of general Hartmann, MSS.

Napier.

After several days' reconnoitring, Massena became convinced that he had no chance of success in an attack upon the lines, and disposed his troops so as to form a species of blockade. To collect provisions sufficient to supply the wants of his army until reinforcements reached them, he foraged the country in his rear, which lord Wellington sought to prevent by drawing down upon him all the militia of the north.

Journal of colonel von Linsingen, MSS.

To aid these a brigade of cavalry, consisting of the first German hussars, and the tenth light dragoons, together with a Spanish battalion, were moved, on the 22d, to Ramalhal, from whence patroles were sent, the enemy's outposts alarmed, and his foraging parties driven back. On one of these occasions, corporal Cristoph Meyer, with twenty hussars, attacked a strong detachment of the enemy, consisting of both cavalry and infantry, which were posted on a height, overthrew them, and brought in one officer, five horsemen, and fifteen foot soldiers prisoners. The gallant corporal was, for this exploit, the next day promoted to the rank of sergeant.

Guelphic archives, MSS.

On the 1st of November a squadron consisting of one troop of hussars and one of the sixteenth, were sent under captain von Linsingen to Obidos, which place had been garrisoned, and lay in rear of the enemy's position. This detachment sent patroles nearly up to the enemy's posts, harassing his foraging parties, and making many prisoners, without, however, being engaged in any serious affair. 1810. November. Journal of colonel von Linsingen, MSS.

Massena commenced his retreat from before the lines on the night of the 14th, but this movement was not discovered until the following morning; and lord Wellington, doubtful of his intentions, did not march in pursuit until the 16th, when it was ascertained that the French had retreated in two columns by Rio Mayor and Santarem. On this day the squadron of cavalry at Obidos rejoined the brigade, which advanced and followed the retreat of the column that was directed upon Santarem. The following day they marched by Alcoentre to Atalaya, through fields which had been devastated by the enemy, and an atmosphere reeking with the effluvia of the unburied bodies of men and animals. About one hundred and eighty prisoners were taken by the light cavalry brigade on this and the succeeding days. Napier. Journal of colonel von Linsingen, MSS.

Massena's main column halted at Santarem, and lord Wellington prepared on the 19th to attack what he conceived to be the rear-guard of a retreating army; but the French marshal had no intention of yet leaving the formidable position Napier.

1810.
November.
Napier.

and fertile country which he now commanded, and lord Wellington, therefore, judged it prudent to remain on the defensive, and to keep Torres Vedras still occupied in force. The allied army was therefore disposed in such a manner as to prevent any sudden irruption of the enemy from Santarem, as well as to secure all routes to the lines between the Tagus and the Monte Junta.

CHAPTER XX.

LEAVING Massena in his strong-hold at Santarem, we will now turn towards Cadiz and the isle of Leon, in the vicinity of which two squadrons of the second hussars of the legion under major von dem Bussche, were, about this period, conspicuously engaged. 1811. January.

This detachment had arrived from England in the preceding May, as a re-inforcement to the small British force, which under general Graham formed part of the allied army in Cadiz and the Isla. These places had been for some time blockaded by a French army under marshal Soult, who, towards the end of the year, had completed a strong line of investment, and threatened the allies with an attack.

But just when the operations of the marshal had become formidable, he was called off by Napoleon to the assistance of Massena in the north, and Victor assumed the command of the investing force. General Graham, being made aware of this circumstance, and of the removal of a corps of the French army from Seville, thought the opportunity favourable to an operation against the investing army, Napier.

1811. January. and he undertook, in concert with the Spaniards, to drive Victor from his lines.

Napier. It was accordingly arranged that a corps embarking at Cadiz should land at Tarifa, and march upon the rear of the enemy's camp at Chiclana, that a bridge was to be thrown over the Santi Petri, which separates the Isla from the main, and that the Spanish irregular troops and those of Ballasteros should assist these operations, by threatening Seville and the French under Sebastiani in the province of Granada.

Narrative of general von dem Bussche, MSS. The embarkation of the troops at Cadiz was commenced on the night of the 17th, but there was so heavy a sea, and such bad accommodation had been provided for the horses by the Spanish authorities, that the shipment of the hussars was not completed until the 19th, and few horses were got on board uninjured. Contrary and violent winds prevented the fleet leaving Cadiz until the evening of the 21st, when they sailed, and about noon the next day made Tarifa ; but here it was found impossible to disembark ; for the wind and current setting in the same direction, caused the vessels to drag their anchors, and carried them into the straits. The idea of landing at Tarifa was, therefore, given up, and they made sail for Algesiras, reaching which on the 23d, the troops landed and arrived the next day at the port for which they had been originally destined.

The corps was here joined by some reinforcements, which made the infantry and artillery under general Graham about four thousand one hundred men and ten guns. With the exception of two companies of Portuguese, the whole of these were choice British troops; but the cavalry consisted of the German squadrons only, and did not exceed one hundred and seventy horses. 1811. January. Narrative of general von dem Bussche, MSS.

About five hundred Spanish cavalry and six thousand infantry arrived on the 28th, under don Manuel la Peña. This officer had been appointed captain general of Andalusia, and commander of the troops in the isle of Leon, by the Cortes, and general Graham consented to act under his orders during the ensuing operations. Napier.

The German hussars and the Spanish cavalry were now formed into a brigade and placed under brigadier-general Whittingham, an Englishman who had raised a Spanish regiment for that service. The vanguard and centre were composed of Spaniards under Lardizabal and the prince of Anglona, and the British formed, with two Spanish regiments, the reserve under general Graham. The whole having been reviewed on the 29th, moved off in the evening of the 1st of March, on the road to Medina Sidonia. Narrative of general von dem Bussche, MSS.

Towards morning the advanced guard came upon the enemy's fortified post of Casa-Viejas, from which a few cannon-shots were fired; but the cavalry surrounding the place, the garrison fled,

x 2

1811. January. Narrative of general von dem Bussche, MSS.

leaving behind two guns and some provisions. A detachment of the hussars under lieutenant Cleve followed in pursuit, and the greater part of the fugitives were cut down. Major Bussche's squadrons were now pushed forward towards Medina; but general la Peña, hearing that that place was entrenched, decided upon moving by the sea-coast, and the hussars were ordered back to the Casa, where they bivouacked for the night, having been thirty-four hours on duty.

Napier.

This day la Peña was joined by considerable reinforcements of infantry and irregular cavalry, increasing his force to eight hundred horse, twelve thousand infantry, and twenty-four guns.

Narrative of general von dem Bussche, MSS.

On the 3d the corps moved upon Vejer, but owing to the ignorance or inattention of an aide-de-camp of general la Peña, the troops were led six miles out of their road. The delay thus occasioned was still further increased by the difficult passage of a stream which the corps reached about four o'clock in the afternoon. The water was rather deep, and a narrow dam which led across was the only means that offered for crossing it. But the dam was both in bad condition and flooded, and when the Spaniards came to the edge, they hesitated, their generals in particular exhibiting much uneasiness at the prospect of such a line of march. General Graham now came up, and seeing the cause of delay, instantly sprang from his horse, dashed into the water, and scrambled over the dam to the other side. A gun was then got across, and the Spaniards became satisfied that the passage was practicable. Much delay, however, was occasioned by the impediment, and it was midnight before the troops reached Vejer.

1811. March. Narrative of general von dem Bussche, MSS.

At five o'clock the following afternoon they were again in march, the German hussars in advance. The route was continued towards the coast, and led through the town of Conil, soon after passing which, the van-guard came upon a French cavalry piquet. Some skirmishing ensued, and a few men fell on both sides; but the corps moved on, and early on the morning of the fifth reached the heights of Barosa.

This ridge is situated about a league from the sea-coast, six miles from Chiclana, and four from the mouth of the Santi Petri. A wide plain, bounded, at the distance of about four miles and a half, by the forest of Chiclana, extends itself on the right; broken ground, covered for the most part with cork-trees, lies in front; a low ridge running for about two miles further in the direction of the coast, unites this with another chain called the heights of Bermeja, and these hills interrupted by the Almanza creek extend to Chiclana and the San Pedro river.

The troops having been much harassed by the fatiguing marches which they had made, came up in a straggling manner, and although la Peña had promised general Graham not to approach the

Napier.

1811. March. Napier. enemy except in a concentrated mass, he sent off Lardizabal with the vanguard and some reinforcements before the rest had arrived, direct to the mouth of the Santi Petri. A bridge had been thrown over here by Zayas on the 2d, but he was afterwards forced back into the Isla, and Lardizabal lost three hundred men in re-establishing the communication.

La Peña now ordered the British division to the heights of Bermeja, and general Graham, after in vain expostulating with the Spaniard on this injudicious disposition of the troops, proceeded to comply with the command. The British general, however, concluded that the centre division of the army and the cavalry would at least be kept on the Barosa position, which offered so good a key to the movements of the allies, and leaving a few companies to guard the baggage, he entered the wood in front, with the rest of his troops. But scarce had the British marched off in this direction, when la Peña carried away the main body of his army for the same point, leaving four guns and five battalions to guard his baggage, and directed the cavalry to follow by the coast.

Meantime marshal Victor, with nine thousand men and fourteen pieces of cannon, concealed by the forest of Chiclana, keenly watched the movements of the allies, and general Whittingham had not yet withdrawn the cavalry when his columns came forth. Lieutenant von Gruben, who was reconnoitring in this direction with a small party of the hussars, immediately sent a report of the enemy's approach to Major Bussche, and it was not long before the reconnoitering party became engaged. The report was forwarded to general Graham, and now two strong columns were seen in rapid march over the plain on the right. The one led by Victor in person, and preceded by two squadrons of cavalry, moved along the reverse of the Barosa position, and threatened the right flank of the allies, while the other, commanded by Laval, marched against the centre. Major Bussche, observing that the French cavalry made for the coast, and thus threatened both the rear and right of the allies, begged that general Whittingham would allow him to retain one of his squadrons to check this movement. The general, who had made every arrangement for a retreat, reluctantly acceded to this request, and major Bussche, mounting the heights with the hussars, led them in a direction parallel to the enemy's cavalry, which, after a short time halted; their infantry column continuing its march. As this approached, some of the Spanish guns opened a fire, and two of their battalions advanced and skirmished; but as soon as the enemy's balls came near, they dispersed, and left the German squadron alone to meet the enemy.

1811. March.

Narrative of general von dem Bussche, MSS.

Napier.

Narrative of general von dem Bussche, MSS.

An orderly retreat was the most that major Bussche could hope to accomplish, and to secure

1811. March. Narrative of general von dem Bussche, MSS.

this, he retired by alternate half-squadrons, charging the enemy's cavalry with one troop while the other retreated. The French dragoons invariably retired behind their infantry when the hussars charged; but the squadron then becoming exposed to a shower of musket-balls, suffered considerably, and several men and horses were wounded. Major Bussche was thus engaged, alternately charging and retreating for more than a quarter of an hour; meantime some of the Spanish battalions were got together again, and the squadron much exhausted retired behind them.

Leaving this part of his detachment in charge of captain Werner von dem Bussche, the major now set off to look after his other squadron, which, with the exception of lieutenant von Gruben's party (still remaining in observation), he found behind the wood in front of the Barosa heights, in attendance upon general Whittingham. The British troops under Graham, who had rapidly counter-marched on receiving the report of the enemy's movements, had by this time arrived at the foot of the position, and were about to engage in a most unequal contest with the French divisions. Major Bussche begged, therefore, that he might be permitted to remove the squadron from a position where it could not possibly act, and endeavour to co-operate with general Graham. This was repeatedly but vainly urged: although three

Spanish squadrons were at genreal Whittingham's disposal, he kept this body of hussars, amounting to nearly one-half of the detachment, marching about in a place where they could be of no service, exposed to a heavy cannon fire, and without any apparent plan or meaning!

1811. March. Narrative of general von dem Bussche, MSS.

Thus were the two German squadrons circumstanced, when an aide-de-camp reached general Whittingham with an account of the total discomfiture of the French by the gallant English brigades, and the retreat of Victor; and at length the general consented to be deprived of his escort, which was quickly hurried away by major Bussche in pursuit of the enemy. Meantime the first, and Gruben's party of the second squadron, had been taken off by colonel Ponsonby, who, leading them round the right flank of the allies, came upon the enemy's rear-guard of cavalry, just as it was about to charge the exhausted British battalions.

A loud shout from the English infantry saluted the Germans as they passed, and the squadron, led on by captain Werner von dem Bussche, charged the French dragoons, which much exceeded them in number, with such impetuosity, that breaking through the cavalry, they captured the commandant and two guns, and coming suddenly on the columns in rear, many of the enemy laid down their arms. The steadiness of a few companies, however, restored order, and the progress of the hussars was checked.

At this moment another shout from the British

1811. March.

Narrative of general von dem Bussche, MSS.

proclaimed the arrival of major von dem Bussche and the rest of the Germans; but general Whittingham had consented too late to their removal; for the French cavalry had withdrawn, and their columns entering the wood were covered by a strong rear-guard of grenadiers and riflemen. The arrival of this detachment of hussars ten minutes sooner, would probably have led to the capture of the greater part of the French infantry, and the allies had cause to complain of the misapplication of a force, which, timely employed, would have crowned a victory which British bayonets had so nobly won.

Napier.

The French lost two generals, six guns, an eagle, two thousand men, and four hundred prisoners, in this short but sanguinary battle. The loss of the British amounted to fifty officers, sixty serjeants, and above eleven hundred men.

La Peña, with twelve thousand infantry and eight hundred cavalry under his command, looked idly on during the whole of the action, nor did he even seek to profit by the result; general Graham, therefore, after waiting some hours on the heights, marched his troops into the Isla on the following morning, and the Spanish general continuing his inertness, Victor returned to his lines on the 8th, when the former withdrew altogether, and the blockade was renewed.

The hussars had to mourn the loss of captain von Voss, a brave officer, who much distinguished him-

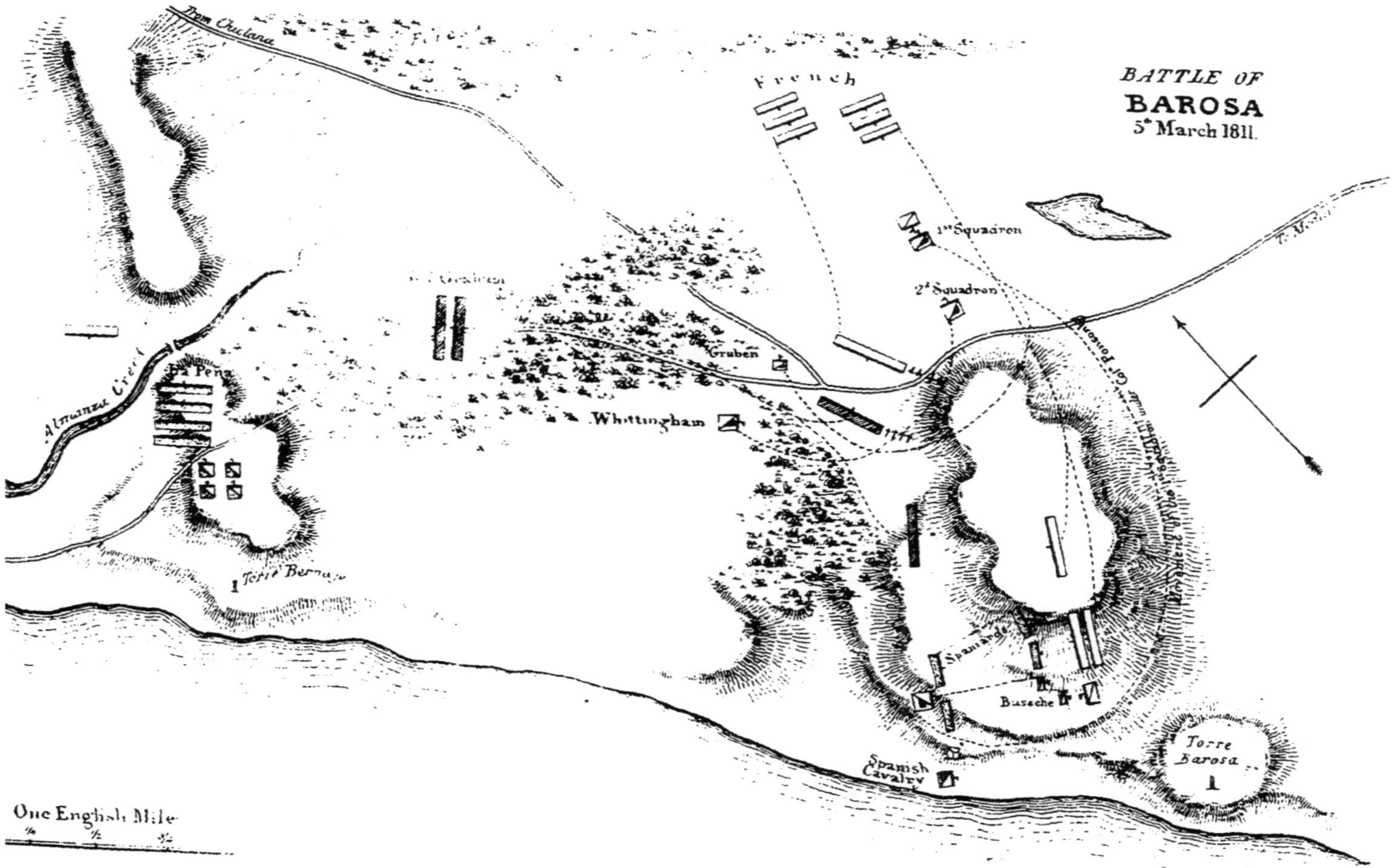

BATTLE OF
BAROSA
5th March 1811
French
From Chiclana
1st Squadron
2d Squadron
Col Ponsonby
Gruben
Whittingham
La Pena
Almanza Creek
Torre Bermeja
Spaniards
Busche
Spanish Cavalry
Torre Barosa
One English Mile
¼
½
¾

self in the principal charge against the French cavalry. Lieutenant von Bock, thirty-one men, and forty horses were wounded, and one man and six horses were killed. 1811. March.

CHAPTER XXI.

1810. November. CONSTANT rains in the north of Portugal during the winter months had prevented any operation of importance from being commenced by either commander after Massena's removal to Santarem, and the main bodies of both armies remained tranquil. The cavalry at the outposts, however, were kept in activity.

Journal of colonel von Linsingen, MSS.

At seven o'clock in the morning of the 22d of November, the first hussars of the legion were attacked in force, and driven behind the bridge of Celariçe. The skirmishing lasted the entire day, and lieutenant Ernest Poten, who had been sent with a strong patrole early in the morning towards Tremeo, was nearly being cut off; this party, however, although closely followed by the enemy, was so admirably covered by its little rear-guard of ten men, under sergeant Bergmann, that lieutenant Poten was enabled to bring off his detachment with the loss of only one man and horse. The gallant sergeant, in securing the passage of a river for the main body, had his horse shot under him, but sword-in-hand on foot he rallied his men, then about to give way, and keeping back the enemy, enabled lieutenant Poten to cross the stream in safety.

Guelphic archives, MSS.

The hussars suffered much during this period of outpost duty, from the continued inclemency of the weather, and the want of almost every necessary that could contribute to preserve the condition of their horses, and being obliged to go into cantonments, encreasing vigilance was indispensable. Little affairs with the enemy's outposts were of daily occurrence, in which they frequently made prisoners with trifling losses, and towards the latter part of the year, they suffered much more from sickness than from the attacks of the enemy.

1810. November. Journal of colonel von Linsingen, MSS.

Some reinforcements reached the British army about the middle of January, and the French general apprehended that it was about to be concentrated at Alcoentre. This induced marshal Junot to drive in the outposts at Rio Mayor on the 19th of January, in order to ascertain the fact. On this day he advanced with a considerable force of cavalry and infantry, and driving the third squadron of the Germans out of Rio Mayor, occupied the place. The marshal, in his eagerness to gain information, came forward with the skirmishers, and was unfortunate enough to receive a wound in his face, from the carbine of a hussar named Dröge, which disabled him for a considerable time. The following day the enemy retired, and the hussars occupied their old quarters. For the rest of January and the whole of February, nothing more important occurred than occasional rencontres with the enemy's foraging parties and piquets, in which the allied

Napier.

Guelphic Archives, MSS.

1811. January. Guelphic Archives, MSS.

cavalry had almost uniformly the advantage.* Some of these little affairs exhibited strong instances of enterprize and intrepidity on the part of the German hussars. A serjeant named Westermann, patrolling with four men towards Alcobaca on the 23d of February, was daring enough to attack a piquet of twenty-four chasseurs commanded by an officer, and cutting several of the enemy down, he brought off seven men and eight horses prisoners. Cornet von Strenuwitz of the hussars, also, made some successful attempts to surprise the enemy's outposts.

Despatch of lieutenant colonel von Arentschild.

On the night of the 9th of February, a party of about nine or ten men under the command of this officer, cut down the greater part of a cavalry piquet which he had surprised in front of Alcan hede, about eight or ten of an infantry support which was formed in the rear, and caused a reserve of infantry, said to be fifty in number, to take to their heels. One officer and eleven men and horses became his prisoners without any loss to the hussars. On the night of the 20th the same

* The French were not the only assailants at this period. A hussar piquet was one night led to turn out by the repeated firing of one of the videttes, who soon came galloping in, with a countenance expressive of the greatest alarm and anxiety. But his foe had been a wolf! The animal had, he stated, made several springs at him and his horse, and he was induced to fire in self-preservation; but neither pistol nor carbine could divert the ravenous animal from its prey, and he had ridden off at full speed, as the only means of safety. The officer who commanded the piquet, doubting the truth of this story, went to the point at which the man had been posted; and here the tracks of the assailant, as well as the marks of the bullets, verified the statement of the hussar.

officer dexterously led the enemy's piquet, consisting of an officer and twenty chasseurs, and the same number of infantry, into an ambuscade, formed of thirty of the sixteenth light dragoons and hussars, near Ferragoas. These fell upon the enemy, and the whole of their infantry with the officer were taken or cut down. Several of the chasseurs were likewise cut down, and three were taken; but the rest escaped. The officer, who was also wounded, proved to be an aide-de-camp of general Clausel, and had been for several days, with parties in ambuscade, lying in wait for the British patroles; the fortune of war now brought him in with seventeen of his party, a prisoner.

1811. February.

Despatch of sir W. Erskine.

At length Massena, the condition of his army no longer enabling him to continue at Santarem, decided upon a retreat, and falling back by Torres Novas and Thomar on the night of the 5th of March, he made for a position in front of Pombal.

Napier.

At day-light on the 6th, lord Wellington proceeded to follow the enemy. General William Stewart crossed the Tagus at Abrantes with the greater part of marshal Beresford's corps, while the first, fourth, and sixth divisions and two brigades of cavalry were directed on Thomar, to which place general Stewart marched on the 7th; but Massena taking the direction of the Mondego, the troops at Thomar were ordered to halt, and the light division, hussars, and royal dragoons to follow the eighth corps. While these were in pursuit, the

1811. March. Napier. third and fifth divisions moved from the lines upon Leiria, and the second and fourth divisions and some cavalry were directed to return from Thomar to the left bank of the Tagus to relieve Badajos.

But Massena, instead of continuing his retreat, concentrated the sixth and eighth corps and Montbrun's cavalry in front of Pombal, where the advanced squadron of hussars under captain von Müller, with whom were lieutenants Krauchenberg and Bergmann, charged a strong column of the enemy's cavalry with great success, defeating several efforts which they made to deploy at the entrance of a defile, by driving the leading squadron back upon the column. A party of the sixteenth came afterwards to the support of the hussars, and the enemy retired, but continued skirmishing until nearly evening. The enemy lost one officer and eleven men and horses in prisoners. The hussars had three horses killed, and one sergeant, five men, and five horses wounded.

Narrative of major von Müller, MSS.

Napier. Lord Wellington, finding that Massena was disposed to make a stand here, countermanded the march of the fourth division and the heavy cavalry to the Alemtejo, but he could not concentrate a sufficient number of troops at Pombal before the 11th. Massena had, however, retired during the night, but was so closely followed by the light division, that his rear-guard under Ney was obliged to be drawn up on a height behind the town to check the pursuit, and a detachment was placed in the castle. Massena's line of retreat was now in danger of being cut off; but darkness came to his assistance, and the operation terminated with a sharp skirmish at Pombal, from whence the French were ultimately driven with some loss. The marshal continued his retreat in the night, and on the morning of the 12th his rear-guard was found most skilfully disposed at Redinha. Here a combat ensued in which the British had twelve officers and two hundred men killed and wounded, and the enemy as many; and some masterly movements and dispositions were made by both leaders; but Ney eventually fell back upon the main body, then at Condeixa, ten miles in the rear.

1811. March. Napier.

The pursuit was renewed on the 13th, and Massena, led by the judicious dispositions of general Trant to relinquish his original design of retiring on Coimbra, changed his line of march to that of the Puente de Murcella, to secure which, he sent a division to a village five miles on his left. This was turned by the third division, and the enemy evacuated Condeixa and hurried to Casal Nova. From hence they retired in the night, and on the morning of the 14th took up a strong position, occupying the heights above the Deuca river and the defiles of Miranda de Corvo. Here an engagement ensued in which the light division, having been much exposed, suffered considerably. Massena passed the Ceira that night, and was obliged to destroy a

1811. March. quantity of ammunition and baggage to lighten his march.

Napier. The allies reached the Ceira in the evening of the 15th, and found that Ney had taken up a strong position there, having his left upon the village of Fons d'Aronce. Against this lord Wellington sent the third division, which surprised and overthrew the enemy in the first charge, causing them to fly in disorder towards the river, where many were drowned and others crushed to death on the bridge, and Ney was forced to abandon his position with considerable loss.

Massena retired in the night behind the Alva, leaving a rear-guard on the Ceira under Ney. The following day the allies halted, much exhausted from the want of provisions and the great privations which they had suffered.

On the 17th, Ney, having withdrawn his rear-guard the preceding evening, the allies passed the Ceira; but the enemy were again in position behind the Alva and on the Sierra de Moita, where Massena intended to halt for several days. Lord Wellington's admirable dispositions, however, obliged him to re-commence his retreat. The pursuit was renewed on the 20th through Penhancos with the light division and the cavalry, and the communication opened with Wilson, Trant, and Silveira. Captain Aly's squadron of the German hussars, which formed the advanced guard, on this day made, under the protection of a fog, a most extensive capture, consisting of one captain, three subalterns, and five hundred and twenty infantry, twelve hundred sheep, twelve bullocks, and ten horses. The loss of the squadron was only one corporal, one hussar and horse killed, and three horses wounded. 1811. March. Journal of colonel von Linsingen, MSS.

The third and sixth divisions of the army followed the advanced corps in reserve, but the remainder halted at Moita for provisions which were to come from Lisbon. The French reached Celerico on the 21st with two corps and the cavalry, and Regnier occupied Guarda with the second corps, while at the same time their communication was opened with Almeida as well as Celerico by detachments of cavalry on the Pinhel. These were, however, soon after abandoned by the enemy, whose sixth corps then took up a position at Guarda, the second going to Belmonte, and the eighth corps and cavalry to the eastern valleys of the Estrella. Napier.

On the 28th the British troops came up from Moita, as also reinforcements which had arrived from England, and these were formed into a seventh division. Early on the following day the allies moved upon Guarda, and a battle was expected; but the appearance of the columns threw the French into confusion, and they abandoned a nearly impregnable position without firing a shot. Upwards of a hundred prisoners were captured by the cavalry, to which were added, on the following Journal of colonel von Linsingen, MSS.

1811. April. day, three hundred more of Regnier's corps, which had quitted Belmonte in the night.

Napier. On the 1st of April the allied army reached the Coa, on the right bank of which the French general was in position. Here, on the 3d, was fought the sanguinary battle of Sabugal, where, in less than an hour, the British had nearly two, the French more than fifteen, hundred killed and wounded! and Regnier, overthrown, was obliged to retreat.

Journal of colonel von Linsingen, MSS. The first division having been this day held in reserve, the infantry of the legion were not engaged; but the hussars were active in the pursuit, and captured, principally under captain Aly, four officers, ninety men and horses, and twenty-five mules, besides the entire baggage of marshal Soult, losing only two men and three horses in killed, wounded, and missing.

CHAPTER XXII.

Massena was soon in full retreat for Ciudad Rodrigo. On the 5th he passed the frontier of Portugal, and fell back with coolness and good order across the Turones; but the British light cavalry and artillery pressed close upon his rear; and when he finally escaped over the Agueda at Barba del Puerco, his loss amounted to three hundred men killed, wounded, and prisoners. Here his army became augmented, but he was yet unequal to shew a front to the allies, and he fell back on Salamanca. Lord Wellington then invested Almeida, establishing his head-quarters at Villa Formosa: the light division occupied Gallegos and Espeja, and the rest of the army were disposed in villages along the Coa. 1811. April. Napier.

The German hussars now resumed their old duty on the outposts, which were pushed forward towards the Agueda and Ciudad Rodrigo. Upon the provisioning of this fortress and that of Almeida, Massena was intent. One convoy had entered on the 13th, and information having been received that another was to enter on the 16th, general Spencer attempted to intercept it; and, accordingly, before day-break on that morning, he crossed the Agueda with eight thousand men. The hussars were in advance, and Journal of of colonel von Linsingen, MSS.

1811. April. when they reached St. Felices, about four miles from Rodrigo, their commander heard that the convoy had already passed. Receiving no counter-order, however, he proceeded on his march, and came upon a detachment of from three to four hundred infantry and twenty cavalry, which formed the enemy's rear-guard. These the hussars cut off from the main body, but could not come up in time to prevent them from securing a position behind an old wall, where they were inaccessible to cavalry. Hoping that a few guns might be sent forward to dislodge the enemy, Arentschild blockaded them in their stronghold for more than an hour. The British general, however, having heard of the escape of the convoy, did not proceed, and a strong body of the garrison coming to the relief of the rear-guard, the hussars retired with the loss of a few horses.

Journal of colonel von Linsingen, MSS.

Napier.

Towards the end of the month Massena, having been considerably reinforced, determined upon making an effort to relieve Almeida, and put his army in motion for that purpose. On the 27th, having made an ineffectual effort to seize the bridge of Marialva on the 23d, he reconnoitred the line of the light division from Espeja to that place; lord Wellington therefore concentrated the main body of his army behind the Dos Casas, and on the 2d of May, the whole French army having been observed coming out of Ciudad Rodrigo, withdrew the light division upon Fuentes Onoro, and through that village across the river.

The English chief was now resolved to abide a battle, and disposed his troops between the Turones and the Dos Casas, the left being at fort Conception, the centre opposite Alameda, and the right at Fuentes Onoro.* Upon a rising ground behind the latter place, the first and third divisions were posted, having five picked battalions in the village, and the blockade of Almeida was covered by the fifth division placed near fort Conception, and the sixth opposite Alameda.

1811. April. Napier.

Fuentes was attacked by the enemy on the afternoon of the 3d with a large force, which, though vigorously resisted, obliged the British battalions to abandon the streets; but reinforcements arriving from the main position, the French were forced back, and after a severe contest, in which two hundred and sixty British and somewhat more of the enemy fell, were driven across the river. The skirmishers of the legion under major Aly of the third line,

* In the course of these movements, a circumstance occurred which deprived one of the legion battalions, for some days, of its colonel. The army were marching through a narrow defile, when lord Wellington wished to halt the head of the column; but the road was so crowded with troops that no staff officer could well get to the front, and colonel B., who was remarkable for his good word of command, volunteered his services to effect the desired object. With a powerful exertion of his lungs he accordingly proclaimed, "the army is to halt by lord Wellington's order," and instantly the column was motionless. But the unusual effort was followed by great exhaustion, and for the only time that he had ever been absent from the command of his regiment, which he had on all occasions most ably led during the whole peninsular war—the gallant officer was obliged to place himself for a few days on the sick report.

1811. were posted to the right of the village, and took
May. an active part in the combat, losing twenty-five in
Correspondence of killed and wounded. The hussars were not engaged;
general Löw, MSS. but in retiring before the enemy's skirmishers into
Journal of colonel von position, had a few of their number wounded, among
Linsingen, MSS. whom was captain Krauchenberg.
Napier.

Massena arrived on the following day, and was joined by Bessieres with further reinforcements. He designed to turn the British right, to protect which lord Wellington extended that flank by placing Julian Sanchez at Nava d'Aver, supported by the seventh division under general Houston, at Poco Velha. In the morning the enemy renewed the action with an overpowering force of cavalry and infantry. The British light division and cavalry hastened to the support of general Houston, and although the left wing of his division was at first driven back, the light division restored the fight. The French cavalry then formed on the plain in front of Nava d'Aver, upon which Julian Sanchez retired across the Turones. The right of the seventh division was next turned, and the British and German cavalry were attacked. These, being little more than one-fifth the number of the enemy's horse, could but offer a partial check to the opposing squadrons, and ultimately withdrew behind the light division with considerable loss. The seventh division, being thus unprotected, was charged before the battalions could form squares, and captain Ramsay's battery of horse artillery was cut off; but

1811. May. Napier.

part of the division taking advantage of a stone wall, made the enemy recoil, and Ramsay gallantly extricated himself. But, meantime, the British right was turned, and it became necessary for lord Wellington to change his position. The right was therefore ordered to be thrown back upon Frenada across the Turones, to which place the seventh division was transferred; and notwithstanding the overpowering mass of Montbrun's cavalry, five thousand in number, supported by fifteen pieces of artillery, this dangerous and critical movement was accomplished with success.

On seeing the new position, the French commenced a heavy cannonade, which did great execution; but on being answered by twelve British guns, its violence abated, and the enemy's cavalry drew off. Fuentes now became the important point of attack, and here the riflemen of the legion together with a piquet of the corps under lieutenant-colonel von dem Bussche, were engaged, and suffered considerably. Both sides fought with great obstinacy and with alternate success until evening, when the lower part of the town was abandoned. The French, however, retired some distance from the stream, while the British maintained the chapel and crags above the town, and, therefore, fairly claimed the victory. The loss of the allies amounted to fifteen hundred men and officers, and that of the French was estimated at five thousand; this estimate is, however, considered to be an exaggerated calculation.

Correspondence of general Löw, MSS.

Napier.

1811. May. London Gazette.

Of the German troops which were engaged in this combat, major Meyer, captain von Gruben, and lieutenant Krauchenberg of the first hussars were wounded, the latter severely; two men and five horses of the same regiment were killed, and forty non-commissioned officers and hussars and twenty horses were wounded.*

Of the line brigades major Beck, captains Müller and von der Decken, and ensign Bachelle were wounded, the three last severely, three men were killed, and fifty-four non-commissioned officers and soldiers were wounded and missing, the latter of whom were all wounded.

Napier.

A fresh attack was expected by lord Wellington on the following day, and part of the English position was entrenched; but the enemy shewed no intention of renewing the fight, and on the 10th retired across the Agueda.

On this night, owing to negligence on the part of some of the British commanders, Brennier brought off the garrison of Almeida with little loss; and joining Marmont, by whom Massena had been now

* The Guelphic Archives record several instances of individual gallantry which were exhibited in this action by the first hussars; among others, sergeant Christoph Meyer, whose deeds as corporal have been already noted, and hussars Ludolph Krauel and Frederick Meyer are particularly mentioned. The latter rescued his captain (Gruben) from the midst of the enemy, cutting down a French officer by whom Gruben had been wounded, and having in the melée lost his horse, he seized and continued the fight on that of his opponent. Sergeant Meyer with six hussars, charged an enemy's detachment of twenty horse commanded by an officer, and brought in seven of the party prisoners.

succeeded in command, the greater part of the French army was withdrawn to Salamanca. Lord Wellington now set out to visit the army in the Alemtejo, which, during his pursuit of Massena, had been engaged under marshal Beresford in the siege of Olivenza, and was now about to commence that of Badajos. 1811. May.

To this part of the allied army major Hartmann and the two batteries of German artillery, now under the command of captains Cleeves and Frederick Sympher, had remained attached, and it was afterwards reinforced by the two light battalions of the legion, which, having recovered from the effects of the Walcheren expedition, were again in the field under their former chief, Charles von Alten, now promoted to the rank of major-general. Narrative of general Hartmann, MSS.

This brigade joined the army of marshal Beresford on the 17th of April, a few days before which Olivenza had surrendered. The operations were now directed against Badajos, and lord Wellington, arriving at Elvas on the 21st, proceeded to reconnoitre the former place on the following day, escorted by the legion brigade and two squadrons of Portuguese cavalry. Journal of major Rautenberg, MSS.

On the march, general Alten learned that a working party, consisting of one hundred infantry and thirty horse, had been sent from Badajos early in the morning for the purpose of cutting timber for pallisades, in a wood which the brigade had just passed. The general immediately sent patroles into the wood to ascertain the fact, but no appear-

1811. May. ance of the enemy presented itself; and lord Wellington not considering the circumstance of sufficient importance to delay his march, the escort proceeded towards the fortress.

When arrived on the surrounding heights, the German light infantry were extended by detached divisions to cover the staff, and lord Wellington proceeded to reconnoitre from the left bank of the river attended by the cavalry.

Narrative of colonel Baring, MSS.

With the exception of a few shots from the place, for some time all was quiet; but suddenly two strong columns, apparently from twelve to thirteen hundred men, accompanied by cavalry and guns, issued from the fortress under cover of its fire, and advanced one towards the staff, the other against captain Bösewiel's company of the second light battalion, which had been detached to some buildings at a little distance from the rest of the brigade; at the same time the convoy from the wood, which, instead of one hundred, proved to be four hundred strong, appeared in his rear. Lieutenant-colonel Halkett, who commanded the second battalion, immediately made an effort to bring up some of the other divisions to the assistance of the detached company, but it was already overpowered, and the French convoy entered Badajos, leaving lieutenant Grant and four men killed, captain Bösewiel and seven men wounded, and taking two officers,* two non-commissioned officers, and thirty-two men of the German brigade prisoners.

Journal of major Rautenberg, MSS.

* Surgeon Nieter and assistant-surgeon Müller of the second light battalion.

Notwithstanding this encounter, lord Wellington effected his reconnaissance; and having expressed his high satisfaction at the conduct of captain Bösewiel's company, ordered the troops to return to Olivenza, where the light brigade arrived at ten o'clock, having been seventeen hours under arms. 1811. May.

Lord Wellington now returned to the northern army, leaving the operations against Badajos to be conducted by marshal Beresford. These were commenced on the 4th of May, when a corps under general William Stewart invested the fortress on the left bank of the Guadiana. General Alten's brigade of the legion formed part of this corps, and partook of its various duties until the night of the 12th, when marshal Beresford, having received intimation of the approach of an army under Soult to the relief of the place, judged it prudent to hold every thing in readiness for an immediate march. He, therefore, ordered the ordnance and stores to be returned to Elvas, and transferred his head-quarters to Valverde. Here he held a conference with the Spanish generals Blake and Castanos, the result of which was a determination to assemble the allied army at Albuera on the 15th, and offer battle to the enemy. General sir Benjamin d'Urban's Report.

The position chosen was a range of gentle heights running nearly parallel to the little rivers of Albuera and Aroya, having the former in front. On the right of this were placed the Spaniards under Blake; in the centre the English, under generals Stewart, Cole, and Lumley; on the left,

1811. May. the Portuguese, under general Hamilton, colonel Collins, and colonel Otway; and the village of Albuera, situated in front of the centre, was occupied by the light brigade of the legion under major-general Charles von Alten.

The whole force of the allies amounted to about twenty-seven thousand infantry, two thousand cavalry, and thirty-eight guns, which were thus brigaded :*—

CAVALRY.

MAJOR-GENERAL THE HONOURABLE WILLIAM LUMLEY.

Brigadier-general Long commanding British and Portuguese.

Four six-pounders, British horse artillery—Captain Lefebure.

1st British brigade .. colonel the hon. George de Grey.
1st Portuguese brigade. colonel Loftus Otway.
2d Portuguese brigade. brigadier-general Madden.
1st Spanish brigade .. brigadier-general Don Casimero Loy.
2d Spanish brigade .. brigadier-gen. count de Penne Ville Mur.

INFANTRY.

SECOND BRITISH DIVISION, HONOURABLE MAJOR-GENERAL WILLIAM STEWART.

Six six-pounders, king's German artillery—Captain Cleeves.

1st brigade .... lieutenant-colonel Colborne.
2d brigade .... honourable lieutenant-colonel Abercrombie.
3d brigade .... major-general Houghton.

Four nine-pounders royal British artillery—Captain Hawker.

* This detail is taken conjointly from the Appendix attached to sir Benjamin d'Urban's Report, and from general Hartmann's Narrative.

FOURTH BRITISH DIVISION, HON. MAJOR-GENERAL COLE. 1811.

Six six-pounders, king's German artillery—captain F. Sympher. May.
1st brigade, (Fuzileers,) lieutenant-colonel sir William Meyers.
3d brigade, (Portuguese) colonel Harvey.

PORTUGUESE.

MAJOR-GENERAL HAMILTON.

Six nine-pounders—Captain Braun, king's German legion.

1st brigade ········brigadier-general A. Campbell.
2d brigade ········brigadier-general A. Luiz Fonseca.

Six six-pounders—Captain Arreaga.

SPANIARDS.

LIEUTENANT-GENERAL DON JOACHIM BLAKE.

Captain-general Don Francisco Xavier Castanos.
Six four-pounders—Colonel Don José de Miranda.

1st division ········marechal de Campo Don José de Lardizabal.
2d division ········lieut.-gen. Don Francisco de Ballasteros.
3d division ········marechal de campo Don José de Zayas.
4th division ········brigadier-general Don Carlos de Espana.

UNATTACHED.

Light infantry brigade, king's German legion, major-general Charles von Alten.

1st light battalion····lieutenant-colonel Leonhardt.
2d light battalion ····lieutenant-colonel Halkett.

Two regiments Portuguese light infantry—Colonel Collins.

MAJOR GEORGE JULIUS HARTMANN, KING'S GERMAN LEGION,

Commanding the allied artillery.

MAJOR DICKSON, ROYAL BRITISH ARTILLERY,
Commanding the Portuguese artillery.

1811. May. The French were in every arm superior to the allies. Thy had twenty-six thousand veteran infantry, four thousand five hundred cavalry, and fifty-two guns, some of which were twelve-pounders.

Sir Benj. d'Urban's Report.

The British cavalry had been concentrated at Zafra and los Santos, and were directed to fall back gradually before the enemy by Santa Martha, upon Albuera; but they were driven in rapidly by the numerous opposing squadrons, and by three o'clock in the afternoon of the 15th, the whole of the opposite bank of the river was in possession of the enemy's horse.

Their infantry began to arrive the same evening, and encamped in a wood opposite the British right. On this flank marshal Soult resolved to make his principal attack, and early on the morning of the 16th formed the élite of his infantry, and a large proportion of his cavalry and artillery in the hollow of a tongue of land which lay between the Ferdia and Albuera streams; but, in order to divert the attention of the British general he at the same time directed the remainder of his troops upon the village and bridge of Albuera, threatening the allied left and centre.

Appendix, No. XIV.

These troops moved out of the wood between eight and nine o'clock in the morning, and general Alten's battalions were soon after engaged. Colonel Colborne's brigade of the second English division, with captain Cleeves's battery of German artillery, were immediately sent down to his support; the Portuguese guns, under captain Braun, answered the enemy's cannonade, and a sharp contest ensued. 1811. May.

But it was soon evident that the real attack was on the right; for two-thirds of the infantry, which were in motion for the bridge, suddenly countermarched to the left, and hastened back to the rear of the main body, while part of the cavalry, crossing the Albuera, galloped up the left bank, and came round the right flank of the allies. Sir Benj. d'Urban's Report.

Marshal Beresford, penetrating the enemy's design, directed general Blake to throw back his right, and the second division to move from the centre to his support, and bringing the Portuguese division and colonel Collins's brigade from the left, formed them in close columns upon the ground which the right of the second division had quitted.

The fourth division was at the same time placed obliquely in rear of the right, forming a reserve for that wing and the centre, and supporting the main body of British and Spanish cavalry which were moved to its front. Captain Sympher's battery of German artillery was posted with the fourth division, that of captain Cleeves accompanied the second division, and the English horse artillery remained with the cavalry. Narrative of general Hartmann, MSS.

With the exception of the Spaniards, these several changes were well and promptly executed. But general Blake, impressed with an idea that the enemy's real attack was on the centre, delayed the Sir Benj. d'Urban's Report.

1811. May. execution of the orders which he had received, and marshal Beresford was himself obliged to move the Spanish troops, who had been scarcely posted when the enemy fell upon them. They made, however, a gallant resistance, and the first brigade of the second British division, accompanied by four guns of captain Cleeves's battery, soon arrived to their support. Captain Cleeves now rapidly ascended the height with his light six-pounders, and unlimbering within ninety yards of the enemy's columns, opened a sharp fire upon the mass. The brigade followed, led up in column by general William Stewart, who attempted to form line as the battalions arrived; but before the deployment could be effected, a body of the enemy's lancers and hussars, which, hidden by a thick mist and rain, had gained the rear and right flank of the brigade, and, when there, were mistaken for Spaniards, came wildly down upon the British regiments, and committed dreadful slaughter among them. The alarmed soldiers flying in disorder through the intervals of captain Cleeves's battery, prevented his men from limbering up the right division of guns before the arrival of the horsemen, and the gunners were cut down and speared by the hussars and lancers. By the great exertions and personal exposure of the non-commissioned officers and men of the two left guns, and more particularly owing to the bravery and presence of mind of sergeants Hebecker and Bussmann, these were limbered up, and were in

Appendix. No. XIV.

Napier.

Lord Beresford's Despatch.

Appendix. No. XIV.

Guelphic archives, MSS.

movement to the rear, when the shaft horses of one gun fell wounded, and the leading driver of the other was shot from his horse. A corporal named Fincke now gallantly jumped from his own horse, and mounting that whose rider had been killed, galloped through the enemy's cavalry and brought off the gun:* the rest as well as three English guns were obliged to be abandoned, and lieutenants Thiele and Blumenbach of the German battery were wounded.

1811. May.

Appendix, No. XIV.

Meantime the British brigade had suffered tremendously, and the thirty-first regiment under major l'Estrange were alone enabled to keep their ground; but the mist clearing off, general Lumley perceived the assailants, and sending four squadrons of the allied cavalry to the spot, the hussars and lancers were fallen upon with fury, and were nearly all destroyed.

Sir Benj. d'Urban's Report.

The third brigade of the second division, led on by marshal Beresford in person, and supported by a corps of Spaniards, now moved up, and the second brigade also gaining the contested ground, the action was renewed with increased vigour. The enemy, reinforced from his reserves, again marched in column against the height, and a deadly conflict of infantry ensued.

It was continued with desperate valour, until not one third of any of the British regiments that had

Napier.

* Fincke's gallantry was afterwards rewarded by lord Wellington with the handsome present of a hundred Spanish dollars. (*Guelphic archives.*)

1811. May.

ascended the height were left standing, and some of their most gallant leaders had been killed or wounded. The force of the second division became at length so diminished that the French were enabled to lodge one of their columns more in advance of their left than they had hitherto done, and marshal Beresford ordered some Spanish battalions to charge this flank. But neither orders nor expostulations could induce the Spaniards to advance, and after in vain dragging a colonel to the front, and offering to lead them on himself, the marshal despatched an officer for a brigade of general Hamilton's Portuguese. These not arriving after some time had elapsed, he proceeded personally to enquire the cause of the delay, and finding that the Portuguese division had been removed towards the left of the line, sent forward colonel Collins's brigade to make the desired attack. The marshal then sent instructions to general Alten, whose light infantry had continued successfully to oppose the enemy's attempts to force the passage of the bridge, to retire from thence, and take post with a view to covering the Valverde road, or supporting the front, as might be required. This position was pointed out; Captain Baring, the general's aide-de-camp, was already engaged in the superintendance of the movement, and the legion had actually been withdrawn from the village, when a countermand arrived—for the French were observed flying before the troops on the heights!

Sir Benj. d'Urban's Report.

Further Strictures on Napier's History of the Peninsular War.

Narrative of colonel Baring. MSS.

General von Alten's Report.

The fourth division, ordered forward at the suggestion of colonel Hardinge, had come to the assistance of the exhausted brigades on the contested ground. While the Portuguese battalions, aided by the British and German artillery, beat off the enemy's horse, the fuzileers appeared on their left, and the third brigade of the second division on their right. These in conjunction with the British troops which had been yet left standing, opposed a new front to the dense columns, and charging simultaneously, the masses broke; the captured guns, with the exception of one howitzer, were recovered, and the French fled precipitously from the field, followed by their victorious opponents. 1811. May. Further Strictures, &c.

The enemy's reserve still offered some resistance, and general Alten's brigade became again engaged; but the French finally retired across the stream to their original position in the wood, and during the night Soult commenced his retreat for Seville covered by his numerous cavalry. Sir Benj. d'Urban's Report.

In this battle, which lasted four hours, the allies lost nearly six thousand men, and the French more than ten thousand. Of the legion light brigade lieutenant Whitney and seven rank and file were killed, major Hartwig, captains Baring, Rudorff, and Arnold Heise, lieutenants Hartwig and Fahle, and ensign Schmalhausen were wounded, captain Heise mortally; and ninety-two non-commissioned officers and soldiers were wounded and missing. The German artillery lost thirty-four horses, two officers Further Strictures, &c. Appendix, No. XV.

1811. May. Appendix, No. XV. Sir Benj. d'Urban's Report.

were wounded, and forty-six non-commissioned officers and men of the two batteries were returned wounded and missing: one howitzer also remained in the enemy's possession.

The allied cavalry and general von Alten's brigade followed the enemy's rear-guard on the 18th, and a part of his chasseurs with their lieutenant-colonel were taken by the Spanish horse under lieutenant-colonel Soto. Badajos was now reinvested, and lord Wellington, arriving at Elvas on the 19th, directed marshal Beresford to follow the enemy cautiously. The second and fourth divisions were, therefore, closed up to the German brigade, and on the 21st the whole moved upon Solana, the enemy's rear-guard being in Fuente del Maestre and Villa Franca.

On the 23d the French quitted these places, and retired upon Usagre, at the entrance of which town on the 25th, generals Lumley and Madden attacked their cavalry, and nearly destroyed two regiments. After this affair the enemy retired to Llerena, and the allied troops were placed in the cantonments which they had occupied previous to the advance of Soult. Marshal Beresford's presence being now required in Portugal, he was relieved from the command of the right corps by General Hill, and lord Wellington proceeded to conduct the siege of Badajos in person.

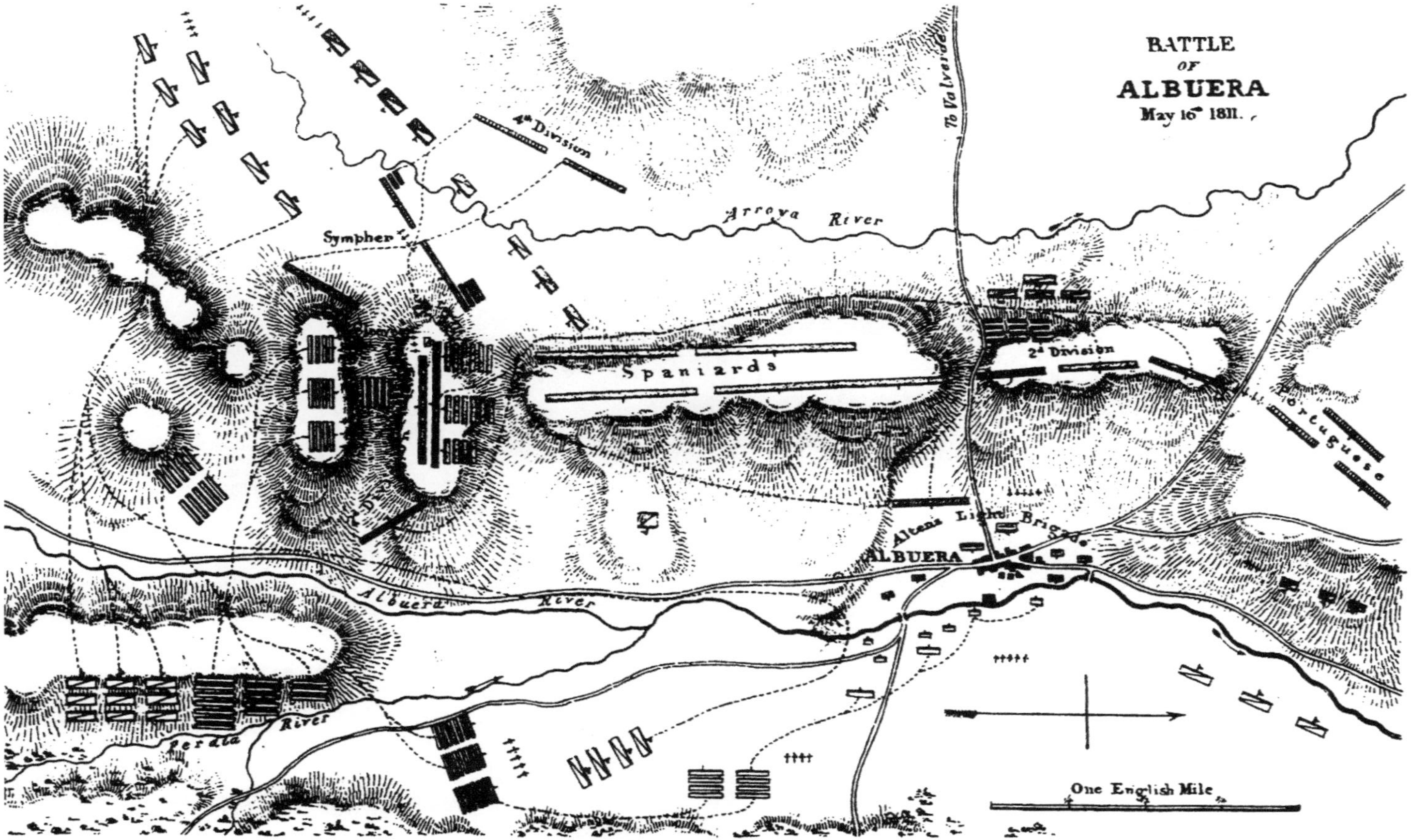

K.L.B. del. L. Hebert Lithog:

London T. & W. Boone June 1832

Printed by B. King 11 Charlotte Str Rathbone Place

APPENDIX.

APPENDIX.

No. I.

Extracts from the Proclamations issued by the Hanoverian Ministry on the 16*th and* 24*th of May,* 1803.

(Translated from the German.)

A.

From the Proclamation of the 16*th of May.*

* * * * * * * * * * *

In order to be prepared before hand for this unexpected occurrence, it is at the present moment indispensably necessary to ascertain exactly, and without delay, the number of our German subjects, who, should the necessity arise, would be able to bear arms in defence of their Fatherland.

Merely with this view, therefore, we require the magistracy of our faithful country, in conjunction with a member of our faithful representative body, *(Landschaften)* accurately and speedily, and as far as the necessary expedition renders it possible, to make out a complete list of those of our German subjects, who stand otherwise in allegiance to us and the Fatherland, and solemnly to engage the same, in case of necessity, *unhesitatingly to suffer themselves to be placed, for the protection and defence of the country, for so long a time as the necessity exists, and the defence of the country demands it, wherever they shall be required to effect this object.*

The tried loyalty and patriotism of our beloved subjects does not allow us to believe that any one of them will be found so forgetful of duty as to transgress this solemn engagement, and by a dishonourable flight from the land criminally to forsake its defence.

Should, however, notwithstanding these favourable expectations, such an event occur, the disgraceful subject who thus withdraws his assistance from his country, at the time of need, shall *infallibly, and without hope of pardon,* after a previous magisterial enquiry, be declared to have forfeited the entire property in our German state, which he may possess, or may expect to inherit. * * * * * * * * *

To the Magistracy at large, &c. &c. &c.

B.

From the Proclamation of the 24th of May, 1803.

* * * * * * * * * * *

Among these entirely incorrect representations, we observe with regret, that one of the greatest is, that many subjects of the state imagine there exists a design to meet the impending invasion with a so-called *levée en masse,* (land-sturm.)

As, however, *this was never intended,* and the sole object of the lists was limited to the ascertaining the number of our subjects fit for service, in order, as has been already done, to be able to call out the same for the completion of the royal army in its required number of men, for the service of the country, *in the capacity of regular troops, for so long a period as the defence of the country from an impending danger, of which it is entirely guiltless, may render it necessary*—

You will, therefore, consider it an urgent duty in every possible manner, and most completely, to set the people right upon this point, and to impress them with a strong assurance that it is by no means the intention to call them out as a so-called *levée en masse* (land-sturm); but *solely and only* as a necessary reinforcement for the regular army in case of danger to the country, consequently to employ them *in the capacity of regular troops.*

* * * * * * * * * * *

To the Magistracy at large, &c. &c. &c.

No. II.

Opinion of the council of war assembled at Haidekrug.

(Translated from the German.)

Under the presupposition that these conditions shall be observed, that, according to them, a new convention shall be concluded, and that no worse conditions be substituted in place of the above named, we the undersigned are agreed that his excellency the fieldmarshal count von Wallmoden Gimborn may conclude a convention for the troops with the French general.

Haidekrug, 4th July, 1803.

(Signed)

L. von Diepenbroick, major-general.
R. von Hammerstein, lieutenant-general.
L. H. A. von Scheither, lieutenant-general.
Br. Linsingen, lieutenant-general.
Kuntze, major-general.
F. von Drechsel, major-general.
J. von Hassel, major-general.
O. Schulte, major-general.
Du Plat, major-general.
C. Pr. von Schwartzburg, colonel.

No. III.

Proclamations, &c. issued by the executive commission at Hanover, prohibitory of recruiting for the English service.

(Translated from the German.)

A.

PROCLAMATION.

It having come to the knowledge of the general-in-chief that in some parts of the country recruiting is carried on for the English service, the magistracy at large are not only warned of the danger to which they expose themselves by in any wise encouraging such recruiting, but the magistracy are required, by the express orders of the general-in-chief, for the preservation of the peace of the electorate, to give information of the hired English recruiting agents.

Hanover, 6th October, 1803.

Signed by the commission.

To the Magistrates of the country at large.

B.

PROCLAMATION.

By order of the general-in-chief, it is herewith made known to the inhabitants of the electorate at large, that every person who concerns himself about recruiting for the English service, or induces others to go over to that service, shall be delivered up to the French military tribunal, and punished according to the severity of the French military laws, agreeable to which, those persons who may be found guilty of the above-mentioned crime, *are punishable with death.*

All persons are therefore warned, and the magistracy are to

consider it their duty to publish every where the present ordinance, and make it universally known in the usual manner.

Hanover, 10th October, 1803.

Signed by the executive commission.

To the Magistrates of the country at large.

C.

NOTIFICATION TO THE CLERGY.

Our, &c.

As the unlimited, public, and most universal notification of the annexed ordinance of the 10th of October, relative to recruiting for the English service, is of the greatest importance to all and every inhabitant of the country, and is therefore to be read from all pulpits on the next three sundays after the receipt of this, a copy of this letter, together with the ordinance itself, is to be immediately communicated to every clergyman for his guidance, and the duplicate of the letter furnished with the *præsentatis* of the clergyman, to be returned here.

We are, &c,

(Signed.) Consistorium of the Country.

Hanover, 13th October, 1803.

To

All general and special superintendants standing under the consistorium of the country, as well as to all religious bodies, charitable establishments, and convents.

D.

PROCLAMATION.

Herewith are annexed some copies of a sentence which has been pronounced by the military tribunal upon sergeant Ahrens, relative to recruiting for the English service, and which, in order to deter others by the example, is to be as much as possible made generally known. It is therefore to be affixed to the amt-offices and posted on the doors of the churches.

Hanover, 8th November, 1803.

Signed by the executive commission.

To the Magistracy of the country at large.

N.B. The verdict referred to, sentences sergeant Ahrens, of the sixth Hanoverian electoral regiment of infantry, in consequence of traitorous recruiting, *(embauchage,) to fifteen years in irons,* (galley-slave punishment.)

(Signed) C. Heise.

No. IV.

Letter of service addressed to his royal highness the duke of Cambridge.

War Office, 19*th December,* 1803.

Sir,

In pursuance of the king's commands, communicated to me by his royal highness the commander-in-chief, I have the honour to acquaint your royal highness that his majesty has directed the independent levies of baron Decken and major Halkett to be discontinued, and has been pleased to order that the men raised under the letters of service granted to those officers shall be formed into a legion to be composed of foreigners, not exceeding five thousand men, which his majesty is pleased to authorize to be raised by your royal highness, upon the conditions hereafter specified.

Article I.—Each recruit is to be enlisted for ten years if possible, but certainly for not less than seven years; and should Great

Britain be at war at the expiration of that term of service, the men are to continue to serve without additional bounty until six months after the ratification of a definitive treaty of peace. No man engaged for a less term of service will be passed at the depôt at Hilsea barracks.

II.—The recruits are not to be under five feet three inches, nor above forty years of age, and must, in every respect, be free from infirmity and fit for service. Young healthy lads who are likely to grow, may, however, be enlisted at five feet two inches high.

III.—No natives of France, Italy, or Spain are to be enlisted under any circumstances whatever; but your royal highness is at liberty to engage abroad, men of all other nations of Europe, and also Poles, Hungarians, Danes, Russians, and Germans residing in this country, but not any of his majesty's British subjects; and your royal highness is also at liberty to engage natives of Holland, taken on board prizes, provided they shall appear from their age and make to be fit for his majesty's service.

IV.—Fifteen guineas will be allowed to your royal highness for each recruit (those men brought from the Continent at the public expense, also those enlisted from on board prizes, and the lads excepted) who shall be delivered at Hilsea barracks, and there approved and accepted for his majesty's service, reserving, however, the sum of three pounds, seventeen shillings, and sixpence, being the like proportion of the bounty, both in money and in necessaries, that is allowed to a British recruit of the line on final approval; the same to be invariably accounted for to your royal highness's recruits at the depôt, under the order of the inspector-general. The man is also to be in possession of all the other articles of necessaries furnished to a recruit of the line on intermediate approval. The bounty paid to the recruit is not, however, in any case to exceed, in money or necessaries, the regulated sum of seven pounds, twelve shillings, and sixpence, now allowed to a British infantry recruit.

V.—For each man brought from the Continent at the public expense, the sum of twelve guineas will be allowed, and those who shall be enlisted from on board prizes, and who shall be approved and accepted of as above stipulated, levy money at the rate of seven guineas will be allowed, and eight guineas for each lad of the description mentioned in article II. with the like reservation of bounty in each case as in article IV.

VI.—No charge whatever will be admitted for any expenses that may be incurred on account of the recruit previous to the man's approval at Hilsea barracks; nor is any expense to be incurred by the public on account of rejected recruits, or of such as may die or desert before approval. The rejected men brought from the Continent are to be subsisted and sent back at your royal highness's expense.

VII.—The pay of the approved recruits will be allowed from the respective dates of their approval at Hilsea barracks, and that of the officers from the date of their commissions.

VIII.—The officers and men will be required to take the oath of allegiance to his majesty, and will be liable to serve wherever his majesty shall think fit to employ them. Each recruit is to sign an engagement accordingly, and to be subject to the same regulations and articles of war as his majesty's British troops.

IX.—The men and lads shall, during the whole period of their term of service, enjoy all such advantages as are or may be granted or allowed to British soldiers wherever they may happen to serve, and shall be subject to all diminutions of pay and allowances which his majesty may think proper to order for the British troops.

X.—The whole of the officers shall be entitled on reduction to an allowance equivalent to British half-pay, provided the legion be kept in the British service for upwards of five years; but in the event of its being sooner reduced, this allowance will be granted to such officers only as shall hold permanent British rank. The rest of the officers will have allowances according to their respective ranks, at the rates specified in the table hereunto annexed, (*A.*)

XI.—When any of the men shall be discharged from the service on reduction or otherwise, they will, if brought from the

Continent, be sent back at the expense of the British government, and an allowance will be made to them in aid of travelling expenses to their respective homes, at the rate of twopence English, or about six *kreutzers* of the empire per league, the same to be calculated from the point of debarkation on the Continent.

XII.—The men who, from wounds or other infirmities, shall become incapable of serving during the period of the term for which they shall have been engaged, will receive from government an allowance for life, not exceeding the Chelsea out-pension, which will be paid to them accordingly if they reside in England, or shall have obtained permission to receive the same on the Continent, but not otherwise.

XIII.—In respect to the supply of clothing and appointments the legion will be on the same footing as British regiments of the line. The arms will be furnished from the public stores.

XIV.—In the first instance, the men already raised are to be immediately formed into two battalions of light infantry, each battalion to consist of the numbers specified in the annexed statement (B.), which battalions will be considered as placed in the establishment of the army from the 19th of December, 1803. The formation of the remainder of the legion will take place in proportion as the men are obtained.

XV.—His majesty, whenever he shall think fit, may discontinue the legion or any part thereof, on the establishment of the army, notwithstanding the period of seven years, or such longer term for which the men shall have been engaged to serve, should not have expired.

I have the honour to be, Sir,
With the most profound respect,
Your Royal Highness's
Most obedient and humble Servant,

(Signed) C. BRAGGE.

To lieutenant-general his royal highness the duke of Cambridge, K.G. &c. &c. &c.

A.

Allowances referred to in Article X.

	s.	d.	
Colonel	7	6	per diem
Lieutenant-colonel and major	5	0	,,
Captain and surgeon	3	0	,,
Adjutant	2	6	,,
Subaltern and assistant-surgeon	2	0	,,

B.

Establishment referred to in Article XIV.

1 Lieutenant-colonel	1 Assistant-surgeon
1 Major	1 Sergeant-major
6 Captains	1 Quarter-master-sergeant
6 Lieutenants	1 Pay-master, do.
6 Ensigns	1 Armourer, do.
1 Adjutant	24 Sergeants
1 Quarter-master	24 Corporals
1 Pay-master	12 Buglers
1 Surgeon	450 Privates
	Total......539

No. V.

DOCUMENT RELATING TO THE AFFRAY AT TULLAMORE.

Extract from a letter addressed by general Floyd to his royal highness the duke of Cambridge, dated Royal Hospital. Dublin, July 28th, 1806.

SIR,

I had the honour of informing your royal highness of an unfortunate affray that happened at Tullamore, and I extremely regret that it is not possible to give you by this post the detailed account.

I must request your royal highness will be pleased to accept of a very abridged, but, as far as it goes, a correct narrative which I gathered on the spot.

On Tuesday the 22d instant, five militia light companies

marched into Tullamore on their way to join their regiments. About seven in the afternoon, as the troops were collecting for roll-call, a boy upon the bridge desired a militia man to beware of the Germans, applying the coarsest epithets to them. A German soldier was then passing, and a militia man knocked him down. Three other Germans accidentally passing unarmed came up to see what was the matter, and were knocked down with a stick. A patrole from the main guard of the first German light infantry came up and seized a militia man who seemed to be a principal rioter. As they carried him off, about twenty militia followed, supposed with intent to rescue. Captain Düring being just then parading his company for roll-call, moved down with it to cover the patrole, and the militia men retreated—faced about—threw stones and then fired, by which five men of captain Düring's company were wounded. Major-general baron Linsingen, hearing a riot, ran out among the militia, entreating them, in the best English of which he was master, to desist; at the same time he ordered a detachment of cavalry to clear the streets of all rioters, which they did effectually, and all was quiet in about a full half-hour from beginning to end. The Germans had no ammunition, but it is said they used some cartridges which they found on the prisoners.

Of his majesty's German legion three officers were wounded, lieutenants Peters, &c. * * * * * *

I spoke to the chief magistrate of Tullamore, Mr. Morris, and to several respectable inhabitants, who all attribute blame to the militia, and were loud in their praises of his majesty's German legion quartered there, and of their exemplary and inoffensive conduct. I must confess I never saw a more orderly, well disposed, or more soldier-like corps than that commanded by colonel baron Alten. * * * * *

(Signed) J. Floyd,
Lieutenant-General.

C.

The EFFECTIVE FORCE *under the command of major-general Frederick baron Drechsel, colonel-commandant seventh line battalion, King's German Legion, in the isle of Rügen and at Stralsund, on the 10th of August,* 1807, *was as follows:—*

	OFFICERS. Commissioned.	OFFICERS. Staff.	Troop quarter-masters, staff, and other sergeants.	Trumpeters and Drummers.	Rank and file.	Horses.
ARTILLERY. 1st battery of horse artillery, 1st, 2d, and 4th batteries of foot artillery; CAVALRY. 2d and 3d hussars; INFANTRY. 1st and 2d light, [of the latter five companies only,] and 3d, 4th, 5th, 6th, 7th, and 8th line battalions	324	81	382	142	7707	1813
This corps proceeded to the Isle of Zealand, and was there joined by the 1st regiment of hussars and 1st and 2d line battalions, making the whole force of the king's German legion on service with the British troops in the isle of Zealand, on the 1st of SEPTEMBER 1807.. Engineers....	7	..	..	..	..	..
Artillery	28	6	21	7	641	508
Cavalry	80	17	132	24	1802	1926
Infantry	347	56	429	155	7464	87
Total	462	79	582	186	9907	2521
Add the numbers absent on the 1st of September, 1807, viz. staff in London........	2	..	..	..	..	..
2d battery of horse and 3d battery of foot artillery at Porchester	11	2	10	3	316	4
1st regiment of dragoons at Tullamore in Ireland	25	6	42	8	597	638
2d do do on the march to Ireland..	25	5	44	8	604	610
three companies of the 2d light battalion at Ramsgate ..	12	2	18	6	296	..
the unattached recruits at Porchester	..	..	..	..	43	..
and the officers of sundry regiments on leave of absence and sick in England and on the continent	18	3	..	..	..	..
Total	93	18	114	25	1856	1252
Grand total of the king's German legion on the 1st of September 1807	555	97	696	211	11,763	3773

13,322 men and 3773 horses.

Hanover, Dec. 22, 1830. (Signed) LEWIS BENNE.

No. VII.

Documents relating to the capture of General Lefebvre Desnouettes.

TRANSLATED FROM THE GERMAN.

A.

Extract from the deposition of Johann Bergmann, late private in the fifth troop of the third hussars, king's German legion, made before the amt at Osterholtz, 8th March, 1830.

Deponent was with the regiment in Spain, in the year 1808, and fought with it at Benavente.

In this affair he cut one French officer from his horse, and made another prisoner; the latter was said to be general Lefebvre.

If he does not err, three charges were this day made against the enemy; the two first were unsuccessful, but at the third charge the French cavalry were overthrown, and driven across the river which runs near Benavente.

It was at the second charge that he came up with the officer whom he cut from his horse. As this officer lay on the ground, he took his sabre and pouch from him.

At the third charge, or in reality the pursuit, he came upon the officer whom he made prisoner. He was one of the first in the pursuit, and as he came up with this officer, who rode close in rear of the enemy, the officer made a thrust at him with a long straight sword. After, however, he had parried the thrust, the officer called out " pardon." He did not trouble himself further about the man, but continued the pursuit; an English hussar, however, who had come up to the officer at the same time with him, led the officer back. * * * * * *
* * * * * * * * * * *

When he maintains that he took general Lefebvre prisoner at the combat of Benavente, he must observe that he does not know this general, and only makes the assertion because it was said to him after the action that he ought to have held fast the man who thrust at him, for it was general Lefebvre. He was then young and did not trouble himself about the matter; he also never saw the man again; he only remembers that he that day wore a dark green frock, a hat with a feather, and a long straight sword.

B.

Deposition of Heinrich Kostermann, late private in the fifth troop of the third hussars, king's German legion, made at Noerten, 23d November, 1829.

Deponent was present at the combat of Benavente, and saw hussar Johann Bergmann take an officer prisoner on the left of the bridge in front of Benavente. This officer was brought off by Bergmann and another hussar; who the other hussar was he does not know, nor to whom or to what place the prisoner was taken; nor can he say whether Bergmann took the officer's sword from him; he heard, however, that the officer was general Lefebvre.

C.

Deposition of farrier Schumburg, late of the third hussars, king's German legion, made at Allershausen, 23d November, 1829.

Deponent was present at an attack near Benavente, in Spain, where a whole troop (*eine ganze schaar*) surrounded the French general Lefebvre; hussar Bergmann was, however, the man nearest to the general, and deponent saw that

Bergmann had got the general's sword, and taken him prisoner; and that the English brigadier commander Stewart received the general. * * * * * * * * * *

D.

Extract from a letter of major-general August von dem Bussche, K.C.H. formerly captain in the third hussars, of the king's German legion, dated Stade, 8th November, 1829.

Johann Bergmann, formerly a private in the third hussars of the king's German legion, no doubt took prisoner the general Lefebvre Desnouettes, in the combat in which that regiment was engaged on the 29th of December, 1808, with the French imperial guard, near Benavente, on the Esla.

This capture was the same day notorious in the regiment, and captain von Kerssenbruch, to whose troop Bergmann belonged, enquired the particulars from him, and some of his comrades; and learned, "that during the individual encounters which took place, the general, being followed by Bergmann, fired a pistol at him, which failing in its aim, he offered him his sword, and made known his wish to be taken to general Stewart; Bergmann, however, did not know general Stewart personally, and while he was enquiring where that general was to be found, a hussar of the tenth English regiment joined him, and led away the prisoner."

No one in the third hussars has ever so much as doubted the circumstance, because Bergmann had shewn himself brave on all occasions, and is an extremely simple fellow, without any sort of boasting. * * * * * * * * *
* * * * * * * * * * *

E.

Extract from a letter of captain George Meyer K.H. of the third Hanoverian hussars, and late of the third hussars, king's German legion, dated Hertzberg, 20th November, 1829.

* * * * * * * * * * *

Hussar Bergmann no doubt took prisoner a French officer of high rank, but gave him over to an English hussar to be delivered up, in order to return again to the fight. He was more brave than shrewd and circumspect; for notwithstanding his acknowledged gallantry and honesty, he was never promoted to be a non-commissioned officer. * * * * * * *

No. VIII.

CORRESPONDENCE RELATIVE TO THE MARCH OF GENERAL VON ALTEN'S BRIGADE FROM ASTORGA TO VIGO.

(From the United Service Journal for 1831. Part III.)

A.

Count Alten to the Editor of the U. S. Journal.

Mr. Editor,—I have but lately read in the second volume of colonel Napier's History of the War in the Peninsula, an assertion that "the British and German troops that marched to Vigo were conducted without judgement, and licentious." Having been honoured with the command of these troops, I feel myself called upon, both in justice to my own character, and to that of the late general Robert Craufurd, who commanded the British brigade of my division, to reply to these animadversions, and hope I shall not be considered unreasonable in requesting a place in your journal for the following statement of facts relative to the march of that corps.

On the 30th of December, 1808, Sir John Moore's army reached Astorga; the brigade then under my command, consisting of the first and second light battalions of the king's German legion, was quartered in the adjacent villages. On the 31st of December, I received a letter from sir John Moore, written the same day, in Astorga, appointing me to the command of the two flank brigades, with which I was directed to make a separate movement upon Orense and Vigo. The first brigade consisted of the first battalions of the forty-third, fifty-second, and ninety-fifth regiments, under colonel Robert Craufurd, and the second brigade of the two light battalions of the king's German legion, the command of which now devolved upon lieutenant-colonel Colin Halkett.

On receiving this letter, I went into Astorga, and waited upon sir John Moore to receive his farther instructions. The general, after confiding to me the outlines of his own plan and intentions with regard to the main body of the army, which he at that time designed should embark at Vigo, informed me that the object of the separate movement which was to be entrusted to me, was, first, to secure the bridge over the Minho at Orense, which place, the enemy being actually nearer to it than the British army were, might be occupied by the French; and, secondly, after securing this point, to proceed to and occupy Vigo, where were assembled the whole fleet under sir Samuel Hood, on which the safety of the army depended. In his letter to me sir John Moore made use of the following identical words:—" I cannot give you any particular instructions, but intrust this arduous service to you, fully relying on your known zeal and judgement."

Conformable to sir John Moore's instructions and intentions, I endeavoured, by every possible exertion, to attain the objects which he had in view. On the 4th of January, I sent forward from Pueblo de Tribez a detachment of three hundred men, consisting of volunteers from both brigades, under the command of major Stuart of the ninety-fifth, which detachment, after forced marches through a most difficult and mountainous country, during inclement weather, occupied Orense on the 6th of January, and I reached that place myself, with the main body of the corps, on the following day.

Forced marches, under such peculiar circumstances, necessarily involve the necessity of leaving behind the sick and stragglers, which, during the latter part of the march, amounted to a considerable number. An officer from each battalion was left behind, on the 3d, to take charge of these men and bring them up, and on reaching Orense, the main object having been secured, I determined to stop there on the 8th, and give the troops a day's rest.

On the morning of the 8th, I again sent forward major Stuart's detachment, with orders to proceed by forced marches to Vigo, and occupy the forts there. The main body followed under my immediate command on the 9th, and proceeding by easy marches, allowing each brigade another halt-day, I reached Vigo on the 12th of January. The first flank brigade was embarked on the same day, and the second brigade on the day following.*

The procuring provisions during this march was attended with much difficulty. The country was poor and thinly inhabited, and the troops arriving late and setting off early, there was seldom time sufficient for baking; however, by sending forward the commissary of general Craufurd's brigade, attended by proper assistants, I succeeded in getting a tolerable supply of meat and wine.

It was at Orense that I received a letter from colonel Múrray, the quarter-master-general, informing me, by command of sir John Moore, of the general's alteration in his plan and intention to embark at Corunna. I was at the same time directed to transmit immediately sir John Moore's orders to sir Samuel Hood for the requisite number of vessels to go round to Corunna. Agreeable to these directions I despatched my aide-de-camp,

* Colonel Robert Craufurd, having the rank of brigadier-general, and being unacquainted with the instructions which I had received from sir John Moore, considered himself called upon to remonstrate with me on the (as he conceived) unnecessary severity of the marches. After first assuring him that he was entirely exonerated from all responsibility to which he might consider himself liable as second in command, I communicated to him part of sir John Moore's instructions, and fully satisfied him of the propriety of the dispositions which I had made. We continued ever after on the most friendly and intimate terms.

captain Augustus Heise, by express to the admiral, and his timely arrival at Vigo enabled the fleet to clear the harbour and to reach Corunna in time to secure the embarkation of the rest of the army.

This was a critical moment; for the harbour of Vigo, beset with high isolated rocks (*estellas*) is most difficult of egress, and but few winds admit of a fleet getting out. On this occasion the ships had scarcely cleared the harbour when the wind changed, and, blowing strong into the bay, rendered it impossible for any vessel to get out. The bay being commanded by a battery of heavy guns, I took measures to render these unserviceable to the enemy, should they reach Vigo before the troops could sail; the forts in the meantime were occupied by a detachment of the German brigade under lieutenant-colonel Halkett.

On the 17th of January, major Martin of the first light battalion king's German legion, who had been left behind at Orense in charge of the sick and stragglers, arrived at Vigo with about six hundred men, which number, according to a fair calculation, may be considered about two-thirds of the whole that were left behind; of the remaining sick and stragglers several came up afterwards, and a good many rejoined their regiments in Portugal. The men of the legion battalions who ultimately never rejoined, were nearly to a man vagabonds of various nations, who had been enlisted in Danish Zealand in 1807, after the taking of Copenhagen. To the best of my belief no Hanoverian was among the number.

While we were wind-bound in Vigo, I was most opportunely joined by brigadier-general Peacock, who was on his way from Lisbon to sir John Moore with part of the military chest. This supply enabled me to issue a month's subsistence to the troops, and to furnish major Martin with money for the conveyance and subsistence of the sick and stragglers, the want of funds for whom had caused major Martin to suffer much *ill-will* and annoyance from the Spanish authorities and inhabitants.

On the 20th of January the fleet sailed, but contrary winds obliged it to put back, and it did not finally clear the harbour until the 23d. On the 25th we arrived off cape Finisterre, where captain Hayes of the Alfred, seventy-four, who commanded the fleet, at first intended to await the further orders of sir Samuel Hood. Captain Hayes was, however, induced, by my taking the responsibility on myself, and giving him an order in writing to that effect, to sail direct for England, where the fleet arrived at the end of January 1809.

Such, sir, are the broad facts of the case, and by these I claim a right to be judged. In obedience to the instructions, and in accordance with the views of sir John Moore, I pressed forward to protect the flank of the main army and secure its intended line of retreat. To effect this, forced marches were indispensable, and the fatigue and suffering which such marches, undertaken under the circumstances that have been described, brought on the troops, necessarily caused many men to be left behind, and consequently occasioned disorder. To repair and prevent these irregularities, I employed all the means that were at my disposal, and had the satisfaction to find that they were as effectual as, under the circumstances, I could possibly expect. Bodies of stragglers, sir, however able the officers who command them may be, will not march with the regularity of close columns; and that instances of indiscipline and licentiousness will occur, is well known to every officer who has served on a retreat. But is the whole march of a corps to be therefore stigmatized as *injudicious and licentious*, and the conduct of the officers by whom it was directed thus held up to censure? Had the assertion which I have sought to refute proceeded from a less distinguished officer or less influential historian than the author of the History of the War in the Peninsula, I should not have thus intruded upon your pages a statement which can have little interest for the majority of your readers—I should have rested satisfied with the flattering testimonials which have been bestowed upon my services in the British army—with the esteem of my peninsular comrades—with the consolations of my own conscience; but when I see myself held up to censure by one whose authority is, in so many respects, entitled to weight, and liable to be handed down to posterity in a point of view unwarranted by the facts, I feel myself called upon to lay before the public the true materials for coming to a right conclusion.

I have to apologize for the length to which this statement has run. More experienced in the use of the sword than that of the pen, I would gladly have avoided engrossing your pages with such a detail, for which I feel myself as unfitted as for any further discussion on the subject.

I have the honour to remain, Sir,
Your most obedient humble Servant,
CHARLES COUNT ALTEN,
General Hanoverian Service.

Hanover, May 1831.

P.S. The testimony of sir George Murray might, if necessary, be brought forward to corroborate those parts of the above statement which came under the cognizance of that general.

*** With reference to this postscript, it appears due to count Alten to quote the following extract from a note of sir George Murray to ourselves.—(ED.)

" As count Alten's anxiety with respect to his professional character has been the cause of his addressing the accompanying letter to you, I think I should be guilty of a very blameable omission if I did not, in returning it, offer my humble testimony at least as to the high character deservedly earned by general Alten during a long course of valuable services, a great portion of which have come under my personal notice. As general Robert Craufurd's name has likewise been mentioned, I should, were it necessary, offer a similar testimony with regard to the ability and the zeal of that officer.

" As to the regiments which marched from Astorga to Vigo under the command of those two general officers, as well the three British as the two Hanoverian battalions, there are, I believe, no corps in any service which have been more remarked than they have both for gallantry and for discipline."

B.

Reply of colonel Napier.

Mr. Editor,

It appears that I have given offence to count Charles Alten by that passage in the second volume of my history which describes the march of our troops from Astorga to Vigo in 1808–9 as licentious and ill-conducted. Hitherto, sir, the attacks that, from time to time, have been made upon my work have been neglected by me, not from any disinclination to meet my opponents, nor from any feeling of weakness, but simply because I have not had leisure; nor would I now have taken the trouble to answer count Alten's observations were it not that the thing is easy in itself, and that I owe him some respect as a brave soldier under whose command I served for a considerable time.

The count, after stating the words of a conversation held at Astorga with sir John Moore, proceeds to show in detail that the instructions he received from that general, namely, "to seize the bridge of Orense and reach Vigo before the enemy," were fulfilled to the letter. I do not dispute it. There was no enemy seen, felt, or heard of during the whole march, and, consequently, there was no difficulty in reaching the points required to be occupied. Were I, indeed, disposed to attack general Alten with any taint of malice, I might observe that the only occasion in which he used his discretionary power, his judgement was at fault. For certainly sir John Moore's intention was to assemble the whole army (after embarkation) in the bay of Vigo with a view to restore order; and there count Alten took the responsibility of making sail for England with that part of the army under his command, before he knew of the catastrophe at Corunna, which would have proved an error if sir John Moore had lived.

I come now to the real point at issue between us. General Alten's observations go to show that he obeyed his instructions, but my remark had only reference to the details of execution, and not upon my own authority as an eye-witness. I have served many campaigns, yet I have never seen " a more licentious and ill-commanded" march, and I trust for confirmation of the assertion to the recollection of the officers who were present. General Alten acknowledges that one detachment of stragglers alone amounted to six hundred men. Now, Sir, the ships waited in Vigo bay, after the troops arrived there, at least ten days, and during the whole of that period stragglers were coming in by two's and three's, as the navy officers who were constantly engaged in bringing them off to the vessels can testify. In addition to this I find by the adjutant-general's returns that about five hundred men were left behind when the ships sailed. Here, then, we have at least one-third of the whole number of troops straggling during a march in which the face of an enemy was never seen, nor the want of provisions ever felt; the troops also sleeping under cover every night, and in good villages; for I must take leave, in opposition to the general's observations, to say that the country, although mountainous, was the reverse of sterile, and with the exception of the two first days' journey, not at all difficult for unincumbered infantry such as ours. General Alten, indeed, is obliged to confess that the stragglers committed excesses, but he excuses it on the score of the forced marches that his instructions obliged him to make. Forced marches is a vague term. I have seen the same troops afterwards make marches double the length of those without leaving a straggler behind, and without a fault, much less an excess being laid to their charge; and the reason they did so was that general Craufurd, (whose ability was never questioned by me, and therefore required no defence from general Alten,) struck by the excesses committed during the march to Vigo, had conceived, and organized, and enforced a system of divisional discipline which will remain a model for the imitation of all soldiers whatever may be their nation.

But to return to the forced marches. They were necessary to fulfil sir John Moore's instructions. Now, general Alten was the senior officer of the two brigades; his interference was certainly not perceived by the British part of the force under his command, but he was, undoubtedly, the commanding officer, and in that capacity had direction of the whole march. Hence, if he thought the forced marches necessary, he should have interfered to prevent general Craufurd from halting nearly two or three times every day, for the purpose of punishing soldiers and thus delaying the march several hours, with a view to establish that discipline by terror which ought to have been established by arrangement. If, on the other side, general Alten thought fit to leave general Craufurd the entire management of his brigade, there seems no reason why he should take offence at an observation in my work where his name is not mentioned. In conclusion, I have only to repeat that, in my opinion, there never was "a worse conducted or more licentious march" than that to Vigo.

I have now only to notice sir George Murray's observations. It is difficult to discover exactly what they are meant for. If to give currency to count Alten's narrative their value is but small, seeing that sir George knows nothing of the march, except from hearsay. If they are to vouch for the accurate memory of general Alten with respect to the parting speech of sir John Moore, that has nothing to do with the matter at issue. If they are to vouch for the characters of the generals engaged, I am not aware that I ever impeached general Alten's zeal or general Craufurd's ability. But if they were meant, without committing sir George Murray to any specific fact, to give currency to an attack on my work, I can understand them.

Having now, Sir, stated as much as I think fitting upon this occasion, I have only to remark that, at a future period, I may possibly endeavour to shew my other opponents that their positions are not so strong as they, perhaps, imagine.

Meanwhile, Sir, I remain, with great respect for the impartiality with which you give publicity to the statements of all parties,

Your obedient servant,

W. Napier.

C.

Captain Christoph Heise to the Editor of the United Service Journal.

MR. EDITOR,

Having read in the thirty-fourth number of the United Service Journal, count Alten's letter relative to the march of the corps under his command from Astorga to Vigo in 1808–9, as well as colonel Napier's reply to this letter in the thirty-fifth number, in which the latter makes use of the following passage:—

" Were I, indeed, disposed to attack general Alten with any taint of malice, I might observe that on the only occasion in which he used his discretionary power, his judgement was at fault. For certainly sir John Moore's intention was to assemble the whole army (after embarkation) in the bay of Vigo with a view to restore order; and then count Alten took the responsibility of making sail for England with that part of the army under his command, *before he knew of the catastrophe at Corunna*, which would have proved an error if sir John Moore had lived."

I beg leave to transmit to you, for insertion in your valuable and impartial journal, the annexed authenticated copy of the letter written by count Alten to captain Hayes of his majesty's ship Alfred, previous to the fleet with the troops under his command sailing for England.

Count Alten, in his letter published in your journal, has expressed his determination not to take up his pen a second time in this matter. However, I myself, having become possessed after the death of my late brother, lieutenant-colonel Augustus Heise, of the official letter-book kept by him in his capacity of aide-de-camp to count Alten during the march from Astorga to Vigo, consider it a duty I owe to truth, and to the character of general Alten, to lay this document before the public, leaving it with them to decide about a *fact* upon which the gallant colonel appears to have been so completely misinformed.

As I do not enjoy the advantage of having been an eye-witness to the military events which have in this instance called forth the censure of the historian of the peninsular war, I must leave the rest of colonel Napier's reply to count Alten's statement of facts, to the judgement of every individual reader who will take the trouble of comparing both. Should I be permitted to venture a remark which has struck me during their perusal, it is this:

That many of the leading events as well as of the minor details connected with military operations are sure to come to the knowledge of the officer in command, and will guide his conduct accordingly, while they will most likely remain at the time a secret to the eye-witness in a subordinate situation; and therefore the latter's opinion may be influenced, or, perhaps, prejudiced to such a degree, as to make it difficult for him to alter it at a subsequent period, and, probably, not the less so should the eye-witness, unfortunately for the responsible superior, happen to be a party interested in upholding his own first impressions.

Having now, Sir, stated as much as I think fitting for me on this occasion, I trust that my reasons for doing so will not meet with any misinterpretation, and that I shall stand exonerated from any selfish motive for thus far trespassing with my humble observations on your pages and the patience of your readers, while I beg leave in conclusion to cite for myself, and to apply, as far as it is applicable to my own situation, the same plea which colonel Napier has brought forward as the main cause for publishing a reply to general Alten's letter, viz.:—

"Were it not that the thing is easy in itself, and that I owe count Alten some* respect as a brave officer under whose command I served for a considerable time, I would not take the trouble to answer," &c. I have the honour to remain,

With the greatest respect, Sir,

Your obedient and humble Servant,

CHRISTOPH HEISE,

Captain Royal Hanoverian Jäger Guards
H. P. late first light infantry batt. K. G. L.

Hanover, *October*, 1831.

* In my own case, I beg, however, to substitute in lieu of *some*, THE HIGHEST.—C. H.

Letter referred to in the foregoing.

H. M. S. Alfred, off Corunna,
January 26th, 1809.

SIR,

In consequence of the notification we received yesterday from captain Seymour of his majesty's ship Pallas, about the disasters which befel the army under the command of lieutenant-general sir John Moore, and their sudden sailing to England which followed it, I beg to request that you will profit of the present fair wind to proceed there with the least possible delay with the corps under my command belonging to the same army, which expeditiousness I feel it my duty to represent to you as highly necessary on account of the symptoms of infectious fevers which have already appeared amongst the troops, owing to the great hardships and fatigues they were exposed to on the late retreat; besides that, the men being, from want of transports, very much crowded on board the ships, would make it, in my opinion, extremely dangerous for the health of the men to wait any longer for the despatches you expected to find from rear-admiral sir Samuel Hood, either off cape Finisterre or off Corunna, and not having received them at either place makes it most probable they are gone to Vigo.

I have the honour to be, &c. &c.
(Signed) CH. ALTEN.

To captain Hayes, H. M. S. Alfred.

Memorandum by captain A. Heise, aide-de-camp.

At the time this letter was written a thick fog had come on, and the wind being at the time contrary to Vigo, no vessel could have gone there and returned within two days; we sailed, after having lain to for eighteen hours.

(Signed) A. H.

I certify that the above letter from general Alten, with the memorandum of captain Augustus Heise, is a correct copy extracted from the official letter-book kept by the latter in his capacity of aide-de-camp to general Alten, during the march from Astorga to Vigo in 1808-9.

G. J. HARTMANN, K.C.B., major-general,
Late lieutenant-colonel K. G. L. artillery.

No. IX.

DOCUMENTS SHEWING THE LOSS OF THE FIRST AND SECOND LIGHT BATTALIONS KING'S GERMAN LEGION, BETWEEN ASTORGA AND VIGO IN 1808-9.

Extract from the returns, in the adjutant-general's office, Horse-Guards, of the number of men who were left in Spain and Portugal by the army under the late lieutenant-general Sir John Moore.

	Sergeants.	Trumpeters and Drummers.	Rank and File.
Forty-third foot	2	..	163
Fifty-second do......................	..	1	126
Ninety-fifth do.	..	5	209
First light battalion king's German legion	1	..	93
Second do. do.	..	..	67
Total........	3	6	658*

The nominal returns of the three English regiments are so imperfect, that it is impossible to collect from them how many men of those regiments were left behind between Astorga and Vigo; but the number must have fallen considerably short of that which is apportioned to each British regiment above, as both battalions are there included. Of the fifty-second regiment

* An additional number of two sergeants and sixty-two men of the forty-third regiment, which is added to the above in the original return, has not been included here, because, from the specifications of the places where the men were left behind, it does not appear that any of them were lost between Astorga and Vigo.

only twelve are returned as left behind on the retreat to Vigo, the rest being stated to have been left on the retreat to Corunna; and many of the forty-third, and the greater part of the ninety-fifth, are returned without any specification of the place where they were left behind. The returns of the German brigade are, however, complete, and the men are thus accounted for:—

First light battalion king's German legion.

	PRIVATES.
Sent to general hospital, in Salamanca, 11th of December, 1808, and not since heard of	2
Ditto at Ciudad Rodrigo	1
On retreat from Villada to Majorga, detached to impress cars for the commissariat, and taken prisoners by the enemy	3
Left sick at Castro Gonzales, and taken prisoner	1
Do. at Palacios, near Benavente, and do.	3
Dropped by fatigue between La Baneza and Astorga, supposed taken prisoners	7
Traced as far as Corunna, but never rejoined battalion	1
Left sick at Astorga, and not since heard of	1
Left sick at Ravanal, supposed dead	1
Conveyed sick on carts as far as Astorga, but from thence the roads through Galicia not admitting of the same conveyance, were placed upon mules, and owing to the exhausted state of the animals, and the deep snow, were prevented from keeping up with the column, and probably perished on the road	6
Left on command at Ponferrada to impress bread for the commissariat, while the division marched on towards Vigo; but owing to the delay of procuring it, and the almost impracticable roads, could not come up again with the division, and were either taken prisoners by the enemy, or killed by the Spaniards	36

Dropped on the different marches between El Burgo and Vigo, and as no conveyance could be procured to bring them on, were left on the road, and therefore either perished, or were taken prisoners	24
Dangerously wounded at the battle of Talavera, 18th July, 1809, and taken prisoners with hospital, (including one sergeant)	6
Do. and taken prisoners in the hospital of Plasencia	2
Total, (1 sergeant)	94

Second light battalion, king's German legion.

Sent into the general hospital, at Salamanca, and not since heard of	2
Left sick at Castro Gonzales, supposed taken prisoner	1
Dropped on the different marches from Majorga to Orense, and as no conveyance could be procured to bring them on, were left on the road, and, therefore, either perished, or have been taken prisoners by the enemy............	46
Left dangerously ill at Ravanal, supposed dead..........	1
Left on command at different places to impress bread for the commissariat, while the division marched on towards Vigo, bnt owing to the delay in procuring it, and the almost impracticable roads, could not come up again with the division, and were either taken prisoners by the enemy, or killed by the Spaniards	17
Total	67

Of these, it will be seen that several were left behind previous to the brigade arriving at Astorga, and that eight men are included in the return of the first light battalion, who were taken prisoners after the battle of Talavera. Deducting these—namely, from the first light battalion twenty-seven, and from the second light battalion three—the total number of men of the legion brigade that were left behind between Astorga and Vigo, and did not rejoin their regiments, will be a hundred and thirty-one; thus

Total as per return, First light battalion		94
Second do. do.		67
		161
Deduct, First light battalion	27	
Second do. do.	3	
		30
Total		131

No. X.

A.

DETAIL OF THE LOSS OF THE TRANSPORT SMALLBRIDGE.

Extract from the evidence of Cornelius Plügge, private in the fourth company of the second light battalion, king's German legion, given before a Court of Inquiry at Arciros de Baixo, in Portugal, December 23d, 1810.

(TRANSLATED FROM THE GERMAN.)

* * * * * * * * * * *

On the 10th of January, 1809, witness embarked in this transport, at Vigo, as servant to quarter-master Willan; he believes the whole number of men of the light brigade, which were also embarked in the vessel, amounted to a hundred and eighty; the officers were:—Captain Wilcken, lieutenant Heimbruch, ensign Augsburg, ensign Riddle, and quarter-master Willan. In the afternoon of the 10th, it came on to blow so hard that one of the cables broke, and the master was obliged to cut the other, and go to sea. On going out the long boat was lost, and the mizen sprung: the rest of the fleet remained in Vigo. After proceeding some distance, the master opened his instructions, and found that his destination was Corunna. On the following morning the weather was very boisterous, and they had lost sight of land; on the second day they fell in with a Spanish brig, from which the master learned that he had long passed Corunna; upon this captain Wilcken, as the ship had suffered much, and little provisions were on board, persuaded the master not to return to that port, but to seek the first English harbour which he could make.

After beating on against violent winds, a private of the third company, named Mühring, saw, about three o'clock in the morning, a light, which appeared to be at the distance of two or three English miles; this he pointed out to the mate, who immediately called up all the ship's company on deck. Upon this the captain said that "he now knew where he was; this light was the light on the Scilly islands." About a quarter of an hour afterwards, high rocks and land were visible, and the vessel lay to; the strong wind, however, continued to drive her nearer the rocks, and in about an hour afterwards she struck, the rudder was carried away, and the ship began to fill. Signals of distress, with guns and small arms, were incessantly fired, but without effect; the pumps broke, and the water rose in the vessel.

Captain Wilcken having, with the rest of the officers, offered up a short prayer in the cabin, now came upon deck, and found the master, with four bladders fastened round his body, and a bundle in his hand, about to abandon the ship. Captain Wilcken immediately posted two sentries upon him with loaded rifles, to prevent his escape; at the same time he directed all the men who could row to get into the boats. Upon this, witness, corporal Rode, and Boxmann, two buglemen, and Cornelius Bogart, of the second light battalion, and Ebeling and Heuer, of the first light battalion, with one sailor (an Italian), got into the jolly boat, while Peters, Nemscheck, Fahrenholtz, Müring, Mezer, Wessel, Stutzer, and Schmidt, of the second light battalion, went into the other boat, with orders to row, if possible, on shore, and send off some help to the ship. During this time the vessel struck violently upon the rocks, and lay over so much on one side that several persons were drowned between the decks. Half an hour after they had left the vessel they could see by the light of the tower that she went down.

After buffetting with the waves for five hours, they came so near the coast, that the people on shore were able to make signals to them with poles, to approach the land which they reached between ten and eleven o'clock, and found that they had landed on the island of Ushant on the coast of France. They were here declared prisoners of war, but were well treated by the inhabitants, who took them the next day to the main land. From hence they were removed to Brest, where they arrived after a march of five hours, and received the usual clothing of prisoners of war. After a few days they were removed to Arras, which place they reached in the course of a month. Eight months afterwards, witness, as well as twenty English sailors and soldiers, made their escape; but fifteen of the party were taken the first day by the *gens-d'armes*. He and six others came, after much difficulty, nearly to Antwerp, where he and one of the Englishmen were taken and brought to Antwerp by the *gens-d'armes*. Here he remained two days, and was then sent back to Arras, where he was forced to serve in the Irish brigade. They promised him a hundred livres bounty, but he never received any. * * * *
* * * * * * * * * * *

On the first of November, 1810, he found the first opportunity to desert, and persuaded his whole mess, consisting of ten men, to do the same; he reached the English army at Sobral in safety, was from thence sent to Belem, and on the 6th of December, 1810, to the detachment at Aveiros de Baixo. * * *

B.

Return of the officers, non-commissioned officers and soldiers of the light brigade of the King's German Legion, *who were lost on board the Smallbridge transport, on the return of sir John Moore's army to England, in January* 1809.

Battalions.	Officers.	Sergeants.	Rank and File.	Total.
1st light battalion, king's German legion	..	..	22	22
2d light battalion, king's German legion	5	7	180	192
Total......	5	7	202	214

RANK AND NAMES OF THE OFFICERS.

Captain Bodo Wilcken.
Lieutenant George von Heimbruch.
Ensign Charles Augustus Augspurg.
Ensign William Riddle.
Quartermaster James Willan.
} 2d light battalion.

(Signed) Lewis Benne.

Hanover, December 22, 1830.

RETURN OF THE CORPS OF THE KING'S GERMAN LEGION *employed in the expedition to the Scheldt, under the command of lieutenant-general the earl of Chatham, K.G. in* 1809.

CORPS.	Colonel.	Lieut-colonels.	Majors.	Captains.	Lieutenants.	Cornets and Ensigns.	Paymaster.	Adjutant.	Quartermaster.	Surgeon.	Assist.-Surg.	Vet. Surgeon.	Troop Quartermaster.	Sergeants.	Trumpeters & Buglemen.	Corporals.	Privates.	Grand Total.	Horses.
2d hussars under command of colonel Victor von Alten—per return of 1st August, 1809, when on board of transports going to the Scheldt........	1	1	2	8	7	8	1	1	..	1	2	1	8	34	8	32	547	662	73 offi-cers. 616 hus-sar.
1st light battalion under command of lieutenant-colonel Ernest Leonhardt	..	1	1	3	12	6	1	..	1	1	1	..	..	37	15	36	669	784	..
2d light battalion under the command of lieutenant-colonel commandant Colin Halkett. The lieutenant-colonel was soon after ordered to England, and major Charles Best received the command of the battalion....................	..	1	2	4	10	5	1	1	..	1	1	..	..	33	16	30	583	688	..
Total................	1	3	5	15	29	19	3	2	1	3	4	1	8	104	39	98	1799	2134	616

Hanover, December 22d, 1830. (Signed) LEWIS BENNE.

RETURN OF CASUALTIES IN THE FIRST AND SECOND LIGHT BATTALIONS OF THE KING'S GERMAN LEGION *during the operations in the Isle of Walcheren in* 1809.

	KILLED.			WOUNDED.		
	Officers.	Sergeants.	Rank and File.	Officers.	Sergeants.	Rank and File.
1st light battalion [On the 7th August, 1809, in the affair before Flushing]	..	..	4	2	1	12
1st do. [Between the 8th and 15th August, 1809, before Flushing]	..	..	..	..	..	7
2d do.	1	..	3	..	..	12
Total..............	1	..	7	2	1	31

Names of the officers killed and wounded.

7th August, 1809.—1st light battalion, Lieutenant Frederick William Augustus du Fay, dangerously.*
Ensign Frederick von Hedemann, do.
14th do. 2d do. Lieutenant Florian Sprecher, killed.

(Signed) LEWIS BENNE.

Hanover, 22d December, 1830.

* This officer died of his wounds [as captain in the 2d light battalion] on the 11th February, 1810, at Porchester.

No. XII.

Return of killed, wounded, and missing, of the King's German Legion, *in action with the enemy on the 27th of September* 1810, *in the position of Busaco.*

CORPS.	KILLED.				WOUNDED.								MISSING.				TOTAL.							
	Sergeants.	Corporals.	Drummers.	Privates.	Majors.	Captains.	Lieutenants.	Ensigns.	Sergeants.	Corporals.	Drummers.	Privates.	Sergeants.	Corporals.	Drummers.	Privates.	Majors.	Captains.	Lieutenants.	Ensigns.	Sergeants.	Corporals.	Drummers.	Privates.
1st light battalion detachment	1	..	..	..	..	..	..	..	1	..	..	10	1	..	..	2	..	..	..	..	3	..	..	12
2d do. do.	..	..	..	1	..	..	1	..	1	..	..	5	..	..	..	..	..	..	1	..	1	..	..	6
1st line battalion	..	..	..	3	..	..	1	..	1	..	..	4	..	..	..	..	..	..	1	..	1	..	..	7
2d do. do.	1	..	..	2	1	..	..	..	..	..	..	6	..	..	..	1	1	..	..	..	1	..	..	9
5th do. do.	..	..	..	1	..	..	..	..	1	..	..	8	..	..	..	..	..	..	..	..	1	..	..	9
7th do. do.	..	..	..	..	..	..	..	..	1	..	..	3	..	..	..	..	..	..	..	..	1	..	..	3
Total	2	..	..	7	1	..	2	..	5	..	..	36	1	..	..	3	1	..	2	..	8	..	..	46

OFFICERS WOUNDED.

RANK AND NAME.	REGIMENT.	REMARKS.
Major von Wurmb	2d line battalion	slightly.
Lieutenant Stolte	2d light battalion detachment	severely.
Lieutenant von Düring	1st line battalion	slightly.

(Signed) S. Löw, *major-general.*

No. XIII.

A.

RETURN OF KILLED, WOUNDED, AND MISSING OF THE KING'S GERMAN LEGION *in action with the enemy on the 3d and 5th of May* 1811, *at and near Fuentes de Onoro.*

CORPS.	On the 3d of May 1811.							On the 5th May 1811.															
	KILLED.		WOUNDED.					KILLED.				WOUNDED.								MISSING.	TOTAL.	
	Rank & file.	Horses.	Captains.	Sergeants.	Drummers.	Rank & file.	Horses.	Sergeants.	Trumpeters.	Rank & file.	Horses.	Majors.	Captains.	Lieutenants.	Ensigns.	Sergeants.	Trumpeters.	Rank & file.	Horses.	Rank & file.	Men.	Horses.
1st hussars	..	1	1	..	..	4	5	1	1	..	5	1	1	1	..	2	1	37	20	..	50	26
1st light battalion detachment	2	..	..	..	..	5	..	..	..	..	..	..	..	..	..	..	..	2	..	1	10	..
2d do. do.	1	..	..	1	..	3	..	..	..	..	..	..	..	..	..	..	..	1	..	1	7	..
1st line battalion	..	..	..	..	1	2	..	..	..	..	..	1	..	..	..	3	..	14	..	1	22	..
2d do. do.	..	..	..	..	..	4	..	..	..	2	..	..	2	..	..	..	..	11	..	2	21	..
5th do. do.	..	..	..	1	..	3	..	..	..	..	..	..	..	..	..	..	..	8	..	3	15	..
7th do. do.	..	..	..	1	..	2	..	..	..	1	..	..	..	..	1	1	..	4	..	2	12	..
Total	3	1	1	3	1	23	5	1	1	3	5	2	3	1	1	6	1	77	20	10	137	26

Memorandum.—The men returned "missing" are wounded and taken prisoners.

B.

Officers of the King's German Legion wounded at Fuentes de Onoro.

Rank and Name.	Regiment.	Remarks.
Major Meyer	1st hussars	slightly.
Captain Krauchenberg	do.	do.
Captain von Gruben	do.	severely.
Lieutenant Krauchenberg	do.	do.
Major Beck	1st line battalion	slightly.
Captain Müller	2d line battalion	severely.
Captain von der Decken	do.	do.
Ensign Bachelle	7th line battalion	do.

No. XIV.

Letter from captain Cleeves to major Hartmann, relative to the loss of a howitzer of captain Cleeves's battery, in the battle of Albuera.

Camp near Albuera,
May 20, 1811.

Sir,

According to your request, to explain the loss of the howitzer in the battle of the 16th instant, I have the honour to state as follows:—

The enemy began the battle with a pretty heavy cannonade on our left, which the battery of artillery under my command opposed. The action getting warm on our centre and right, the first brigade of general Stewart's division (colonel Colborne's) was ordered to the scene of action with four guns of my battery, to the right of the head of the column, and the remaining two followed the rear. Getting near the enemy, I formed line, and came to action on the top of a hill, about eighty or ninety yards distance from the enemy's column (which I imagined was just going to deploy) to cover the formation of our infantry, which formed in the rear of my guns, making the hill nearly the centre of this front.

The left of our line discharged a volley of musketry and charged the enemy, but were repulsed; the right did the same and would have been successful, had not, in this critical moment, our soldiers descried the enemy's cavalry, which tried, *ventre à terre*, to turn our right flank, and our line gave way.

I had then no other chance left to cover our soldiers and save the guns (the men ran through our intervals, which prevented our limbering up) but to stand firm, and to fight our ground. We prevented the cavalry from breaking our centre; but finding no opposition on our right, they turned us, and cut and piked the gunners of the right division down. The left division limbered up, and both guns would have been saved; but the shaft horses of the right gun were wounded, and came down, and the leading driver of the left gun got shot from his horse. Corporal Henry Fincke had presence of mind enough to quit his horse, to replace the driver, and then galloped boldly through the enemy's cavalry; his own horse, which ran alongside of him, secured him from the enemy's cuts and saved the gun, which I immediately made join the fight again. At this moment I was made prisoner, but had the good luck to escape unhurt.

Two guns were nearly immediately retaken; but the howitzer was carried off. Lieutenant Blumenbach was taken and wounded with the left division; lieutenant Thiele and myself were taken with the right; the former badly wounded by the Polish lancers.

I have the honour to remain, Sir,

(Signed) ANDREW CLEEVES,

Captain King's German Artillery.

To MAJOR HARTMANN, &c. &c.

No. XV.

Return of killed, wounded, and missing, of the King's German Legion, *at the battle of Albuera, 16th of May,* 1811. (From the London Gazette.)

REGIMENTS.	KILLED.			WOUNDED.							MISSING.					
	Lieutenants.	Rank and file.	Horses.	Majors.	Captains.	Lieutenants.	Ensigns.	Sergeants.	Rank and file.	Horses.	Lieutenants.	Trumpeters.	Rank and file.	Horses.	Total.	Horses.
1st light battalion	..	4	..	1	2	..	1	3	55	..	..	..	2	..	68	..
2d do. do.....	1	3	..	..	1	..	..	3	28	..	..	..	1	..	37	..
Artillery	..	..	24	..	..	2	..	..	16	..	1	1	29	10	48	34
Grand total ..	1	7	24	1	3	2	1	6	99	..	1	1	32	10	153	34

OFFICERS WOUNDED.

RANK AND NAME.	REGIMENT.	REMARKS.
Major Hartwig	1st light battalion	slightly.
Captain Baring (aide-de-camp)	do.	do.
Captain Rudorff	do.	do.
Captain Arnold Heise	2d light battalion	mortally.
Lieutenant Hartwig	1st do.	slightly.
Lieutenant Fahle (adjutant)	do.	do.
Ensign Schmalhausen	do.	do.
Lieutenant Thiele	artillery	severely.
Lieutenant Blumenbach	do.	slightly (missing.)

Memorandum.

The greater number of officers and men returned "missing" rejoined their regiments.

END OF VOL. I.

RETURN

SUMMARY RETURN shewing all the Casualties which have taken place in the Corps of Officers of the late King's German Legion from its forma
Captain LEWIS BENNE, of the Staff of th

KILLED IN BATTLE.

CORPS OF THE KING'S GERMAN LEGION.	Brigadier Generals	Colonels	Majors	Captains	Brigade Majors	Lieutenants	Second Lieutenants	Cornets	Ensigns	Adjutants	TOTAL
PERMANENT STAFF,	„	„	„	„	2	„	„	„	„	„	2
CORPS OF ENGINEERS,	„	„	„	„	„	„	„	„	„	„	„
REGIMENT OF ARTILLERY,	„	„	„	1	„	2	1	„	„	„	4
CAVALRY,	„	„	„	5	„	6	„	3	„	1	15
INFANTRY,	1	1	2	19	„	18	„	„	3	1	45
TOTAL,	1	1	2	25	2	26	1	3	3	2	66

DIED OF WOUNDS.

CORPS OF THE KING'S GERMAN LEGION.	Lieutenant Colonels	Majors	Captains	Lieutenants	Ensigns	TOTAL
PERMANENT STAFF,	„	„	„	„	„	„
CORPS OF ENGINEERS,	„	„	„	„	„	„
REGIMENT OF ARTILLERY,	„	„	„	„	„	„
CAVALRY,	1	1	6	2	„	10
INFANTRY,	3	1	11	12	2	29
TOTAL,	4	2	17	14	2	39

LOST AT SEA, OR DROWNED BY SHIPWRECK.

CORPS OF THE KING'S GERMAN LEGION.	Major Generals	Lieutenant Colonels	Captains	Lieutenants	Ensigns	Chaplains	Adjutants	Quartermasters	TOTAL
PERMANENT STAFF,	„	„	„	„	„	1	„	„	1
CORPS OF ENGINEERS,	„	„	„	„	„	„	„	„	„
REGIMENT OF ARTILLERY,	„	„	„	„	„	„	„	„	„
CAVALRY,	1	„	3	„	„	„	„	„	4
INFANTRY,	„	2	5	7	7	„	1	1	23
TOTAL,	1	2	8	7	7	1	1	1	28

DIED FROM ILLNESS OR ACCIDENTS.

CORPS OF THE KING'S GERMAN LEGION.	Colonels	Lieutenant Colonels	Majors	Captains	Brigade Majors	Second Captains	Lieutenants	Cornets	Ensigns	Paymasters	Adjutants	Quartermasters	Surgeons	Assistant Surgeons	Veterinary Surgeons	TOTAL
PERMANENT STAFF,	„	„	„	„	3	„	„	„	„	„	„	„	„	„	„	3
CORPS OF ENGINEERS,	„	„	„	1	„	„	„	„	„	„	„	„	„	„	„	1
REGIMENT OF ARTILLERY,	„	„	„	1	„	1	2	„	„	„	„	„	„	„	„	4
CAVALRY,	„	1	3	10	„	„	2	5	„	2	1	„	„	„	2	26
INFANTRY,	1	4	4	22	„	„	29	„	12	„	„	5	1	3	„	81
TOTAL,	1	5	7	34	3	1	33	5	12	2	1	5	1	3	2	115

Placed on the Reduced Allowa[nce] (provided by the Letter of Service, having become unfit by Infirmities, f[or] further Military Duty.

CORPS OF THE KING'S GERMAN LEGION.	Brigadier Generals	Colonels	Lieutenant Colonels	Majors	Captains	Lieutenants	Cornets	Ensigns	Paymasters	Surgeons	Assistant Surgeons
PERMANENT STAFF,	„	„	„	„	„	„	„	„	„	„	„
CORPS OF ENGINEERS,	„	„	„	„	„	„	„	„	„	„	„
REGIMENT OF ARTILLERY,	„	„	„	„	„	„	„	„	„	„	„
CAVALRY,	„	1	1	1	3	1	1	„	1	„	„
INFANTRY,	1	„	2	4	5	6	„	1	„	1	1
TOTAL,	1	1	3	5	[illegible]	[illegible]	1	1	1	1	1

RETURN of the number of Officers of the King's German Legion, who were placed upon half-pay at the expiration of two months, after the Disbandment of their respective Corps.

Rank and Names of the different Colonel Commandants at the disbandment of the King's German Legion.	Description of the Corps of which the King's German Legion was composed.	Colonel in Chief	Colonel Commandant	Lieutenant Colonels	Majors	Capts of troops & companies	Brigade Majors	Second Captains	Lieutenants	Second Lieutenants	Cornets	Ensigns	Captain Commissary	Paymasters	Chaplains	Adjutants	Quartermasters	Surgeons	Assistant Surgeons	Veterinary surgeons	TOTAL
	Permanent Staff, *a*.	1	„	„	„	„	7	„	„	„	„	„	„	„	5	„	„	„	„	„	13
	Corps of Engineers,	„	„	„	„	4	„	4	2	„	„	„	„	„	„	„	„	„	„	„	10
Lieutenant-general Frederick von der Decken,	Regiment of artillery,	„	1	1	2	8	„	8	16	16	„	„	1	1	„	1	1	1	4	1	62
Major-general Sir William von Dörnberg, K.C.B.	1st regiment of dragoons,	„	1	1	2	10	„	„	10	„	10	„	„	1	„	1	1	„	2	1	40
Major-general Augustus von Veltheim,	2d ditto,	„	1	1	2	10	„	„	10	„	10	„	„	1	„	1	1	1	2	1	41
Lieutenant-general Charles count Linsingen, K.C.B.	1st regiment of hussars,	„	1	1	2	10	„	„	10	„	10	„	„	1	„	1	1	1	2	1	41
Major-general, Victor von Alten,	2d ditto,	„	1	1	2	10	„	„	10	„	9	„	„	1	„	1	1	„	2	1	39
Colonel sir Frederick von Arentsschildt, K.C.B.	3d ditto,	„	1	1	2	12	„	„	11	„	11	„	„	1	„	1	1	1	2	1	45
Major-general Charles count Alten, K.C.B.	1st battalion of light infantry,	„	1	1	2	10	„	„	11	„	„	10	„	1	„	1	1	1	2	„	41
Major-general sir Colin Halkett, K.C.B.	2d ditto,	„	1	1	2	10	„	„	12	„	„	10	„	1	„	1	1	1	2	„	42
The colonel-in-chief, field-marshal his R. H. the duke of Cambridge, K.G. &c	1st battalion of the line,	„	„	1	2	10	„	„	18	„	„	10	„	1	„	1	„	1	2	„	46
Major-general Adolphus von Barsse,	2d ditto,	„	1	1	2	10	„	„	19	„	„	10	„	1	„	1	1	1	1	„	48
Major-general sir Henry von Hinüber, K.C.B.	3d ditto,	„	1	1	2	10	„	„	13	„	„	10	„	1	„	1	1	1	2	„	43
Major-general Sir Siegesmund von Löw, K.C.B.	4th ditto,	„	1	1	2	10	„	„	16	„	„	10	„	1	„	1	1	1	2	„	46
Lieutenant-colonel commandant Lewis von dem Bussche,	5th ditto,	„	„	2	2	10	„	„	14	„	„	10	„	1	„	1	1	„	2	„	43
Major-general Augustus von Hohnstedt,	6th ditto,	„	1	1	2	10	„	„	15	„	„	9	„	1	„	1	1	1	2	„	44
Lieutenant-general Frederick von Drechsel,	7th ditto,	„	1	1	2	9	„	„	20	„	„	10	„	1	„	1	1	1	2	„	49
Major-general Peter du Plat,	8th ditto,	„	1	1	2	10	„	„	14	„	„	10	„	1	„	1	1	1	2	„	44
Colonel Claus von der Decken,	Foreign veteran battalion,	„	1	1	1	10	„	„	10	„	„	9	„	1	„	1	1	1	2	„	38
	TOTAL,	1	15	18	33	173	7	12	231	16	50	108	1	17	5	17	16	14	35	6	775

a. As the other officers employed upon the staff of the Legion, held also regimental commissions, they are returned with the corps to which they belonged.

Total as detailed in the Return above,	775
Killed in battle,	66
Died of wounds,	39
Lost at sea or drowned by shipwreck,	28
Died from illness or accidents,	115
Placed on the reduced allowance, (provided by the letter of service) having become unfit by infirmities, for further military duty,	29
Placed on half-pay on account of wounds, or other infirmities contracted in the service,	59
Resigned and retired without receiving any allowance,	136
Superseded, being absent without leave,	28
Dismissed his majesty's service by sentence of general courts martial,	7
Officers who were gazetted, but whose appointment did not take place, as they never joined the corps,	24
Officers who left the Legion, either by promotion or transfer to British regiments or appointments upon the staff of the army,	44
Grand Total of all the officers, who served in, or were appointed to, the late King's German Legion,	1,350

Return

18th December, 1[8]0
9th January, 1804,
17th March, „
30th April, „
14th June, „
3d Sept. „
15th Nov. „
14th Jan. 1805,
3d April, „
24th Aug. „
14th May, 1806,
1st Aug. „
1st Dec. „
1st July, 1807,
1st Dec. „
1st June, 1808,
1st Dec. „
1st May, 1809,
25th Dec. „
25th June, 1810,
25th Dec. „
25th May, 1811,
25th June, 1812,—
1st Oct. 1813,—
25th Jan. 1814,—
25th Nov. 1814,—
25th Dec. 1814,—
25th May, 1815,—
25th Dec. 1815,

A.

tion, November 1803, to its Disbandment, 24th February 1816, extracted from the official Records of that Corps, by Brigade Major, late King's German Legion.

Total	Placed on Half-pay on account of Wounds or other Infirmities contracted in the Service. Lieutenant Colonels	Majors	Captains	Lieutenants	Cornets	Paymasters	Adjutants	Quartermasters	Surgeons	Assistant Surgeons	Total
"	"	"	"	"	"	"	"	"	"	"	"
"	"	"	"	"	"	"	"	"	"	"	"
"	"	"	1	"	"	"	"	"	"	"	1
9	1	7	5	2	2	1	"	1	1	"	20
20	2	5	17	8	"	1	1	1	1	2	38
29	3	12	23	10	2	2	1	2	2	2	59

RESIGNED AND RETIRED WITHOUT RECEIVING ANY ALLOWANCE. Lieutenant Generals	Major Generals	Lieutenant Colonels	Majors	Captains	Second Captains	Lieutenants	Second Lieutenants	Cornets	Ensigns	Captain Commissary	Paymasters	Adjutants	Quartermasters	Assistant Surgeons	Total
"	"	"	"	"	"	"	"	"	"	"	"	"	"	"	"
"	"	"	"	1	1	"	"	"	"	"	"	"	"	"	2
"	"	1	1	2	"	"	1	"	"	1	"	"	"	1	7
1	1	"	3	8	"	13	"	17	"	"	1	"	"	1	45
"	"	2	2	11	"	47	"	"	11	"	1	1	3	4	82
1	1	3	6	22	1	60	1	17	11	1	2	1	3	6	136

SUPERSEDED BEING ABSENT WITHOUT LEAVE. Lieutenant Colonels	Captains	Lieutenants	Cornets	Ensigns	Assistant Surgeons	Veterinary Surgeons	Total
"	"	"	"	"	"	"	"
"	"	"	"	"	"	"	"
"	"	"	"	"	"	"	"
1	"	1	6	"	1	1	10
1	2	5	"	10	"	"	18
2	2	6	6	10	1	1	28

Dismissed his majesty's service by sentence of General Courts Martial. Captains	Lieutenants	Paymasters	Quartermasters	Total
"	"	"	"	"
"	"	"	"	"
"	"	"	"	"
"	"	1	"	1
1	2	1	2	6
1	2	2	2	7

Officers, who were gazetted but whose appointment did not take place, as they never joined the corps. Lieutenant Colonels	Lieutenants	Cornets	Ensigns	Total
"	"	"	"	"
"	"	"	"	"
"	"	"	"	"
1	"	7	"	8
"	1	"	15	16
1	1	7	15	24

Officers, who left the Legion either by promotion or transfer to British regiments, or appointments upon the staff of the army. Captains	Brigade Majors	Lieutenants	Cornets	Ensigns	Adjutants	Surgeons	Assistant Surgeons	Veterinary Surgeons	Total	Total decrease in the corps of officers.
"	1	"	"	"	"	"	"	"	1	7
"	"	"	"	"	"	"	"	"	"	3
"	"	"	"	"	"	"	1	"	1	17
1	"	2	6	"	1	7	2	1	20	168
2	"	6	"	7	1	5	1	"	22	380
3	1	8	6	7	2	12	4	1	44	575

of the strength of the King's German Legion at different periods.

		Officers.	Troop-quarter-masters and serjeants.	Trumpeters and Drummers.	Rank & file.	Troop horses.
3, at Weymouth ...... cavalry,	 400					
Hilsea, artillery,	 74					
Hilsea, 1st light battalion,	 486					
Hilsea, 1st line ditto,	 356					
Porchester Castle, 2d light battalion,	 246	....			2397	
Cumberland Fort	 227					
Lymington,	 468					
On the road to join,	 140					
....	....	53	87	42	2273	74
....	....	135	151	64	2871	542
....	....	159	176	71	3404	658
....	....	202	208	83	3558	765
....	....	224	230	90	3884	972
....	....	256	258	97	4840	1128
....	....	294	294	112	5292	1276
....	....	309	318	118	5445	1522
....	....	346	366	133	6044	1710
....	....	607	648	193	11933	2457
....	....	653	677	205	11885	2731
....	....	660	697	211	11807	3309
....	....	653	698	210	11739	3359
....	....	651	688	209	12607	3471
....	....	653	701	214	12273	3306
....	....	657	701	243	12301	3227
....	....	658	701	214	12230	2985
....	....	659	693	206	11363	3092
....	....	665	697	201	10993	3085
....	....	662	703	201	11694	3142
....	....	655	702	217	12081	3203
(exclusive of 8 officers, 1 serjt. 17 rank and file, prisoners of war,)	....	663	814	242	14175	3050
inclusive of foreign veteran battalion, (368 heads) but exclusive of 10 officers and 218 men, prisoners of war, and about 100 invalids,)	....	735	878	261	14025	3712
inclusive of foreign veteran battalion, 18 officers, 24 serjeants, 8 drummers, 667 rank and file, but exclusive of 254 officers and men, prisoners of war, and invalids,		775	834	260	13780	4064
inclusive of foreign veteran battalion, but exclusive of a number of invalids and prisoners of war,	....	814	838	240	11770	3670
inclusive of foreign veteran battalion, but exclusive of invalids and prisoners of war,	....	815	850	236	11567	3614
exclusive of 139 men, who were not yet returned from prisoners of war,	....	817	855	222	10163	3541
......	....	782	765	239	10442	3558

Return of the effective strength of the King's German Legion, on the 25th May, 1815.

	Officers	Troop-quarter-masters and sergeants.	Trumpeters and Drummers.	Rank & File.	Troop horses.
Permanent staff, (brigade majors and chaplains, ...	11	0	0	0	0
Engineers, (in different countries,)	10	0	0	0	0
Artillery,—in the north of Germany, in England, Portugal, Sicily, the Netherlands, &c.	61	30	10	958	501
1st dragoons, in the Netherlands, &c.	39	55	10	498	514
2d ditto, ...	42	42	10	518	504
1st hussars, ditto, ...	41	55	10	618	626
2d ditto, ...	41	54	6	564	675
3d ditto, ...	47	62	11	789	721
1st light battalion, ditto, ...	50	64	14	487	0
2d do. ditto, ...	51	51	16	434	0
1st line battalion ditto, ...	50	49	12	411	0
2d ditto, ...	50	50	14	500	0
3d ditto, ...	50	47	13	555	0
4th ditto, ...	50	49	9	474	0
5th ditto, ...	49	47	16	454	0
6th ditto, at Messina in Sicily, ...	50	50	20	729	0
7th dttto, Palermo, do.	50	54	20	801	0
8th ditto, in the Netherlands, ...	50	46	16	526	0
Veteran battalion, (25th Jan. 1815) Antwerp, ...	25	35	11	638	0
The corps had no regular depots at this time, but had invalids in England and other places, about	0	16	4	209	0
Total, (exclusive of 139 men, who were not yet returned from prisoners of war)	817	855	222	10,163	3,541

Return of the effective strength of the King's German Legion, on the 25th December, 1815.

	Officers	Troop-quarter-masters and sergeants.	Trumpeters and Drummers.	Rank & File.	Troop horses.
Permanent staff, (brigade majors and chaplains), ...	12	0	0	0	0
Engineers, ...	10	0	0	0	0
Artillery in Genoa, (3d company of foot), France, &c.	62	39	13	1189	619
1st dragoons at Onaing in France, &c.	41	49	10	450	420
2d do. Lieu St. Amand near Bouchain in France, ...	41	38	9	387	401
1st hussars.—on the 24th Dec. 1815, at Berlincourt in France, broke up for Hanover on the 25th Dec. 1815, ...	41	51	7	521	552
2d do. at Trièpval in France, &c.	40	50	6	497	571
3d do. Boiry Bequerelle in France, &c.	45	55	10	611	611
1st light battalion, at Jupille near Liege, ...	41	43	19	495	0
2d do Chateau Frelous, &c.	42	32	11	418	0
1st line battalion, at Leigne, &c.	47	39	11	351	0
2d do. Neerwende in Brabant, &c.	48	45	16	495	0
3d do. Linden, near Louvain, &c.	43	35	17	470	0
4th do. Horpmeal, in Holland, &c.	46	37	14	404	0
5th do. Alleur, in Brabant, ...	44	34	15	380	0
6th do. Genoa, &c.	45	53	19	601	0
7th do. Genoa, &c.	50	45	21	721	0
8th do. Villers L'Eveque, &c.	44	31	19	466	0
The depots of the 1st and 2d dragoons, and 1st, 2d and 3d hussars at Norwich barracks in England, under command of major Moritz von Müller, of 1st hussars, ...	0	10	1	441	378
[N.B.—The 11 officers are returned with their respective regiments, a detachment of 7th line battalion, on the march from France, ...	0	9	0	22	0
A detachment of 1st and 2d light, and 1st, 2d, 3d, 4th, 5th and 8th batt. of the line, under command of major Ernest von Düring, at Neinburg and Verden, (the 28 officers returned with the respective battalions),	0	15	1	670	0
Foreign veteran battalion at Antwerp, per state of men of 28th Nov. 1815,	40	55	20	853	0
Total, ...	782	765	239	10,442	3,558

Signed,

L. BENNE.

HANOVER, *Dec.* 22, 1830.

www.ingramcontent.com/pod-product-compliance
Ingram Content Group UK Ltd.
Pitfield, Milton Keynes, MK11 3LW, UK
UKHW021935170225
455227UK00002B/25

9 781474 540599